PUBLIC OPINION AND THE MILITARY ESTABLISHMENT

PUBLIC OPINION
and the MILITARY
ESTABLISHMENT

Edited by CHARLES C. MOSKOS, Jr.

Volume I (1971)
SAGE RESEARCH PROGRESS SERIES
ON WAR, REVOLUTION, AND PEACEKEEPING

 **SAGE PUBLICATIONS** *Beverly Hills, California*

For information address:

SAGE PUBLICATIONS, INC.
275 South Beverly Drive
Beverly Hills, California 90212

Printed in the United States of America

International Standard Book Number 0-8039-0115-1 (C); 0-8039-0116-X(P)

Library of Congress Catalog Card No. 70-151672

First Printing

CONTENTS

INTRODUCTION   i x

I. MILITARY EDUCATION AND CIVILIAN VALUES

Laurence I. Radway   3

RECENT TRENDS AT AMERICAN SERVICE ACADEMIES

Peter Karsten   37

"PROFESSIONAL" AND "CITIZEN" OFFICERS: A
   COMPARISON OF ACADEMY AND ROTC
   OFFICER CANDIDATES

Nona Glazer-Malbin   63

THE ROTC: MILITARY SERVICE ON THE COLLEGE
   CAMPUS

William A. Lucas   99

ANTICIPATORY SOCIALIZATION AND THE ROTC

II. CIVILIAN RESPONSE TO MILITARY ROLES

Bernard Beck   137

THE MILITARY AS A WELFARE INSTITUTION

David Sutton   149

THE MILITARY MISSION AGAINST OFF-BASE
   DISCRIMINATION

Leon Bramson   185

THE ARMED FORCES EXAMINING STATION: A
   SOCIOLOGICAL PERSPECTIVE

Robert B. Smith   221

DISAFFECTION, DELEGITIMATION, AND CONSEQUENCES:
   AGGREGATE TRENDS FOR WORLD WAR II, KOREA
   AND VIETNAM

III. **THE EMERGENT MILITARY ESTABLISHMENT**

Morris Janowitz   255

THE EMERGENT MILITARY

Charles C. Moskos, Jr.   271

THE NEW ESTRANGEMENT: ARMED FORCES AND
   AMERICAN SOCIETY

PUBLIC OPINION AND THE MILITARY ESTABLISHMENT

INTRODUCTION

PUBLIC OPINION AND THE MILITARY ESTABLISHMENT
Charles C. Moskos, Jr.

Public attitudes as well as academic definitions of the
American armed forces fluctuate between two poles. At one end
are those who see the military as a reflection of dominant
societal values and an instrument entirely dependent upon the
lead of civilian policy makers. Conversely, others stress how
much military values differ from the larger society and the independent influence the military has come to exert in civil society.
In a real sense, these two emphases differ about whether the armed
forces or society is primary. Yet, neither conception is wholly
wrong nor wholly accurate. Rather, the issue is more one of the
simultaneous interpenetration and institutional autonomy of the
military and civilian spheres.

At the outset, moreover, it should be made clear that the conceptual question of the independent versus dependent relationship
of the military and civilian orders is not intrinsically an ideological issue. Indeed, we find diverse viewpoints on the conceptual question crisscrossing political positions. Thus, supporters of the military organization have argued both for and
against greater congruence between military and civilian structures. Likewise, the harshest critics of the armed forces have
variously claimed the military establishment is either too isolated or too overlapping with civil society. The point here is
that at some level a conceptual understanding of the armed forces

and American society can be analytically distinguished from a
political position. In fact, of course, this is not always so
readily apparent when one gets down to concrete cases. But, it
is my personal statement that an ideological position must ultimately lead to social science analyses.

In any event, we can readily observe even in the relatively
short time since the start of the Second World War four different
and more or less discrete public portrayals of the American military establishment. The first period includes the year immediately
following the conflict. A second period begins with the Korean
War (1950) and ends in the middle 1950s. This is followed by a
Cold War period which for our purposes can be dated from the
middle 1950s through the early 1960s (although, of course, the
Cold War historically speaking predates the Korean War and per-
sists into the present). The current or Vietnam period starts
from about 1964 and continues into the time of this writing (1971).
In each of these periods, the mission and the organization of the
military required different emphases and forms. This in turn
resulted in different kinds of modal service experiences and
corresponding changes in public attitudes toward the armed forces.

Americans gave the Second World War unparalleled backing. No
other military conflict in which the United States has been
involved, before or since, has equaled it. The Japanese attack
on Pearl Harbor followed immediately by Germany's declaration of
war united the American nation as nothing else could have done.
The only organized opposition to the war--but without the
slightest indication of support for the Axis powers--was that of
small religiously-based pacifist groups and the "nonsupport"
policies of minuscule Trotskyist groups. It is within the context
of the widespread support for the Second World War--at elite,
intellectual, and mass levels--that we can appreciate the absence
of any serious criticism of the American military. Even the most
horrific acts--the Allied fire-bombing of German cities and the
atomic obliteration of Hiroshima and Nagasaki--were excused as
steps to shorten the war and thereby save the lives of American

servicemen. What is often forgotten, however, is that the
nation's unquestioning commitment in pursuing victory was exceptional rather than typical.

The Korean War, on the other hand, followed the normal American historical pattern of ambivalence toward the nation's war
involvement. From its initial outbreak, the Korean War was
plagued by political indecision. After the Chinese intervention,
this was further compounded by reversals on the battlefield which
aggravated the schism in America's political thinking concerning
the war's aims. Conservatives generally took the hard line of
extending the war directly to China in the quest for total victory.
Most liberals and moderates, while still supporting anti-Communist
policies, favored a compromise solution. Some opposition to the
war existed within Left-wing groups, but such radical voices were
so weakened by the Joseph McCarthy era as to be hardly heard at
all. The eventual stalemate of the Korean conflict contributed
to adverse account of American troop behavior: prisoner-of-war
collaboration, the lack of troop motivation, and the deterioration
of military discipline.

During the ensuing Cold War period, the military did not
escape embroilment in political controversy. Such controversy
was centered on issues of military leadership and the institutional role of the military. Command policies at the highest
level were subjected to conservative charges in two major Senate
hearings. The military establishment found itself on the defensive in countering charges of being soft on Communism in both the
McCarthy-Army hearings of 1954, and in the 1962 hearings resulting from the cause celebre following Major General Edwin Walker's
relief from command (for sponsoring troop information programs
with extreme conservative content). During the same period,
intellectuals on the Left emerged from their quiescent stance and
began critically to attack the military establishment from another
direction. Deep concerns on the nature of the military-industrial
complex in contemporary American society were raised--an issue
which was to achieve a fruition of sorts over a decade later. By

and large, however, the Cold War attacks on the military were relatively mild and in basic respects the armed forces maintained the high regard of the American public.

If the debates concerning the military establishment were generally muted in peacetime, this was not to be the case once America intervened massively in Vietnam. Although there was a brief spate of glory attached to the Green Berets, opposition to the war soon led to negative portrayals of the armed forces. Indeed, as the antiwar movement gained momentum it began to generalize into a frontal attack on the military system itself— particularly within elite cultural and intellectual circles. The 1967 March on the Pentagon crossed a symbolic threshold. Not only was the war in Vietnam opposed, but for a growing number the basic legitimacy of military service was brought into open question. Adding to the passion of the antimilitarists were the revelations of American atrocities in Vietnam, the physical and ecological devastation being perpetuated throughout Indochina, and the sometimes heavy-handed repression of troop dissent. Conversely, advocates of the war tended to label all peace proponents as physically betraying the American soldier in combat. As the war in Indochina ground on, separating the substantive and ethical issues of the war from contradictory stereotypes of the American military became increasingly difficult. By an involuted leap of reasoning, whether one had a favorable or unfavorable conception of the American military was becoming the defining characteristic of how one stood on the war in Southeast Asia.

The contrast in political evaluations and public reactions toward the American military establishment over three wars is revealing. In the Second World War, the American military was almost universally held in high esteem in a popularly supported war. Conservatives and isolationist sectors of American public opinion were quick to fall in line behind a liberal and interventionist national leadership. In the wake of the Korean War, defamatory images of the American serviceman were propagated by Right-wing spokesmen. Liberal commentators, on the other hand,

generally defended the qualities of the American fighting man. In
the war in Southeast Asia a still different pattern has emerged.
Although initially an outcome of a liberal Administration, the war
has come to be primarily defended by political conservatives in
terms of "support the boys." At the same time, the severest
attacks on both the behavior of American soldiers and the military establishment now emanate from the Left.

Operating somewhat independently of events in Vietnam has
been a host of other developments serving to tarnish the American
military's image in the most recent period: the capture of the
Pueblo, racial strife within the armed forces, the inequities of
the draft, reports of widespread drug abuse among troops, corruption in the operation of post exchanges and service clubs, astound-
ing cost overruns in defense contracts, and military spying on
civilian political activists.

But even beyond Vietnam and factors unique to armed forces and
society in the United States, the public decline of the American
military establishment may well be part of a more pervasive
pattern occuring throughout Western parliamentary democracies.
Researchers on contemporary armed forces in Western Europe, the
United Kingdom, Canada, and Australia, have all noted the sharp
depreciation of the military's standing in these societies. Indeed,
although it seems somewhat far afield, the possibility suggests
itself that Vietnam may be a minor factor in explaining the
lessened prestige of the American military establishment. This is
to say that the American military like its counterparts in other
Western (post-?) industrialized societies is experiencing an
historical turning point with regard to societal legitimacy and
public definition. The essays in this volume, then, address themselves to a fundamental question--what is the sociological import
of public attitudes, civilian values, and societal definitions of
the military establishment. This set of studies was assembled
under the auspices of the Inter-University Seminar on Armed Forces
and Society sponsored by the Russell Sage Foundation. The present
collection constitutes the first volume in the Sage Research

Progress Series on War, Revolution, and Peacekeeping. Subsequent
volumes will similarly be collections of essays having a unit in
theme. In most instances these will be hitherto unpublished
studies. In some cases, however, there will be inclusion of
reprinted or revised articles originally appearing in publications
not usually read by students of military sociology. The purpose
of the Research Progress Series is to bring to the attention of a
relevant audience studies demonstrating both intellectual continuity and new approaches in the analyses of armed forces and
society.

The studies in this volume on <u>Public Opinion and the Military
Establishment</u> fall easily into three topical headings. The first
section deals with civilian values and military education. Laurence
I. Radway discusses recent trends at American service academies by
highlighting the conflict between academic values and military
programs. Although the situation varies from academy to academy,
Radway documents the gradual ascendance of academic professionalism
over traditional military training. The study by William A. Lucas,
based on data from eight different ROTC programs, shows how formal
ROTC training does not inculcate militaristic values among ROTC
students. Rather, Lucas shows, attitudes toward military life are
generally shaped before the future officer arrives on campus.
Peter Karsten compares academy cadets and ROTC students and finds
the ROTC students consistently less militaristic than the cadets.
Moreover, Karsten finds no evidence that ROTC militarizes its
students and concludes that the abolishment of ROTC on cosmopolitan campuses can only result in insulating the military from
civilian values. The piece by Nona Glazer-Malbin treats the
situation of ROTC and the university as a microcosm of ambiguous
civil-military relations. Although Glazer-Malbin finds no evidence
that ROTC socializes its students into acceptance of militaristic
values, she, nevertheless, points to other undesirable consequences
of a military presence on campus.

The second topical section examines civilian responses to
various military roles. Bernard Beck applies "labeling" theory to

the welfare role of the military. Beck argues essentially that
the military has been successful in its welfare role precisely
because it is legitimated on other than conventional welfare
grounds, e.g., national defense, manly honor, espirit de corps.
Leon Bramson's treatment of the Armed Forces Examining Station
shows how entrance into the military system can be regarded as
rite de passage in American society. Highly critical of militaristic values, Bramson suggests ways to implement an alternate
form of civil religion. David Sutton presents a case study which
reveals why the military's official policy to implement off-post
racial nondiscrimination has been a failure. (Sutton's study anticipated belated Pentagon efforts to overcome off-post discrimination.) He also shows, however, how the presence of black troops
does cause changes in racial stereotypes in off-post communities.
The study by Robert B. Smith is a detailed exmination of changes
in public attitudes toward American involvement in World War II,
Korea, and Vietnam. Although there are some notable differences
between the wars, Smith's presentation of longitudinal survey data
shows some striking similarities in rates of disaffection for all
three wars.

The concluding section of this volume is concerned with the
nature of the emerging military establishment in American society.
The essay by Morris Janowitz argues that there must be a period
of intensive "institution building" on the part of the American
military over the next two decades. The armed forces must move
toward a constabulary concept in which organizational goals inhere
in the minimum use of force. For Janowitz, the essential problem
in the near future is to establish organizational procedures which
will closely articulate the military profession with civilian
society. My contribution presents a model by which we may ascer-
tain whether the armed forces and society are moving toward convergence or divergence. An examination of various indicators
suggests that the generation-long convergence of the military and
American society which began in World War II has reversed itself
and we are moving into an era in which the military will become

increasingly isolated from the society at large.

Throughout all of the essays there runs the theme that the American armed forces are undergoing a significant redefinition. Although this state of affairs is becoming more and more apparent, public discussion on the role of the military in American society is too often dominated by either antimilitary polemicists or apologists of the warfare state. If our society is ever to fulfill its democratic promise, the relationships between its civilian and military structures require especially informed and sustained attention. This volume represents a commitment on the part of the contributors to proceed toward that goal.

ACKNOWLEDGMENTS

Leon Bramson, "The Armed Forces Examining Station." By permission of Prentice-Hall, Inc., where a shorter and somewhat different form of this article appears in Human Nature and Collective Behavior --Papers in Honor of Herbert Blumer, and edited by Tamotsu Shibutani, (C). 1970.

Peter Karsten, "'Professional' and 'Citizen' Officers: A Comparison of Academy and ROTC Cadets." By permission of Foreign Policy where a shorter and somewhat different form of this article appears in Volume 1, No. 2 (February, 1971).

Part I.

MILITARY EDUCATION AND CIVILIAN VALUES

RECENT TRENDS AT AMERICAN SERVICE ACADEMIES

Laurence I. Radway

Although the academies produced only 3 per cent of all newly commissioned officers in 1969,[1] these officers continue to set standards for the profession of arms; they are far more likely to devote their careers to military service;[2] and they will eventually hold the predominant share of rank and responsibility in the armed forces. The primacy of academy graduates is most evident in the Navy, least evident in the Air Force. Because the Army stands between the other two, its case may be taken as representative, and in the Army 80 per cent of all major generals are West Pointers. If one examines only generals in posts so important that they are authorized to report directly to the chief of staff, still more are West Pointers.

The number of Academy graduates has increased. Before the Air Force Academy opened (1955), academy enrollments totalled about 6,200. They are now approximately 13,000, in part because a third institution has been added, in part because West Point has been expanded to the size of Annapolis. This increase of more than 100 per cent will enable the academies to supply a significantly larger part of the post-Vietnam regular officer corps.

The impact of these institutions on state and society is indirect and deferred in the sense that it is made through the men whom they shape for later responsibilities. Their contemporary influence rests largely on what they were like when today's military leaders were still students, and their mark on the next generation of admirals and generals will depend on what they are like today. In each case impact varies with the kinds of students they attract and the kinds of experiences these students undergo. I believe the first of these variables counts for more than the second, i.e., that self-selection into an academy is a more important determinant of future attitudes or values than anything that goes on there.[3]

THE RAW MATERIAL

The following is based largely on West Point, since I have more information on that institution than on the other two.

Army leaders no longer come from rural backgrounds. But only 33 per cent of the members of West Point's Class of 1973 were reared in large cities or in the suburbs thereof, a figure not only lower than that for the country as a whole but lower than that for civilian colleges.[4] If inner cities alone are considered, the contrast is still more striking, e.g., 6.8 per cent of West Point entrants were reared in large cities as opposed to from 12 to 27.3 per cent of students at various kinds of civilian colleges. These figures probably reflect the large role of Congress in the appointing process; many Congressional districts lack cities of over 50,000.

Alumni sons constitute only 4 to 7 per cent of an entering class, a proportion smaller than that at many Ivy League institutions; on the other hand 15.4 per cent of the Class of 1973 had fathers who were career military men. Although professional and managerial families predominate, this does not mean that entrants come from families of higher income or status than those of civilian freshmen. West Point actually lags a bit behind the latter in its proportion (25 per cent) of students whose fathers are businessmen, and it lags even more in the proportion (6.8 per cent) whose families earn over $25,000 a year. In the Class of 1973 the largest number of cadets came from families making

$10,000-$15,000, and 30 per cent of the families made less than
$10,000.[5]

These indicators of middle to lower-middle class origin are
supported by data on religion. Only 20 per cent of West Point
plebes belong to denominations which attract high-status families,
e.g., Episcopal, Presbyterian, Congregational. Most belong to
other Protestant denominations (Methodist, Baptist, etc.) or to
the Catholic Church. The proportion of Catholics, which has risen
steadily since World War II, now stands at 35 per cent. One per
cent of all cadets are Jews, a figure well below the national
average for all college students, and even further below the
average (12 per cent) for institutions of comparable selectivity
as measured by entrant's test scores.[6] A drive for black students
is now under way. Between 1870 and 1961, West Point enrolled an
average of less than one each year; Annapolis had even fewer. But
the recruitment of blacks is now a major goal of each academy, and
determined recruitment efforts have brought some results. The
Classes of 1972 and 1973 included more than forty blacks each.
All academies now measure total black students in the dozens,
with most of the increase having taken place since 1966.[7]

Entrants are relatively bright. They are more likely to
have maintained "A" averages in high school than freshmen at most
civilian institutions. In the class of 1973 at West Point, 44.3
per cent stood in the top tenth of their secondary school classes,
again a higher percentage than most civilian institutions could
boast, though below the 53 per cent figure for the comparable Air
Force Academy class. Data for a somewhat earlier period (1964-
67) reveal that Air Force Academy entrants scored particularly
high on College Board mathematical aptitude and achievement tests.
West Point entrants did less well than those at Annapolis or the
Air Force Academy.[8] Compared to highly selective private colleges
on the other hand, the service academies as a whole recruit fewer
entrants in the top tenth of their secondary school classes, and
significantly fewer who score over 700 on College Board aptitude
tests. The difference, in short, is at the topmost rung of the
academic ladder.

With respect to substantive academic interests, the proportion of West Point entrants hoping to major in the social sciences is less than one-half as large as the proportion of students at all civilian institutions except technical institutes, the proportion hoping to specialize in the humanities is only one-fifth as large.[9]

Leadership and athletic credentials are impressive. West Pointers are much more likely than civilian freshmen to have been elected president of a high school organization; they are more likely to have won a varsity letter (75 per cent), to have been captain of a team (33 per cent), to feel it important to become an outstanding athlete, and to have considered the athletic program of the institution a major reason for choosing it.[10] In the Class of 1973 at West Point, nearly 40 per cent had won a varsity letter in football.

The portrait that emerges is one of upward-mobile youngsters from medium-sized cities who have to depend on their merits to achieve success and who, in Lovell's words, have already met the challenge of academic work, peer-group relations, and athletic competition.[11] They are more ambitious, forceful, hard-driving and dominant than civilian undergraduates, and admission into an academy promises them a good education and leadership status in an historic profession. Members of West Point's Class of 1973 were more likely than their civilian peers to want to keep up with public affairs, assume administrative responsibility, become community leaders, and obtain recognition from others.[12] Only a distinct minority of cadets can be described as moody, arty, or shy. More tend to see themselves as outgoing friendly people who "do the work but are not that serious as students."[13]

It is also clear that West Point entrants are less libertarian than civilian students. Lovell concludes that they are less likely to be "turned off" by an emphasis on authority, conformity, tradition, or patriotism. The differences are not great but they are consistent. The Class of 1973, compared to civilian undergraduates, was less likely to argue with teachers and less

likely to think students should participate in designing curricula
or evaluating faculty. It was more likely to support the regulation of student publications, guest speakers, and off-campus
behavior. It was more likely to attend religious services.

The expressed political preferences of cadets were also distinctive. On a five-point scale, they were more likely than civilian students to describe themselves as "strongly conservative"
(5.4 per cent) or "moderately conservative (33.8 per cent), and
less likely to describe themselves as "liberal" (20.4 per cent)or
"left" (0.9 per cent). And while civilians expected to get more
liberal during four years of college, cadets expected to become
less so! Cadets were less inclined to want to liberalize divorce,
legalize marijuana, coddle criminals, abolish capital punishment,
or concede the right to publish all scientific findings. They were
less interested in Federal protection of consumers or aid for the
disadvantaged; they were more interested in Federal control of
student activists. During their high school years significantly
fewer had protested against racial discrimination or against
American military policy.[15]

With the reservation that the data are about ten years old,
material is also available to indicate that cadets hold moderately
"hardnosed" views on foreign affairs. When West Pointers were
compared with a group of Dartmouth undergraduates heavily weighted
by the inclusion of ROTC students, more of them felt total war
likely in the next fifteen years. Although the differences were
less, cadets led in attributing neutralism to lack of moral fibre
or to communist influence in neutral nations. More felt that the
Korean War illustrated the desire of communists to conquer the
world and that American forces were unnecessarily denied victory
in that conflict.[16]

To be sure, none of the foregoing means that cadets are out
of the mainstream of American opinion. As Lovell noted shrewdly,
a comparison with Gallup poll figures on the likelihood of major
was suggests that it was the Dartmouth students who were deviant
and the West Point cadets who were closer to adult opinion.

Nevertheless, the comparisons made abot become significant when it is recalled that graduates of institutions like Dartmouth often hold senior posts in the national security establishment. For the same reason it is important to note other differences between senior civilian officials and the cadets who are destined to become senior military officials. Civilian Federal executives are far more likely to come from urban or suburban upper-middle class families. More than 50 per cent of the under secretaries and assistant secretaries appointed by President Kennedy were born in metropolitan areas.[17] In a larger group of political executives who served between 1933 and 1965, over 20 per cent had attended one of eighteen famous residential preparatory schools in the East; if the analysis is confined to national security agencies, the proportion rises to 30-40 per cent.[18] The civilian appointee is less likely to be Catholic, twice as likely to belong to a high-status Protestant denomination, and twice as likely to be a Jew.[19] Since many political appointees are lawyers--44 per cent in the survey just cited--they tend to rank high in verbal skill, and this is one attribute in which West Point entrants score below students in university-related colleges.

Finally, modest but suggestive data are available on differences between entering cadets and new Foreign Service Officers. While there is little difference in economic status, FSO's are more than twice as likely to come from urban areas, six times as likely to come from New England, and far less likely to come from the South.[20] They are half as likely to be Catholic. In describing themselves they employ such phrases as "cultured", "Intellectual," "sophisticated", "less likely to be middle-brow", "rebellious", and "less likely to be cooperative".[21] This is not the image which West Point cadets have of themselves; and while the latter are much younger, it is unlikely that the passage of four or five years would increase significantly their tendency to resort to such language. Finally, Harr notes that 75 per cent of all mature FSO's describe themselves as "somewhat liberal" or "liberal" in political orientation.[22]

THE CHALLENGE TO COMBAT VIRTUES

No one really knows what effect the service academies have on entering students.[23] My hunch is that before World War II they were more likely to exaggerate the differences noted above, and, more generally, to widen the gap between military and civilian undergraduate experience; and that the converse has been true in more recent years. The argument here is speculative and complex. It begins with an analysis of professional and institutional aims, and especially of their growing complexity.

Armed forces leaders have always required two sets of virtues. One consists of skills and attitudes useful in battle, the other of skills and attitudes useful in coping with the larger social and technological environment.

Combat leadership requires an ability to inspire a special category of men under special conditions. Particularly in the army, combat units draw personnel of little education and low social status. Even if few will ever hear a shot fired in anger, all must be taught to persevere in the face of confusion and danger; for the influence exerted by the prospect or memory of battle is not greatly diminished by the rarity of the contingency itself. And human beings must be trained to overcome egoism and fear; it does not come naturally. Hence adamant insistence on loyalty, unity, courage, obedience. hardiness, and zeal. In no man are such qualities much enhanced by long study or reasoned argument, least of all in the underclasses who loom so large in combat outfits. They are enhanced instead by discipline, by symbol and, above all, by personal example. Moreover, in a nation where Spartan attributes are in short supply, any institution which feels a need for them must seek some protection by isolating itself from civilian society.

The converse is true of ability to cope with the larger environment. In Janowitz's terms, this rests on "managerial" rather than "heroic" qualities.[24] But it illuminates some issues of military education to introduce a further distinction between what is required to deal with the scientific and technological environment.

In both cases the civilian world is likely to value the necessary
skills more highly than it values combat virtues, and it more
often tries to develop them by education. Accordingly, military
institutions which also want to develop them are more likely to
try to stay in touch with civilian society.

The relative emphasis given to combat skills, and to what I
shall call techno-social skills, depends on several factors, among
them rank,[25] echelon, and type of unit. The pressure for intrepid
conduct is felt more strongly by paratroopers than by members of
a sterilization and bath company, and more by Marine fighter pilots
and platoon leaders than by flag officers at higher headquarters.
Less obviously, it has varied with social class. The aristocrats
who led European armies gloried in "a hard gallop, a gallant fight,
and a full jug".[26] They preferred brawn to brain, and character
to intellect, especially because they judged character to be an
elusive virtue which they alone shared--like ignorance, a mark of
birth! Education, on the other hand, was a weapon of the rising
middle class, an accomplishment to be scorned, or a threat to be
fought. Thus in England the staff-college graduate was not favored
so much as "that splendid chap, the regimental officer"; and until
well into the 19th century naval officers were trained by taking
youngsters between the ages of twelve and fourteen and putting
them on ships.

The history of military education, Barnett notes, has been a
tug-of-war between two images: one conceives of the soldier as a
fighting man, the other as a manager. The claims of the manager
are now pressed vigorously. Given more highly educated enlisted
personnel, given the nature of modern conflict with its sophisticated and costly weapons and inexorable political constraints, it
is hard to preserve the priority accorded to combat virtues in an
earlier age. Yet it is just as obvious that those virtues are not
obsolete. So the tug-of-war continues. Within the service academies it is reflected in competing codes of behavior. As an Air
Force Academy statement put it:

"The Academy must fuse two potentially conflicting

values: on the one hand the spirit of intellectual
integrity and inquiry, which may downgrade deference
to authority unless rationally supported, and on the
other hand, the spirit of military loyalty and discipline, which sometimes accents deference to authority
without rational justification."[27]

The tug-of-war is also reflected in continuing dialogue
between commandants, who are responsible for the military program,
and deans, who are responsible for the academic program. "Doers"
are contrasted with "thinkers". Partisans on one side insist that
the function of the faculty is to motivate and inspire, not merely
to educate. They worry lest students grow "sicklied o'er with
the pale cast of thought." Their opponents correlate promotion
to the grade of general officer with early prowess in differential calculus. The width of the gap should not be exaggerated
since earnest efforts are made to bridge it from both sides, but
it is never wholly closed. It becomes a matter of consequence
when, as at the Air Force Academy in the mid-1960's, proposals
are advanced to make the Dean, not the Commandant, next in line
to the Superintendent, or to transfer certain subjects of instruction from the Commandant (or from the Director of Athletics) to
the Dean.[28]

Each of the parties to the dialogue has external allies.
Commandants, especially at West Point and Annapolis, derive support from senior officers who are out with the fighting fleet or
the field armies, and from those retired officers who are concerned
that professional military training remain tough and realistic.[29]

A striking case of external intervention was a wide ranging
inquiry led by Representative F. Edward Hebert (D., La.) of the
House Armed Services Committee in 1967-68. As Hebert said
candidly:

"The reason this committee sits is becuase of information
that has come to us which indicated, particularly in the
area of the Air Force Academy, it was concentrating on
academics and subordinating military training."[30]

In the course of the hearing Representative Hebert expressed
satisfaction that the Naval Academy, in his words, was moving

from "the academic left" to the "professional right"; he recommended that academic deans, who had customarily served until
retirement, be limited to four-year renewable terms; he worried
that curricular studies were being made by men concerned more with
academic content than with military training; he endorsed the
rigors of the "plebe system"; and he fought to bring academy football teams to the Sugar Bowl and comparable shrines.

Supporters of the academic program also have powerful external allies. Sometimes an individual intervenes, the most notable
example is probably Admiral Rickover. Beginning in 1959, Rickover's acidulous criticism influenced key members of Congress as
well as civilian appointees in the Navy Department. Annapolis
graduates, he argued, were two years behind graduates of good
engineering schools. He called for "a sharp change in the
objectives and the curriculum of the Naval Academy", with purely
military features deferred until one year after graduation.
Other targets were anti-intellectualism, "juvenile" hazing, the
suppression of individuality, the use of deprecatory nicknames
for the social science and humanities departments ("Bull," Dago"),
overemphasis on routine at the expense of independent thought,
on practical skill at the expense of liberal arts, and on descrip-
tive engineering--detailed facts about particular valves, pumps,
and circuits--at the expense of basic theory. He also urged the
appointment of a civilian dean.[31]

In other cases support for the academic program comes from
external Boards of Visitors established by law or from ad hoc
or standing advisory committees appointed by superintendents.[32]
But the process of influence is more subtle than it appears. Such
bodies may serve to endorse changes already planned, or to give
superintendents courage to defy opposition within their institutions. Occasionally, the mere process of preparing for the visit
of an external group prompts a self-examination which leads to
academic change.

Certain additional forces help to prevent undue subordination
of intellectual pursuits to athletics, military training, or

character-building activities. Entering students are more demanding, partly because high schools are improving, partly because
service academy admissions procedures are more rigorous. The
Superintendent of the Air Force Academy stated that the most
important reason for the introduction of academic majors and M.A.
programs was to provide an incentive for better students. Faculty
members are also increasingly demanding. In the case of military
faculty, inadequate educational standards lead more quickly to
low morale; in the case of civilian faculty, resignation. A third
potent force is service rivalry. The intensely competitive staffs
of the academies are highly sensitive to each other's standing.
Information is exchanged at many levels and innovations can pass
from one institution to another at stunning speed.

Also important is the growing trend to graduate study. Most
of today's service academy students eventually will earn an
advanced degree; and while in the past graduate work was rarely
started until mid-career, beginning with the Air Force Academy in
1963 each institution now places top students in Master's programs
shortly after graduation.[33] Of the midshipmen who completed Annapolis in 1968, about one hundred proceeded directly to such
universities as Berkeley, Cal Tech., Columbia, M.I.T., Michigan,
North Carolina, Princeton, and Stanford. Of the Air Force Academy
Class of 1969, one hundred and twenty--including 90 per cent of
the top tenth of the class--went to graduate school. The career
plan for Army officers is such that fewer West Pointers begin
advanced study immediately, but 75 per cent will eventually proceed to the Master's level or higher.

The armed forces would clearly find it intolerable if the
bulk of these students flunked out. Yet they are rarely able to
provide preliminary remedial work, because this would increase the
cost of the enterprise and prolong the student's absence from the
mainstream of his service career, thereby damaging his promotion
prospects. Inevitably, therefore, the academies feel obliged to
offer an undergraduate program which will enable their men to

compete with civilian graduate students, an endeavor in which
they seem to have been reasonably successful.

One indicator of the prevailing ethos at the academies is that
commandants, whose staffs in times past were citadels of anti-
intellectualism, are now assigning prospective "company officers"
to graduate school to study behavioral science, either because
they feel they must dangle such bait to attract quality men (who
will often be in demand by academic departments as well) or out
of a growing conviction that good training officers need a
knowledge of human relations, testing, counseling, and the like.
Another sign of the times is the response of seadogs at Annapolis
to the discovery that midshipmen were slighting professional
courses and summer cruise requirements because performance in
these areas was inadequately weighted in the computation of class
standings. The remedy adopted was to increase the rigor, intellectual respectability, and weight of such work.[34] Thus naval
science itself becomes more of an academic subject.

THE LIBERALIZATION OF CURRICULA

The service academies continue outrageously to overschedule
the time of their students. They require from 15 to 20 per cent
more credit hours than civilian universities, and they pile time-
consuming administrative chores on top of athletics, professional
training, and their mixed engineering--liberal arts curricula.
Voices have often been raised in protest. But efforts to raise
educational standards have simply increased the pressure to add
new material to already jampacked programs. How else to give due
attention to orbital mechanics, systems analysis, modern Africa,
mathematical logic, oceanography, family relations, communications
theory, ethnology, computer science, international organization,
space vehicle design, music, microbiology, advanced Chinese,
industrial psychology and unconventional war?

One response was to reduce the time devoted to military training during the academic year. Another was unofficially to lower
the academic bars. In the mid-1960's, the Naval Academy helped
harassed students by limiting the number who could be given "D's"

or "E's", and by allowing students who flunked to take a second examination. The first practise was particularly objectionable to some of the new civilian Ph.D.'s who had just been recruited to improve the academic program; a minor scandal ensued. A third response was "system beating" behavior by students themselves. Some upperclassmen were content to coast or, as they put it, "to ride the curve." Others, numbed or bored, took to sleeping in class. Still others tried cheating. In 1951, well before the high tide of curricular modernization, ninety cadets were dismissed from West Point for cheating. More than one hundred were dismissed from the Air Force Academy in 1965 in another cheating incident. In each case about two-fifths were varsity football players or other recruited athletes who had to carry a heavy schedule of intercollegiate contests in addition to other requirements. In its official report on the Air Force scandal, the investigating committee rejected the hypothesis that the academy's program made "excessive demands."[35] If the committee intended only to attribute this particular breech of honor to another cause, it may have been correct. If it was attempting to deny that the demands were excessive, it could not have been more wrong. Programs at all three academies make excessive demands on students.

But the most significant response to burdensome and unmanageable curricula were the historic decisions of each institution to modify the traditional policy of a common course of study. To be sure, each continues to prescribe certain subjects. But it now permits students to choose among individual electives and "major" fields of study or "areas" of concentration. This departure from the lock-step system has been dictated by a need to come to grips with the new techno-social environment without demoralizing the young.

It is unwise to attempt to be precise at this point because detailed arrangements change almost annually. The Naval Academy now offers majors in about two dozen fields, e.g., marine engineering, economics, chemistry, and Far Eastern studies. It also offers

the option of two degrees--the Bachelor of Science in Engineering
or the straight Bachelor of Science. The Air Force Academy offers
a slightly larger number of majors, each requiring a somewhat
larger number of courses. The Military Academy has been a trifle
more circumspect. Its alumni continue to favor a generalized
program with stress on mathematics, science, and engineering. It
is also possible, though less certain, that the prospect of
curricular specialization reactivates fear of a divided army.[36]
West Point now offers four areas of concentration--applied science
and engineering, basic science, humanities, and national security
and public affairs. These are divided into 22 "fields". Students
who prefer not to choose any area or field may forego a concentration and select any elective courses whatsoever. A quota
system is used to ensure that no more than 10 per cent of the
cadets will concentrate in the humanities, and no more than 35 per
cent in any other area.

These changes have been accompanied by a great increase in the
number of courses offered. The result is that curricula resemble
those of civilian colleges more than before. So do instructional
methods. Of course, each academy still emphasizes small sections
rather than large lectures. Moreover, prepackaged materials, textbooks, recitations and tests are still more in evidence than at
the strongest civilian institutions. But the use of paperback
books is growing, and there is a trend to fewer and more comprehensive examinations, seminar work, independent research and honors
programs. The Trident Program, adopted by Annapolis in 1963,
enables a few midshipmen to be excused from most senior year courses
in order to undertake a major research project, usually in science
or engineering.

Finally, the departmental structure of the academies, which
has implications for the distribution of power and therefore for
the direction of change, is coming to resemble that of civilian
institutions more closely. It is true that West Point and Annapolis, as recently as 1969, tucked away work in philosophy, music
and art among their offerings in literature.[37] But West Point has

now divorced chemistry from physics, and history from the other
social sciences. Even that giant conglomerate, the Department of
History, English and Government at Annapolis, has now been divided
into two departments.[38]

The existence of more highly differentiated departments
offering more varied and advanced courses has led to so-called
cooperative M.A. programs, first at the Air Force Academy, then
at the Naval Academy. Selected civilian universities are asked
to grant credit toward their Masters' degrees for advanced work
taken at an academy. This can enable some students to complete
the requirements for an M.A. with less than one year in residence
at the civilian institution, especially if it has no thesis
requirement. Not all observers, needless to say, are equally
enthusiastic about such arrangements.

Vying for institutional recognition in the normal American
manner, academy officials frequently debate which school has the
best balanced program and which is the most innovative. In the
past the Naval Academy took pride in its strong emphasis on
science and engineering. As a 1967 study said, "The Navy is
committed to a technological environment . . . This is not a
State Department-sponsored institution."[39]   The Air Force
Academy, on the other hand, has long taken pride in its emphasis
on the social sciences and humanities. Officials there are also
quick to assert that they started earlier and went further in such
matters as electives, majors, number of offerings,[40] number of
specialized departments, graduate credit courses, and the relega-
tion of military training and athletics to a minor place in the
program.

There is no doubt that the Air Force Academy gained from the
lighter hand of tradition. It gained also from the career structure of its service, which permits more specialization. But in
fairness it must be noted that the initial staff of the Air Force
Academy drew heavily upon West Pointers who had discussed these
matters at length; that the Superintendent of the Naval Academy
had requested a study of electives in 1953; and that in a contest

for priority, the palm should probably go to the Royal Military
College of Canada, which had introduced a split curriculum before
World War II. To the detached observer there is enough glory
here for all. It is more important to observe: (1) that liberalization of curricula was an understandable response to problems
shared by all three institutions; (2) that it evolved from long-
standing practices, such as the offering of honors sections in
which abler students passed quickly to topics not included in
standard sections, thereby acquiring de facto or covert electives; and (3) that once the lock-step was broken, the incentive
to innovate increased because departments began to compete for
customers, while resistance to innovation diminished because a
free market of student choice began to supplement the grimly con-
tested allocation of a finite quantity of time by committees of
zealous department heads. At the Air Force Academy, where program flexibility is greatest, one official stated: "It is not
much harder to get a new major approved today than it was to get
a new course approved yesterday." This surely is an exaggeration,
but it makes the point.

PROFESSIONALIZATION OF THE FACULTY

The premium placed on ability to cope with the large techno-
social environment is also reflected in the professionalization
of teaching staffs. Here, too, it is possible to see a growing
convergence between military and civilian education at the undergraduate level. Generalists are being replaced by specialists
better equipped to deal with the new curricula. Although the
process is incomplete its direction is clear; greater insistence
on graduate work prior to appointment; more opportunity to enhance
competence while on the job; and a demand for prerogatives
enjoyed by faculty members at civilian institutions.

The Military and Air Force Academies rely almost wholly on
military instructors. The Naval Academy staff is divided almost
evenly between civilian and military instructors, and for this
reason will be discussed separately.

Department heads at the Military and Air Force Academies keep files on promising junior officers, usually alumni, whom they may eventually wish to add to their staffs. Prior to assignment to an academy such officers are normally sent to civilian universities for graduate work. In selecting those universities, the academies draw on institutions scattered throughout America. There is some emphasis, however, on more prestigious universities. In a typical recent year, for example, out of fifty-four degree holders in West Point's Social Sciences Department, nine had done their work at Harvard, eight at Oxford, six at Columbia, and three each at Stanford and Princeton. To be sure, the degrees are more likely to be M.A.'s than Ph.D's. Washington is not quickly persuaded that military instructors must complete a doctoral dissertation when it is likely that they will spend only a few years in academic life, and when their work appears to require teaching rather than research prowess. Nevertheless, the proportion of doctorates at the Air Force Academy is now 28 per cent, and while it is only 11 per cent at West Point, it has risen rapidly in the last decade and is likely to continue in this direction. Like other institutions not wholly secure about their educational status, the academies count degrees carefully.

Officer instructors are usually assigned for three or four years. Some, however, serve longer, and the number is growing. Most departments at West Point and the Air Force Academy have one or two "permanent professors" whose positions are authorized by Congress and who have tenure until they complete thirty years of commissioned service or until the age of sixty-four, whichever comes later. Congress has now also authorized West Point and the Air Force Academy to appoint a maximum of ten per cent of their faculties as "tenure associate professors." The latter hold five-year appointments which are renewable for the duration of their service careers.

The Naval Academy has no nucleus of permanent officer instructors. Moreover, its transient officer instructors rotate more rapidly than their counterparts at the other schools. Since World War II, department heads have served for an average of about two

years. Annapolis also suffers from the lack of an organized program to provide officers with graduate training before they teach.
Naval officers' land tours are short, and promotion boards are
likely to pass over officers who have spent four or five years in
a combination of graduate study and teaching billets. In response
the Navy contends that continuity and expertise can be provided
by a layer of civilian instructors, and in 1962 the Secretary of
the Navy went so far as to imply that all departments, except
those which dealt with naval science, would eventually be manned
almost wholly by civilians. Although this did not materialize
(there was, indeed, serious opposition from naval officers), the
number of civilians rose 30 per cent in the next five years.

The proportion of civilians, however, is an imperfect indicator of professionalism. In fact, in some departments greater
professionalism obviously awaits the retirement of civilians; for
while close study of the staff reveals many dedicated, and some
truly eminent, senior scholars, it also reveals a large number
who spent an inordinate amount of time at lesser institutions and,
more disturbingly, many who are simply old.[41]

A better indicator of professionalism is interest in research
and one of the most striking changes at the academies in the past
fifteen years is the current emphasis on research. West Point has
created an Academic Board Research Advisory Committee and is
authorized to appoint twelve officers to basic research positions
each year. In addition it has established a Science Research
Laboratory. The Naval Academy has a Research Council and a program of sabbatical leaves. Its Engineering Department includes a
group of young motivated instructors who busily sponsor symposia,
encourage midshipmen to undertake professional activities, and
clearly benefit from access to research funds and Federal laboratories. The Air Force Academy has an assistant dean for research
and its own research fund. In coming years it plans to have one
out of every twenty instructors on full-time research status. At
present it has about eighty officers and over one hundred cadets
in funded research or consulting projects. Military instructors

at all academies also go afield in summers, usually to work on
service-connected high pay-off projects relating to supply, organization, personnel, weapons or tactics.

As faculty members develop their academic expertise, they
simultaneously develop keener interest in professional prerogatives, liberties and amenities. Here they confront the fact that
the service academies are not only educational institutions but
Federal installations, and military ones at that. Civilians at
the Naval Academy are especially likely to be aware of this fact.
As civil servants they accrue annual and sick leave at specified
rates, and they are subject to performance ratings by their
superiors. As members of a military community they are expected
to wear coats and ties in class and to participate in traditional
social activities. Requests for sabbatical leave must be approved
by the Chief of Naval Operations. When they engage in research
and are in doubt concerning the appropriateness of scholarly
conclusions which are critical of current American policy, they
are expected to submit them to higher authority before publishing.[42]

Inevitably, there is tension between the professional drive
for autonomy and the military tradition of centralized command.
In 1966, for example, some recently hired civilian Ph.D.'s at
Annapolis concluded that their superior officers were trying to
tell them how to grade examinations. In the wake of this incident
a new chapter of the American Association of University Professors
was born in Maryland.[43] There have also been complaints of undue
centralization of power at the Air Force Academy in past years.
Some appear to have been directed at the Dean in his relationships with departments, e.g., in the matter of faculty appointments. Others were directed at department heads who allegedly
allowed instructors too little discretion in the design of course
syllibi or the actual conduct of class.[44]

The demand for autonomy implicit in the idea of having
"one's own department" or "one's own class", will no doubt grow at
the academies. So will interest in better office space, more
secretarial staff, sabbatical leaves, opportunity to establish

closer relationships with students, a larger voice in the determination of educational policy, and that hardiest of all peren-
nials, lighter teaching loads. One or another academy already
has a committee on faculty affairs, a faculty forum, a faculty
council, even a faculty junior council. It is safe to predict
that professional aspirations will be aired in such places with
increasing vigor.

STUDENT BEHAVIOR

A parallel to change in the status of faculty is change in
the rigorous regimen formerly imposed on students. Substantial
changes have been made in the system which horrified a visiting
German parliamentarian in the early 1950's--because it struck him
as too Prussian! These changes have been prompted by a realization that it is going to be harder to attract and hold the customer
unless his rights and privileges are liberalized.

Over the "Battle Ramp" leading from the cadet area to the
parade field at the Air Force Academy is the inscription, "Give
Me Men." During the latter half of the 1960's the academies had
cause for concern whether this plea would be sufficiently heeded.
While there has been an upswing subsequently, in February 1969 an
evaluation team at West Point reported a decided decline in
admissions applications.[45] From 1965 to 1968, discussions between
the Superintendent of the Naval Academy and his Board of Visitors
were regularly marked by expressions of anxiety over the volume
of qualified candidates; this was during a period when other major
colleges and universities were deluged. The Air Force Academy
continued to have somewhat more pulling power than its two sister
institutions. One statistic cited to me by authorities was that
it stood sixth on a list of the most desirable institutions in
America in a ranking made by 140,000 male high school students of
high intellectual ability.[46] But while formerly very few appli-
cants declined offers of admission, and then largely to enter such
universities as Stanford, Yale, or MIT, by 1969 the declination
rate had risen significantly, and many withdrew in order to attend
substantial but not especially renowned institutions.

Given the nature of American society, the absence of a post-feudal nobility, and the lure of material values, military life has long been relatively unattractive. Indeed, there is little doubt in my mind that the greatest achievement of the academies, now as in past years, has been their ability to develop a reasonably firm career commitment in a reasonably large number of young men who do not originally have such a commitment. One motive for entering an academy, important in the past, has been weakened by the greater affluence of families and the readier availability of scholarships, including ROTC scholarships, at civilian institutions. Moreover, today's high school students are more demanding, more sensitive to the special characteristics of institutions, more likely to "shop around." Some dislike engineering. Others prefer what one officer called "the California syndrome"--surfing, foreign cars, girls. Many, reared in permissive homes, recoil from what they term "Mickey Mouse" regulations and procedures. Then there is the Vietnam war and the rising antimilitarism of youth.[47] And for wholly unrelated reasons, this time of troubles has coincided with a doubling of the number of spaces the academies must fill to complete expansions planned long ago.

Needless to say, energetic efforts are made to reach prospective candidates. In 1968-69, 615 West Point cadets visited 2,142 high schools to talk with guidance officers and students. During Christmas vacation hundreds of midshipmen go on similar missions. If the Air Force Academy has a football game in Texas, cadets born in the Dallas area are almost certain to speak at Dallas high schools before the game. Recruiting films are carefully designed to portray athletics, dating, the free exchange of views on a controversial issue in class, a car at graduation, folksinging. One academy has some two dozen members on its public relations staff. But in a larger sense everything that is done is now done with an eye to the potential applicant. In the words of one Superintendent, "We have to make this place attractive. We have to be able to tell a young man that he can major in a particular branch of engineering if that is what he wants."

Recruitment difficulties are compounded by attrition during the four-year course. This is a long standing problem; one-third of an entering class may fail to graduate. To be sure, average attrition rates are lower than this, and they have been fairly stable of late, but the stability has concealed disturbing changes in the causes of separations and withdrawals. Formerly the major reasons were academic, now they are motivational.[48]

Understandably, attrition is greatest in the first year.[49] It is during the initial period of adjustment that the student is most distressed by the tempo at which a dizzying number of requirements must be met; by the rituals exacted by upperclassmen; by the compulsion to support the team loudly; by inability to cut classes; by daily room inspection; by tabus against unkempt hair or clothing when personal sloppiness is in high fashion; and by compulsory chapel when contemporaries proclaim that "God is dead." All these shocks are experienced by young men whose initial decision to apply to an academy, if admission officials are correct, is more tentative than their predecessors' ("I'll try it and see if I like it"), and whose parents are no longer so insistent that their sons stick it out.

External critics have encouraged the academies to review their first year systems. In 1963, the Air Force Academy's Board of Visitors criticized the "unproductive harassment" of new students and suggested they be granted Christmas leave. A few years later the Under Secretary of the Navy requested a general review of the first year at Annapolis. All academies now discourage sanctions in the form of corporal punishment, denial of food, or humiliation. Students still face special requirements, but the word has gone out that these are to be somewhat more meaningful, businesslike, and "career relevant." Privileges are related more closely to performance, rewards are substituted for threats. The trials of "Beast Barracks" are now history.

The sensibilities of upperclassmen are also considered more carefully. Reveille comes a bit later at West Point these days; Air Force cadets get a slice of unscheduled time in the evening.

One academy or another now permits students to wear civilian
clothes, drink alcoholic beverages,[50] or drive their own car
under carefully defined circumstances. All academies, moreover,
have begun to be more attentive to student opinion in the formation of educational policy. All are more generous with leave,
including long weekends. Each supports a flourishing program
of extracurricular activities, the most popular of which seem to
be those which enable students to leave the reservation.

The limits of the new permissiveness have been tested by a
number of bearers of the contemporary youth culture who have
secured appointments. At one academy an observer devised a tri-
partite typology of students which, though incomplete and sim-
plistic, is nevertheless suggestive. The first category consists
of "engineers." Less people-minded than thing-minded, they
accept the system phlegmatically. The second consists of "Eagle
Scouts" who accept the system enthusiastically. With positive
attitudes toward a military career, they identify strongly with
the academy, viewing it as "an island of purity in a sea of
"corruption." The third consists of "mods" and rebels. Though
a distinct minority and required to behave circumspectly, this
latter element undoubtedly exists. Each of the academies has had
an occasional incident involving marijuana. Among students
implicated in a cheating scandal at the Air Force Academy in 1967
were some who referred to themselves as "the cool group" and who,
like counterparts elsewhere, sought to distinguish themselves by
their taste in music and their preference for ragged clothes and
long hair.[51]

Aware of how potentially explosive even small incidents can
become, authorities at each academy watch these phenomena with
some foreboding. One summarized his own sense of current institutional priorities by pointing toward the dormitories rather
than the classrooms and stating tersely, "Our biggest problem is
over there."

THE PROCESS AND LIMITS OF CONVERGENCE

My argument has been that the service academies have become
more, not less, like civilian institutions. Convergence, not
divergence, is its main theme, although caution prompts the qualification that this is a generalization about the past two decades
rather than an assumption about the future.[52] Among the unobtru-
sive forces for convergence have been junior faculty members.
Fresh from major universities where, as one put it, "You spend
two years in a dorm with eighty 'gung ho' graduate students,"
they have been extremely sensitive to intellectual trends. A few
years ago they focused on emerging nations; today they are interested in urban violence, poverty, student unrest and race relations. They, and more senior faculty members as well, have
interacted with the faculty of civilian institutions at a growing
number of professional meetings. These have included not only
large, splashy conferences held at the academies themselves[53]
but a great variety of lectures, seminars, and smaller conferences sponsored by their increasingly professional departments.

To be sure, there have been service nuances. But at all
three academies curricular changes have enhanced the influence
of the specialist, sometimes in ways not wholly anticipated. The
advent of electives and majors, for example, has increased the
odds that a given student will take two or more courses with the
same instructor, or that he will come to meet a faculty member as
a research supervisor or departmental advisor. Thus are generated master-apprentice relationships based on shared intellectual
interests.

The growth of extreme ideological positions may also have
been inhibited by sensitivity to standards and practices accepted
by fellow specialists in the larger world. Certainly one cannot
detect any systematic effort to indoctrinate students in controversial political, economic or social issues. Indeed, the
academies have occasionally invited speakers with whose views
they may strongly disagree. The keynote address at a recent West
Point conference was given by a man who condemned the Secretary

of State's conduct of foreign affairs, castigated the regime in
Saigon, doubted that the Soviet invasion of Czechoslovakia posed
a threat to NATO, and described the government of Haiti as "much
worse than any Communist government could possibly be."[54] But at
the official level the academies have projected what can only be
described as an official view--a conventional, if not actually
bland, Establishment perspective. In domestic policy this has
been reflected in the reassurance quickly given to a Congressman
who inquired whether an academy taught any "radical new social
concepts."[55] In foreign policy it has been reflected in the
galaxy of figures who have attended West Point's SCUSA conferences since 1949. The names of Acheson, Dulles, Harriman, Nitze,
Rockefeller and Rusk are supplemented by those of highly senior
officers, academicians and foundation officials.

The possibility that students have been affected by such an
avalanche of moderation is at least consistent with Lovell's findings on differences between men in their first and last years at
West Point. Fewer graduating students believed in the inevita-
bility of all-out war; fewer believed that Korea illustrated a
communist intent to dominate the world; and fewer thought that
neutralism was a result of lack of moral fibre. More broadly, a
shift occurred during the four years from "absolutist" to "prag-
matic" strategic perspectives.[56]

Lovell has also reported a shift from "heroic" to "managerial" orientations. If the Air Force Academy's position is
representative, all institutions now officially encourage such a
shift. A draft of its 15-Year Plan, January 7, 1970, states:

"The combat-model leadership in which a quality
example is offered and unhesitating, unquestioning obedience is demanded, will become more and
more rare. Effective leadership will be increasingly predicated upon respect for job knowledge
and competence accompanied by the ability to
offer sound, rational reasons for the course of
action required. The enlistment of voluntary,
eager cooperation will be the mark of the leader

> of the future, rather than the use of fear as a
> goad to performance. The soldiers and airmen of
> the future will be more highly educated, more
> questioning, and more suspicious of authority than
> in the past."

Finally, recent research at the Air Force Academy reports a com-
plementary shift from "concrete" to "abstract" intellectual and
emotional orientations. The former are identified with extreme
and polarized value judgments, greater dependence on status and
formal authority, greater intolerance of ambiguity, and more
reliance on stereotypes. The latter are identified with less
pessimism, dogmatism, and moral absolutism.[57]

It would be imprudent to speak too confidently about what all
this portends for the impact of future military leaders on
national policy. I have argued that many forces within the
academies have operated to soften the differences between them
and civilian educational institutions. Yet, as noted at the outset, the academies draw a special cross-section of American youth
and the distinctiveness of this cross-section may well increase
in the near future. In 1970, some academies reported an increase
in applications. It is reasonable to assume that a number of
students applied to them because they were troubled by the
unsettled conditions at so many civilian universities; 41 per cent
of West Point's Class of 1973 testified that campus unrest had
been a factor influencing their desire to pursue a military
career.[58] Parents, too, are likely to be influenced by this
factor, especially by the uncertain future of ROTC at other institutions; and studies reveal that West Point entrants discuss
career plans with parents more than do civilian students.

Since it is most unlikely that the average high school senior
is more interested in military service today than he was a year or
two ago, the conclusion seems unavoidable that the young men who
choose to enter a service academy at this time have a special
capacity to be undaunted by the prevailing surge of anti-militarism
among their contemporaries. This capacity is likely to be still
more evident in academy students who survive the scowls or jibes

they may receive from the same contemporaries when they are home
on leave.

If differences in their respective raw materials limit the
likelihood that military and civilian schools will produce men of
identical outlook, other factors external to the service academies
limit the degree to which graduates of one are likely to possess
the same values or interests as graduates of another. To state
this proposition is to raise the issue of convergence vs. divergence not as it relates to civil-military but to inter-service
relationships, and to inquire what impact, if any, a service
academy education has on those relationships.

Once more, one can only speculate. It seems sensible to
begin by recalling that dedication to the combat virtues exemplified by classical heroes is particularly strong among senior
commanders. The ethos of such commanders continues to be
extremely influential in the decisions of promotion boards. As
graduation approaches, the upward-mobile academy student grows
increasingly aware of this fact of life and increasingly interested in choosing a line or combat specialty associated with "the
charismatic leaders whose exploits liven the annals of military
history."[59] Such choice is frequently a cause, as well as a consequence, or relatively strong identification with a particular
military service; for its combat specialties are close to the
vital heart of each service, and those who practice them are
especially likely to feel that they are useful and respected
members of their respective establishments.

To the extent that service pride may be transformed into
service bias, it now becomes relevant to observe that the academies
have not significantly inhibited the formation of such bias or,
to put it the other way around, that they have not laid a very
strong foundation for interservice collaboration. Shortly after
World War II, there was much bold talk about merging the institutions, but little has come of it except some exchanges of
instructors and students supplemented by periodic conferences at
the command and supporting staff levels. With the physical con-

struction of the Air Force Academy and the expansion of the other two, the separation of the institutions has quite literally been set in concrete.

This is not to say that blind loyalty to service is nourished on the playing field or in the classroom, or even that it is on the increase. Service rivalry results from technological change, financial pressures, and the management philosophies and temperaments of ranking civilian and military leaders. But if it continues to be generated by such forces, little that happens at the service academies is likely to alleviate it. To the contrary, the organizational skills and commitments which students acquire there --and the resourcefulness and solidarity which they come to develop--are likely to make them formidable advocates of the institutional interests of their services in tomorrow's bureaucratic politics. With this important reservation, the impact of the service academies on American life is likely to depend less on their own acts of omission and commission than on the kind of young men who decide to apply to them in the future.

NOTES

Acknowledgment is made to Twentieth Century Fund and Harper & Row for permission to use data from Adam Yarmolinsky, The Military Establishment: Its Impact on American Society. Copyright 1971 by the Twentieth Century Fund, New York. Published by Harper & Row.

[1] Report of the President's Commission on an All-Volunteer Armed Force (Washington: Government Printing Office, 1970), p. 72. The Navy drew 6 per cent of its officers from service academies, the Air Force 3.5 per cent, the Army 1.9 per cent.

[2] "Between 80 and 90 per cent of service academy graduates can be expected to remain in the service upon completion of their obligated tour of active duty (now 5 years), as opposed to less than 50 per cent for ROTC scholarship graduates and under 25 per cent for OCS graduates." Ibid., p. 77.

[3] Cf. John P. Lovell, The Cadet Phase of the Professional Socialization of the West Pointer, University of Wisconsin doctoral dissertation, 1962. See also Morris Janowitz, The New Military (New York: Russell Sage Foundation, 1964), p. 21. It is true, of

course, that what goes on there has a great bearing on self-selection.

[4]Walter E. Hecox, A Comparison of New Cadets at USMA with Entering Freshmen at Other Colleges, Class of 1973 (West Point, New York: Office of Research, United States Military Academy, 1970), p. 7. The comparable figures were 37 per cent for four-year liberal arts colleges, 41 per cent for technical institutes, 41 per cent for colleges forming part of public universities, and 54 per cent for those forming part of private universities.

[5]Ibid., p. 10.

[6]Ibid., p. 3.

[7]In 1969-70, the cadet wing at the Air Force Academy included 64 Negroes, 26 Orientals, 31 American Indians, and 26 Spanish-Americans.

[8]Administration of the Service Academies, Report and Hearings of the Special Subcommittee on Service Academies of the House Armed Services Committee, 90th Congress, First and Second Sessions, 1967-68, p. 10384. Hereinafter cited as Hebert Hearings.

[9]Hecox, p. 19.

[10]Arthur E. Wise, A Comparison of New Cadets at USMA with Entering Freshmen at Other Colleges (West Point, New York: Office of Research, United States Military Academy, 1969).

[11]Lovell, p. 96.

[12]Hecox, p. 31.

[13]Gary Spencer, A Social-Psychological Profile of the Class of 1973, USMA (West Point, New York: United States Military Academy, 1969), pp. 5-6.

[14]Lovell, pp. 96-98.

[15]Data in the preceding two paragraphs are taken from Hecox, pp. 20-33.

[16]Lovell, pp. 155-160.

[17]Dean E. Mann, The Assistant Secretaries (Washington, D.C.: The Brookings Institution, 1965), p. 291.

[18]David Stanley, Dean E. Mann, and Jameson Doig, Men Who Govern (Washington, D.C.: The Brookings Institution, 1967), p. 20. The closest comparison, and it is not wholly satisfactory, is that 2.2 per cent of the West Point Class of 1973 came from private

secondary schools which were neither military nor denominational. John W. Houston et al, Characteristics of the Class of 1973 (West Point, New York: United States Military Academy, 1969), p. 5.

[19]Stanley, Mann, and Doig, p. 14.

[20]Hecox, p. 5. Data on the geographical origins of FSO's are from John E. Harr, The Professional Diplomat (Princeton, New Jersey: Princeton University Press, 1969), pp. 174-193.

[21]Ibid.

[22]Ibid., p. 183. The proportion of mature officers describing themselves as "moderately liberal" or "liberal" ranged from one-fourth in the Navy to one-third in the Air Force.

[23]But the question is being studied seriously. See, e.g., Gilbert R. Kaats, "Development Changes in Belief Systems During a Service Academy Education," Proceedings of the 77th Annual Convention of the American Psychological Association, 1969, p. 651.

[24]Morris Janowitz, The Professional Soldier (Glencoe, Illinois: The Free Press, 1960).

[25]Because rank is regarded as important in this regard, some observers thought the fundamental character of the Naval Academy might be changed when, in 1960, its mission was restated to omit specific reference to the preparation of junior officers.

[26]The phrase is Corelli Barnett's, and the material that follows immediately is taken from his stimulating essay, "The Education of Military Elites," in Rupert Wilkinson, ed., Governing Elites (New York: Oxford University Press, 1969), pp. 195-96.

[27]Five-Year Plan for the United States Air Force Academy, Headquarters, United States Air Force Academy, May 1968, pp. 7-8. The 1969 draft plan restated this dilemma: "Cadets learn that their effectiveness as leaders is enhanced to the degree that a rational justification for their decisions is communicated to their subordinates. But they also learn that loyalty and respect for authority are crucial in military organizations, and that ungrudging compliance with disagreeable directives marks the truly professional officer."

[28]For interesting parallels, see Richard A. Preston, Canada's RMC (Toronto: University of Toronto Press, 1969).

[29]Whenever a prestigious service school has an attractive location, a number of senior officers retire in the vicinity so that they may enjoy its amenities and continue to keep in touch. In

1969, nearly three dozen retired flag rank officers of all services lived near the Air Force Academy; six were four-star
generals of the Air Force.

[30] *Hebert Hearings*, p. 10892.

[31] Vice Admiral Hyman B. Rickover, *Report on Russia*, Hearings
before the Committee on Appropriations, House of Representatives,
86th Congress, 1st Session, August 18, 1959.

[32] The report of the 1959 board at Annapolis included an
unusual minority statement by its senatorial members some of whom
had been in contact with Admiral Rickover. They recommended
optional courses for brighter students, more civilian instructors,
including exchange professors, and the transfer of practical drill
to summer. *Ibid.*, p. 72.

[33] By allowing students graduate credit for advanced courses
in its own curriculum, the Air Force Academy enabled them to earn
an M.A. at selected universities in less than one year. This plan
was a compromise after earlier plans to authorize the academy to
give its own M.A. were opposed by its Board of Visitors, the
Defense Department, and the American Council on Education.

[34] *Report of the Professional Training and Education Committee*,
United States Naval Academy, November 20, 1967.

[35] Special Advisory Committee on the United States Air Force
Academy, *Report to the Secretary and the Chief of Staff of the Air
Force*, Washington, D.C., May 5, 1965, p. 90. Hereinafter cited as
White Committee Report.

[36] Turn-of-the-century struggles to establish the authority of
a chief of staff still linger in the collective unconscious of the
Army officer corps.

[37] The Air Force Academy has a separate Department of Philosophy and Fine Arts.

[38] West Point separated history from English in 1926, while
history, political science, economics and English have always been
separate departments at the Air Force Academy..

[39] *Report of the Professional Training and Education Committee.*

[40] In subjects such as psychology, sociology, and anthropology,
the Air Force Academy in 1969 had about three times as many courses
as the Military Academy.

[41] In 1967-68, the average age of full professors in Mathematics and Foreign Languages was 58; only one professor in each
department was under 50.

[42] Faculty Handbook (Annapolis, Maryland: United States Naval Academy, undated) 2nd ed., pp. 24-33.

[43] J. Arthur Heise, The Brass Factories (Washington, D.C.: Public Affairs Press, 1969), pp. 114-120.

[44] See White Committee Report, pp. 31-32; Heise, Chapter 3; Hebert Hearings, passim.

[45] Middle States Commission on Institutions of Higher Education, Report to the Superintendent, the Academic Board, the Faculty and the Board of Visitors by an Evaluation Team, West Point, New York, p. 6.

[46] The first five, in order, were said to be California Institute of Technology, Massachusetts Institute of Technology, Rice, Stanford, Harvard.

[47] For a frank recognition of such rising anti-militarism, see Report of the Board of Visitors, United States Military Academy, May 5, 1969, p. 5.

[48] On the drop in the academic flunk-out rate between 1958 and 1968, see Hebert Hearings, p. 10311. No doubt students and instructors grew better during the decade, but officials may also have decided they could not let academic attrition continue at the old rate in view of rising motivational attrition.

[49] Recent West Point figures were 11 per cent in plebe summer; 7-9 per cent more in the remainder of the first year; and an additional 10 per cent in the last three years. The Air Force Academy has reported a total of 25 per cent for the four years.

[50] Maryland statutes make it unlawful to give or sell alcoholic beverages to midshipmen within five miles of Annapolis.

[51] Hebert Hearings, pp. 10909-13.

[52] Cf. Charles C. Moskos, Jr., The American Enlisted Man (New York: Russell Sage Foundation, 1970). Moskos concludes that while the culture of the officer corps, especially in the Air Force, may be converging with civilian culture, that of the enlisted man is diverging. Moreover, he implies that for the military establishment as a whole, the process of convergence has passed its peak. Op. cit., p. 38; 170.

[53] E.G., West Point's Student Conference on United States Affairs, the Air Force Academy's Assembly, and the Naval Academy's Foreign Affairs Conference.

[54] Proceedings of the Twentieth Annual Student Conference on United States Affairs, United States Military Academy, December 4-7, 1968. The speaker was Bill D. Moyers. Delegates included 216 students from 89 universities.

[55] Hebert Hearings, p. 10582.

[56] Op. cit., pp. 149-162. See also the summary in John P. Lovell, "The Professional Socialization of West Point Cadets," in Janowitz, The New Military, pp. 119-157. "Absolutists" believe communists are intent on world conquest, nuclear war is likely, massive retaliation is the best policy, neutrals are unreliable, if not potentially hostile. "Pragmatists" believe the communists are expansionist, some kinds of conflicts are likely, America must be prepared for all contingencies, graduated deterrence is the best policy, and allies may be essential.

[57] Gilbert R. Kaats, "Development Changes in Belief Systems During a Service Academy Education," Proceedings of the 77th Annual Convention of the American Psychological Association, 1969, p.651.

[58] Spencer, p. 11.

[69] Lovell, in Janowitz, The New Military, p. 125.

"PROFESSIONAL" AND "CITIZEN" OFFICERS: A

COMPARISON OF SERVICE ACADEMY AND

ROTC OFFICER CANDIDATES*

Peter Karsten

For the past few years the Reserve Officer Training Corps (ROTC) has been under considerable attack on the nation's campuses. Compulsory ROTC is being criticized on virtually every campus where it still survives. On several campuses credit for ROTC courses has been removed, and, in some instances, ROTC has been formally asked to leave. In other instances falling enrollments, broken windows, burned-out offices, a generally hostile environment has led one or another of the Services to cancel their program themselves. In short, ROTC is beseiged.

Those seeking its departure have made much of the indoctrinary nature of its curriculum, the presence of external, government control of the program, and the militarization they feel that the ROTC student experiences--all occuring within an academic setting with the contrary design of liberating and stimulating the students' powers of inquiry.

Defenders of ROTC have warned that the uncompromising removal of such programs from the nation's campuses would severely injure the efficiency of a military that has increasingly come to depend on the technical and managerial skills that the ROTC graduate can offer. ROTC officers not only staff the military's reserve system, they also comprise a majority of career officers in the services. As Gene Lyons and John Masland put it over a decade ago, it is

"essential" that "the armed services can secure their share of
the annual crop of college and university graduates."[1]

Such an argument does not constitute a very telling blow to
the case of the critics of ROTC. Indeed, many of these critics
are quite satisfied with an arrangement which may weaken the
ability of the government to prosecute its policies in Southeast
Asia, at the same time that it rids the campuses of an alien spirit.
But some ROTC defenders (such as Harvard's President Nathan Pusey,
and Jack Freeman, a former Air Force officer now the Executive
Assistant to the Chancellor at the University of Pittsburgh) have
offered an argument that does alarm some of the critics.

These defenders have argued that the demise of ROTC would
result in an increase in the number of officers recruited from the
enlisted ranks and an increase in the size or number of the service
academies. In the former case--recruitment from the ranks--it
has been established that the average enlisted man, often the product of an authoritarian social background, with less than a
college education, scores higher on attitude scales measuring
authoritarianism, acceptance of military ideology, and aggression
than does the average college-bred officer candidate.[2] These same
ROTC defenders have then claimed (without verifying the claim) that
the latter case--an increase in the number of service academy
graduates--would have the same effect. The average academy
graduate, they argue, is less flexible than the average ROTC or
Officer Candidate School (OCS) officer. ROTC and OCS officers may
provide a desirable "leavning," a counter-balance, they suggest,
to the more absolutistic and aggressive values of academy graduates
and "rankers." As the Association of State Universities and Land-
Grant Colleges put it recently: "The continued presence in substantial numbers in the Armed Forces of officers from a wide variety
of civilian educational institutions and backgrounds is one of the
best guarantees against the establishment in this country of a
military caste or clique. . . ."[3]

For those critical of the presence of formally accredited ROTC
programs on campus, the suggestion that the death of ROTC would

result in expansions in service academies and enlisted-oriented
OCS programs should provoke some reflection and serious recon-
siderations. If the "citizen" officer defenders are correct, any
changes in present recruitment that would result in a significant
increase in the flow of professional soldiers from the enlisted
and academy ranks might prove counter-productive. That is, the
demise of ROTC would only temporarily dislocate military leadership plans. And any increase in the percentage of authoritarian,
absolutistic, aggressive "leaders" would, we submit, be undesirable. But are the "citizen" officer defenders correct?

The question is one that concerns the nature of the "citizen"
officer--ROTC and college-grad OCS types who serve for two or
three years as platoon and company grade officers or pilots and
then either stay on as careerists or (in most cases) resign.
Some "citizen" officers rise to high command, but all, whether
they stay on or not, may be faced as lieutenants, due to the
nature of modern, dispersed military deployment, with awesome on-
the-spot decision. For the inhabitants of many a Vietnamese
hamlet or river village, survival may well depend on the attitude
of the platoon leader, gunboat skipper, or helicopter gunship
pilot approaching, guns trained, on their homes.

We know that the average ROTC or college grad OCS student
scores lower on F-scale (authoritarianism) measurements than the
average enlisted man or noncollege peer.[4] Thus, for those concerned about the attitudes and values of individuals placed in
positions of military authority and responsibility, the ROTC or
college grad OCS officer would appear to be a safer bet than one
acquiring his commission without first acquiring a college degree,
a phenomenon that may be illustrated by the Mylai incident, as we
shall see. It is probably not simply the fact of the college
experience that makes the difference. Less advantaged youths,
after all, receive a different moral "education" in their environments than do the college-bound, suburban children of the middle
and upper-middle-classes. But, for whatever reasons, the differ-

ence between the two potential military leader groups is a known, and significant, quantity.

What is unknown is just how such ROTC students compare with their service academy counterparts. Are the ROTC types more "flexible" than the academy types, as claimed? One leader of the anti-ROTC movement at Harvard thinks not: "An officer trained at Princeton kills on orders as quickly as an officer trained at the Point."[5] Is there any significant attitudinal distinction between the two types at all?

One way of probing such a question would be to measure the attitudes of the two groups in the field, a year or two after graduation or commissioning. But the Defense Department does not appear ever to have conducted such an investigation, and our own research capacities did not allow for such an analysis. We had to be satisfied with administering an attitude questionnaire (with a near 100 per cent response) in the spring and fall of 1970, to 90 randomly selected service academy (Annapolis) students, 177 ROTC students (110 AFROTC and AROTC students from the university of Pittsburgh and 67 NROTC students from Ohio State University), and 117 male non-ROTC college undergraduates.[6] Such a comparison may be of limited value if Lyons and Masland are correct when they claim that ROTC graduates quickly adjust to and adapt the codes and mores of the professional military. But such a claim is highly moot, and even if a certain amount of adjustment and adaptation does occur, if significant differences between ROTC and academy types exist upon entry into the officer corps, it seems reasonable to expect that some of those differences would persist?

Attitude questionnaires have been used to analyze service academy students, and they have also been used to compare ROTC undergraduates to non-ROTC undergraduates. But to the best of our knowledge service academy and ROTC students have never been systematiclly compared. C. J. Lammers has compared the socialization of Royal Netherlands Naval College midshipmen and Candidate Reserve Officers, but the circumstances of that socialization process are not altogether the same as those we are dealing with.

And furthermore Lammers is concerned only with "the socialization process," not attitudes. John Lovell has, at one point in his study of "the professional socialization of the West Point cadet," compared West Pointers to a sampling of Dartmouth students, 82 per cent of whom expected to perform military service upon graduation, but the sample does not appear to be exclusively composed of ROTC students, and Lovell does not pursue the attitudinal comparison very far. R. W. Gage and William A. Lucas have compared the attitudes of ROTC and non-ROTC students, and both have concluded that ROTC students are significantly more accepting of authority and military ideology than non-ROTC students, but neither has included a sampling of service academy students. In 1969 Isabella Williams, a former student of one of the present authors, administered an attitude questionnaire to students at the Pennsylvania Military College and University of Pittsburgh ROTC and non-ROTC students.[8] But Pennsylvania Military College, as Isabella Williams realizes, cannot be equated to a service academy inasmuch as it graduates many students who will never serve as military officers, and inasmuch as it is a private institution. Moreover, due to circumstances beyond Isabella Williams' control, some of her samples were too small to stand every test for statistical significance. Thus the need for our own study.

Our three sample groups do not spring from precisely the same social background. In terms of family income, parent's level of education, and father's occupation, our Annapolis respondents come from families with slightly higher incomes, better educated parents, and more professional fathers than either the non-ROTC students, who were next, or the ROTC students, whose social origins were slightly more humble than either of the other groups. But these differences in social origins are not relevant to the differences we found in the attitudes of members of our three groups—that is, there was no difference in the response of representatives of one level of social origin from those of any other level.

This surprised us, since one would expect lower-class respondents to be somewhat more authoritarian than those whose parents were

college graduates and professional people. And this would probably have been the case if our respondents had been sampled at
random from the public at large. But Annapolis students were
over-represented in the upper echelons. And since these same
Annapolis students were consistently more authoritarian, absolutistic, and militaristic than either of the other two groups, the
class differentials were neutralized.

R. W. Gage found that ROTC students were more "patriotic" and
accepting of military discipline than non-ROTC college students,[9]
and we found that ranking to apply with every respect of aggressiveness, absolutism, "patriotism", and military discipline tested
for. But our service academy students were consistently more
aggressive and absolutistic than our ROTC sample. When asked
what their reaction might be if, while walking with their girl
friend, someone were to make "a vulgar, obscene comment about
her," nearly half (49 per cent) of our sample of Annapolis
officers-and-gentlemen-to-be indicated that they would offer some
form of physical response, typically: "I'd kick his teeth in."
Only 31.6 per cent of the ROTC sample, and only 23 per cent of
non-ROTC group, gave similar responses (see Table 1). No less
than 66 per cent of the Annapolis respondents indicated that, if
given the choice, they would prefer to serve in a "combat" capacity,
while only 32 per cent of ROTC students preferred "combat" duty to
the alternatives offered: administrative or technical work.[10] The
question was more hypothetical for the non-ROTC male undergraduates,
many of whom will see no service at all, but, for what it is worth,
predictably, only 8 per cent indicated that they would prefer combat service to the other less belligerent options. (Incidentally,
by substituting "Pennsylvania Military College" for "Annapolis"
here, the responses to Isabella Williams study would appear virtually identical to those of our own.)

John Lovell noted that West Point students "tend to be more
'absolutistic' in their strategic perspectives than their Dartmouth
peers."[10 a] Our study revealed the same distinction between our
Annapolis and our Pittsburgh-Ohio State sample (see Table 2).

TABLE 1*

	Offer Physical Response to Insult to Girl Friend % Number	Prefer Combat Duty % Number	Prefer Administrative or Technical Service % Number
Annapolis (90)	49.9 (44)	66.7(60)	25.5 (23)
ROTC (177)	31.6 (56)	32.0(57)	64.0 (113)
non-ROTC "control" group (117)	23.0 (27.)	8.0(9)	69.0 (81)

*Figures do not always total 100 per cent because some respondents had "no opinion" or "no preference."

TABLE 2

	Agree that War is the inevitable result of Man's Nature % Number	Military Takeover Might be Justified % Number	Regard "First-Strike" Use as Acceptable % Number
Annapolis	77 (68)	33.3 (30)	28.0 (25)
ROTC	55.3(98)	19.5 (34)	16.0 (28)
non-ROTC "Control" group	39.0(46)	18.0 (20)	.8 (10)

Seventy-seven per cent of the Annapolis sample agreed with the statement, "war is the inevitable result of man's nature," while only 55.3 per cent of the ROTC, and 39 per cent of the non-ROTC sample agreed. And twice as many Annapolis students (24 per cent) agreed strongly with that statement as their Pittsburgh-Ohio State peers. No less than one in every three midshipmen could conceive of circumstances in which a takeover of the United States government by the military would be justified, while only 19.5 per cent of ROTC, and 18 per cent of non-ROTC students, were of the same

mind. Only 8 per cent of the non-ROTC "control" sample felt that
the U.S. should ever use nuclear weapons in situations other than
retaliation. A larger percentage (16 per cent) of ROTC students,
and a still larger percentage (28 per cent) of Annapolis students
were "first-strikers."

While only 39 per cent of our combined sample of academy and
ROTC officer candidates indicated that they would obey orders
morally repugnant to them (see Table 3), nearly half (48 per cent)
of all our officer candidates who indicated a preference for
combat duty, and 44 per cent of those who indicated that they
would offer physical violence to one who insulted their girl
friend, would obey such orders. The same positive correlation
between aggressive propensities and what we regard as undesirable
behavior exists with regard to our questions about the use of
nuclear weapons. Less than one in every five (19.5 per cent) of
our combined samples of officer candidates felt that the United
States should ever strike first with nuclear weapons. But 31.5
per cent of those showing a preference for combat duty, and 28 per
cent of our "physical force" group, were "first-strikers."

Our heroic fighter samples were not the only ones to correlate positively to "first-strikers." We asked our subjects whether
or not they agreed that "the practice of war is a science best
left to professionals." Of those who agreed, 28 per cent were
also "first-strikers" (Table 3). One West Point cadet may have
spoken for this group when he recently observed that "small tac
nukes" could be of considerable value in suppressing revolution
in Latin America: "Well, you have got to hold the spread of
Communism [which he defined as "sedition, and so forth"] down,
and keep whoever is in government there." That's what's important.[11a]

Moreover, as in the case of our fighter group, no less than
53.6 per cent of those who agreed that war was a science best left
to the control of pros indicated that they would obey morally
repugnant orders. Over half (51.7 per cent) of all officer candidates agreed with that pre-Nuremberg canon of the ardent Statist,
"My Country, Right or Wrong," but no less than 67.2 per cent of

TABLE 3

	Total Number	Would Obey Morally Repugnant Orders		Consider "First Strike" to be Acceptable		Agree with "My Country, Right or Wrong"	
		%	Number	%	Number	%	Number
Combined Officer Candidates	267	39	(105)	19.5	(52)	52	(138)
Officer Candidates Preferring Combat	117	48	(56)	27.3	(32)	63.2	(74)
Officer Candidates Offering Physical Force Response	100	44	(44)	28	(28)	69.0	(69)
Officer Candidates Feeling War a Science for Professionals	125	53.6	(67)	28	(35)	67.2	(84)
Annapolis Sample	90	41	(67)	28	(25)	74.0	(67)

those feeling war to be a science best left to professionals, and approximately the same percentage of "fighter" types, found this conscience-evading dogma attractive.[11b]

For one familiar with Morris Janowitz's distinction between "heroic" and "managerial" professional military officers[12] this high correlation between "fighters," "professionals," service academy students (see Table 3), and undesirable propensities may be somewhat surprising, unless one is also familiar with John Lovell's research. Lovell could find no statistically signifi-cant difference at West Point between "heroic" fighter types and "managerial" types (our "pros") in terms of absolutism.[13] "Pros" are just as dangerous to have around as "fighters." How did our three categories of students like the "pro" and "statist" tenets?

No less than 72 per cent of Annapolis respondents agreed with the remark that war was a science best left to professionals (with 33.3 per cent agreeing strongly), whereas only 47.5 per cent of our ROTC "citizen" officer candidates, and only 18 per cent of the non-ROTC "control" group, agreed. And the same pattern held for the dogma found to be so attractive to our "pros." Almost three or every 4 Annapolis students sampled (74 per cent) found the adage of Captain Stephen Decatur, U.S.N., "My Country, Right or Wrong," to be attractive, whereas only 40 per cent of the ROTC, and 19.5 per cent of the non-ROTC, students approved of this pre-Nuremberg code of conduct.

These attitudinal distinctions occurred again when our subjects were asked their opinions about the military budget and the war in Vietnam. Only a few non-ROTC students and only a handful of the ROTC sample, felt the military budget was too small (Table 4) but 39 per cent of the Annapolis sample felt the budget inadequate.[13a] On questions relating to the Vietnam war, however, ROTC students were closer to their fellow officer candidates than they were to their non-officer-bound peers. Four of every five non-ROTC students objected to the war in Vietnam, while only 36.7 per cent of ROTC, and 28 per cent of Annapolis students found the war objectionable (results very similar to those obtained by Isabella Williams). Only ten per cent of our sample of non-ROTC students expressed a willingness to volunteer for service in Vietnam, while 40 per cent of the ROTC, and 60 per cent of the Annapolis samples indicated that they would "volunteer" for that war, (figures also similar to those of Isabella Williams' study). Only one of every four non-officer candidate respondents imagined that he would obey a direct order morally repugnant to him; no less than 38 per cent of the ROTC sample and 41 per cent of the Annapolis sample indicated that they would obey such an order. Only 18.7 per cent of non-ROTC students felt that the atrocities committed at Mylai were "extremely rare" in Vietnam, but the same percentage (37 per cent) of the ROTC and Annapolis samples considered Mylai "extremely rare."

It could be argued that our officer candidate groups, having once committed themselves to military service, have become victims of an epidemic of cognitive dissonance. That is, they may find Vietnam tolerable and Mylai exceptional largely because they recognize that they must live with a decision to serve that may one day thrust them into a Southeast Asian rice paddy or river delta. It could be argued that they have come to regard the military budget as inadequate in part because of their introduction to the military's traditions, mores, and missions--the military's point of view. But we think it more likely that they were always more positive toward the war and the military than those who avoided the officer candidate programs. We feel that

TABLE 4

	Military Budget Too Small		Object to Presence of U.S. Troops in Vietnam		Would Volunteer for Vietnam		Consider Mylai "Extremely Rare"	
Annapolis	%	Number	%	Number	%	Number	%	Number
	39	(35)	28	(25)	60	(54)	37	(32)
ROTC	10	(18)	36.7	(65)	40	(71)	37	(67)
non-ROTC "control" group	4	(5)	78.5	(92)	10	(12)	18.7	(22)

the reasons for the persistent additudinal differences between those who are officer candidates and those who are not lie primarily in the process of self-recruitment by which means they selected military futures in the first place, and less in the process of military socialization taking place as they prepare for command or even the subtle reinforcing combination of the two. Our reasons are two-fold--(1) self selection and (2) the impotence of "militarization."

SELF-SELECTION

William Lucas and C. J. Lammers have both maintained that

there is a self-selection process at work in both the American
ROTC and the Dutch naval officer corps. "Militaristic" young men
elect at age 17 or 18 to pursue a course that will make them
officers.[14] Moreover, Lammers notes that the regular academy
midshipmen, many the sons of naval officers, are considerably
more accepting of military ideology than their reserve officer
candidate counterparts.[15] That seems to be the case with our
service academy and ROTC samples, and the reason may well be
rleated to the reasons they gave for selecting Annapolis or ROTC.
Nearly half of the Annapolis sample (48 per cent) indicated that
one of their reasons for seeking appointment was a desire to "be
a career officer." Only 17 per cent of the ROTC sample indicated
that such ambitions had motivated them (Table 5). Nearly three
in every four (73 per cent) of the ROTC sample confessed that a
prime motive for joining the program was a "preference to serve
as an officer versus an enlisted man" (a few wrote in "to dodge
the draft"). Slightly more Annapolis (26 per cent) than ROTC
(19.2 per cent) students indicated that an important reason for

TABLE 5

REASONS IMPORTANT IN DECISION TO SEEK COMMISSION

	Desire to Make a Career of Military		Due to Belief in Military Traditions and Methods		Desire Training For Responsibilities in Future Civilian Life		Prefer to be Officer Rather than Enlisted Man	
	%	Number	%	Number	%	Number	%	Number
Annapolis	48	(43)	26	(23)	36.5	(31)	56	(49)
ROTC	17	(29)	19.2	(34)	47.5	(84)	73	(130)

joining was a "belief in military traditions and methods." Conversely, nearly half (47.5 per cent)of the ROTC sample said that
an important reason for seeking a commission was a desire to
secure "training for assuming positions of responsibility in
civilian life," while only 36.5 per cent of career-bound Annapolis

midshipmen gave a similar response. In short, the ROTC students
appear to have more limited and "practical" reasons for service
than the more professional-minded middies. As one anonymous
Annapolis ditty puts it:

Some join for the love of the Service,

Some join for the love of the Sea,

But I know a guy who's in ROTCIE:

He joined for a college degree.

Similarly, just as Lammers found disproportionate numbers of
naval officers' parents in his sample of Royal Netherlands Naval
College midshipmen, we found that the fathers of 33.3 per cent of
our Annapolis, 12.4 per cent of our ROTC, and only 2.3 per cent
of our non-ROTC samples had been commissioned officers. Moreover,
when we added those whose fathers had served in a noncomissioned
status we got similar results (see Table 6), confirming results
obtained by Isabella Williams. Apparently many of the sons of
military officers seek programs that will allow them to emulate
their fathers.

THE IMPOTENCE OF "MILITARIZATION"

Once in the programs, a buttressing of prejudgments, values,
and goals may occur. C. J. Lammers and William Lucas both maintain
that officer candidates "socialize" one another over time, and
Lammers sagely hypothesizes that where initial motivation is low,
such "socialization" may actually serve to drive the student out
of the program.[16] But when we asked respondents to recall views
held on entering college, or created an ersatz time-lapse by
comparing various school years, we did not find evidence of any
significant shifts on the part of either officer candidate groups
in a direction away from that the non- officer candidate group
might be taking. All three groups, for example, showed a slight
increase, from freshmen to seniors, in opposition to the war in
Vietnam, a slight "shift" from conservative to moderate, or from
moderate to liberal views, and a slight "movement" toward a
critical view of the size of the military budget. In the case of
immoral orders, to offer one illustration (see Table 7), fewer and

TABLE 6

Father's Military Service

	Father A Commissioned Officer		Father Served in Military in Some Capacity		Results from the Williams' Survey on Fathers Serving in Military in Some Capacity
	%	Number	%	Number	Per Cent
Annapolis	33.3	(30)	89	(80)	(1969 Pennsylvania Military College)
20.9			7.3		92
ROTC	12.4	(22)	81.7	(145)	1969 Pitt AROTC 71.5
non-ROTC "control" group	10.1		13.5		
	2.3	(3)	68.2	(80)	(1969 Pitt non-ROTC) 65.5

fewer officer candidates indicated a willingness to obey immoral orders with each succeeding class. Not all of these differences were statistically significant, but they all point in the same direction as John Lovell's study of West Pointers, the Feldman-Newcomb study of college undergraduates, and the Campbell-McCormack study of Air Force Academy classes.[17] Thus we feel that while there may be some reinforcing of previously held values taking place within the officer candidate programs that we did not detect, we doubt that there are many new values being created. Surely some traditions, mores, attitudes are "learned" by officer candidates--particularly by those at the "closed-circuit" service academies--but our data leads us to claim that the differences between our three subject samples are less a function of in-house "militarization" or "humanization" than they are a function of a self-selection (or joint-selection) process occurring when young men of 17 decide whether to seek (and recruiters decide to authorize); a professional military career, a program that offers leadership training for future civilian life and a

chance to serve as an officer rather than an enlisted man; or no
voluntary military service at all. It is this decision that
separates the "fighters" and "pros" from the "citizen soldiers"
and "civilian types." The "liberal arts" environment of academe
may have something to do with the fact that ROTC students are less
absolutistic, less aggressive, less militaristic than service
academy students, but our data could not prove it. Furthermore
if ROTC units on campus do not significantly "militarize" any of
those who volunteer to take their programs, neither do we find any
evidence suggesting that the "liberal arts" environment of academe
does any "liberalizing" of ROTC students. The responses of freshmen ROTC students fall between those of their Annapolis and non-
ROTC peers, and so do those of sophomores, juniors, and seniors.
College education, four years of relative insulation from the
school of hard knocks, apparently "humanizes" all three groups at
approximately the same pace. If pre-college self-recruitment is
the key factor, then the particular college environment may make
very little difference, since our evidence, as well as the Lowell

TABLE 7

	Would Obey Order Morally Repugnant	
	%	Number
Combined Officer Candidate Freshmen (78)	48.5	(38)
Combined Officer Candidate Sophomores (55)	42.0	(23)
Combined Officer Candidate Juniors (62)	35.5	(22)
Combined Officer Candidate Seniors (70)	30.0	(21)

and Campbell-McCormack studies, suggest that there may be a progressive softening of many of the "hard-line" views held as freshmen by members of all three groups.

POLICY IMPLICATIONS

In the fall of 1969, a veteran attending college, one Ronald

Ridenhour, precipitated an investigation into the March, 1968,
massacre of the villagers of Mylai by elements of the "Americal"
Division. Before the dust had settled, two generals, three colonels,
nine other officers, and six enlisted personnel faced courts mar-
tial.

Of the 20 men involved, facing charges ranging from mass mur-
der to suppressing evidence and false official statements, one
(Major General Samuel Koster) was a West Pointer. One (Brigadier
General George Young) was a graduate of Columbia Military Academy
and The Citadel, "the West Point of the South." Twelve, including
six of the officers, had entered the Army as enlisted personnel.
These included Captain Ernest Medina (charged with murder), Captain
Eugene Kotouc (charged with murder), Captain Kenneth Boatman,
Captain Dennis Johnson, Major Robert McKnight, Colonel Robert Luper
(all charged with suppressing evidence or making false official
statements), and the six enlisted personnel, four of whom were
charged with murder. Of the remaining six officers all had
attended colleges in the South, several for only a year or two.
These were First Lieutenant William Calley (charged with murder),
who had attended one year of junior college, Captain Thomas
Willingham (charged with murder), a graduate of Murray State
College, Kentucky, Major Charles Calhoun, a Clemson graduate,
Lieutenant Colonel William Guinn, who had attended the University
of Tennessee and the University of Alabama, Lieutenant Colonel
David Gavin, a graduate of Mississippi Southern College, and
Colonel Oran Henderson, who attended military base extension
centers of the University of Maryland and George Washington University. Captain Willingham, the Murray State graduate, was the only
one of the eight charged as principals in the massacre who was a
college graduate.

When word reached West Point of the charges against General
Koster, head of the "Americal" in 1968, and Superintendent of the
Academy in 1970, the Corps of Cadets were assembled to hear Koster
tell them that "throughout my military career the cherished prin-
ciples of [our Academy's] motto--Duty, Honor, Country--have served

as a constant guide to me." The Corps gave Koster a 90-second ovation. As one plebe put it, "everybody [here] seemed to sympathize with the general."[18]

Simultaneous with word of Koster's implication came word of the first recorded case of a West Point graduate ever to request a discharge on the basis of selective conscientious objection to a war. First Lieutenant Louis Font, 23, had been attending Harvard Graduate School in Government at the time.[19]

While our data was being assembled, in late May, 1970, the Army charged two officers, Captain Vincent Hartmann and First Lieutenant Robert G. Lee, Jr., with attempted murder and manslaughter for ordering their men to conduct "target practice" on a number of Vietnamese huts in 1969. One woman eventually died of wounds inflicted during this "target practice;" her nephew was wounded. Neither officer had ever attended college.[20]

In early 1968 Lieutenant Commander Marcus Aurelius Arnheiter, a graduate of the Naval Academy, was relieved of command of the U.S.S. Vance. Several junior officers of Arnheiter's command, Lieutenant (j.g.) William Generous (a NROTC honor graduate, Phi Beta Kappa, from Brown University), Lieutenant (j.g.) Edward Mason (an OCS college graduate), and Ensign Luis Belmonte (another OCS college graduate), had complained that Arnheiter had hazarded his vessel, had falsified its location while entering prohibited areas, had sought to draw enemy fire on his ship, and had generally taken the vessel, as Arnheiter put it, "where the action is."

At one point, the junior officers claimed, he ordered Lieutenant (j.g.) Mason, in an armed motor whaleboat, to fire at a number of Vietnamese ashore. Mason refused. "I can't see shooting a bunch of civilians or even shooting at them," he told Arnheiter. Mason says he feared that Arnheiter would "interpret my shooting as somebody else's shooting and start shooting himself." The Vietnamese turned out to be refugees from a coastal village bombed-out by American air strikes. As one crewman put it, "that kind of guy (Arnheiter) could start World War III."

Arnheiter's Executive Officer, Lieutenant Ray Hardy, another

product of the Naval Academy, remained loyal to his chief and
enforced Arnheiter's often bizarre orders. (Hardy acquired an
ulcer in the process.) All of those who came to Arnheiter's
defense (Rear Admiral Walter Baumberger, Rear Admiral Daniel
Gallery, and Captain Richard Alexander) were Academy graduates.
Admiral Gallery referred to the non-Annapolis critics of our verit-
able Captain Queeg as "odd-ball officers who should have been
wearing beads and picketing the White House." Arnheiter himself
called them a "bunch of dissident malcontents . . . a Berkeley-
campus type of Vietnik/beatnik."[21]

What are the lessons of our experiment in attitude-behavior
analysis and our impressionistic excursion into the backgrounds of
officers involved in "alleged misconduct" in Vietnam?

Certainly one conclusion could be that those critics of ROTC
who have suggested that "an officer trained at Princeton kills as
quickly on orders as an officer trained at the Point" may be incorrect. ROTC (and probably college-graduate OCS) officers appear to
be less absolutistic, less belligerent, and less militaristic than
either the non-college or the service academy officer. (Indeed,
one Ohio State NROTC student went so far as to note that he had
joined ROTC to "work constructively to 'pacify' the military.")
This is not to say that the ROTC student is the ideal officer candidate; we would prefer officers from a still more humanistic mold,
but we are not likely to get a lottery drafting of college graduates for Officer Candidate School for some time, and in the meantime, the apparent contrast of service academy and ROTC student
values suggested by our analysis ought to provoke those intent on
driving ROTC from the liberal arts campus to some serious second
thoughts. We do not feel it proper that there be any formal
relationship between the military and the academic community. ROTC,
like OCS and the Marine Corps' summer training program for officer
candidates, could well go "off campus." But it should be allowed--
indeed, it should be encouraged--to "stick around." Since we are
of the opinion that the military is going to be around in the
United States for some time, we feel that any "reform" that makes

it difficult for a Princeton English major or a Pittsburgh philosophy major to become an officer is most undesirable. Major
William Muhlenfeld recently put it nicely when he argued that it
was

> . . . of utmost importance that [our] armies be led by just
> and compassionate men--men who understand that as leaders
> they are also public servants who have a profound respon-
> sibility to minister to the welfare of those they command,
> to serve with . . . the wisdom to see beyond their actions
> to the effects their actions wreak. This kind of leader-
> ship must come from the university. . . . The paradox is
> that we must wait for the professors to learn.

One senior officer was more explicit: "[Lieutenant] Calley
never would have become an officer if we were not so short-handed.
Why are we short-handed? Because the bastards at Harvard wouldn't
. . . step up to their responsibilities."[22] Our own notion of the
"responsibilities" of "Harvard bastards" may differ somewhat from
the Army's, but, in any event, for the benefit of the American GI,
as well as the Vietnamese villager, we hope that college graduates
continue to serve as officers.

Which leads us to our second conclusion. We feel that English,
Philosophy, "humanities" majors should be encouraged to become
military officers (and probably, for that matter, policemen, social
workers, and government officials as well). Why "humanities"
majors? Because these were the types who consistently gave the
"best" responses to our questionnaire. Those who indicated that
they were "humanities" majors[23] were less willing to obey immoral
orders than were "social science," "natural science," or "engineering" majors (Table 8); they were the least willing to use nuclear
weapons; they were the least likely to respond physically to
insult; they were the least capable of imagining a situation in
which a military take-over of the United State government would
be justified; they were the least interested in endorsing "My
Country, Right or Wrong"; and they were the most critical of the
size of the military budget.[24]

The trouble is that "humanities" majors do not appear to be
very enthusiastic about joining the military, nor are they the

bemedalled recruiting officer's dream-come-true. Isabella Williams
found them to be less interested than any of the other majors in
joining ROTC, and more insistent than others on "the right of the
soldier to criticize his superior officer and/or government
policies without facing sanctions for his dissent." Very few
(less than 5 per cent) of our ROTC sample were "humanities" majors.
But they were disproportionately represented in that group of respondents who feel that the military, as an organization, constitutes one of the "most dangerous" threats to the American system
of government (see Table 8).

Many military men, concerned as they are with "leadership,"
body counts, power, and discipline, are probably quite satisfied
with any system that allows Yosarians, Peter Seegers, and Staughton
Lynds to stay clear of the military. The advocates of a "volunteer" (standing) professional army argue the virtues of such a
self-selection process. We are not as convinced of the advantages of any system that can do without the "citizen" officer or,
for that matter, the "citizen" soldier.

Which brings us to our third conclusion. If you don't like
the way the military functions, you cannot expect it to improve by
insulating yourself from it. What we feel ourselves is that the
"citizen" officer should represent the noblest attitudes and
values in American society--values which we (quite subjectively)
maintain would include a refusal to obey immoral orders, a reluctance to sling nuclear weapons around, and a strong disinclination
for any military coup or other invasion of the political process.

Some will say that we are naive--that one officer is as power-
less as the next to effect any significant check on the ways of a
military which, after all, takes its orders from civilians in
Washington. We admit that having "good" officers does not mean
that they will receive "good" orders. We concede that if a sensitive officer distinguishes between combatants and noncombatants,
"moral" and "immoral" orders, he may still kill the combatants,
may still obey the "moral" orders. But we have seen infantry
lieutenants in Cambodia wearing peace symbols on the TV news,

telling reporters of how they had deliberately led their men clear of the combat zone. We have seen young Army doctors refusing to collaborate, young Army lawyers demanding justice, and young junior officers protesting the war. In the past few years we have seen the movement invade the military itself. A "volunteer" army would end all of that. The most significant changes must occur higher up the ladder of authority (which is why we suggested politics and government service for "humanities" majors). But the vicissitudes of the anti-war movement have demonstrated the difficulties that dissenters will have in penetrating the political process. The military and the police are more accessible. We must all work towards the day when war, armies, and inequity no longer exist, but in the meantime, for the villagers at Mylai and those under the guns of Arnheiter, Mason, and Vance, the presence of a "good" officer counts.

Which is why we were chagrined to find that 84 per cent (31 of 37) of those who felt the military is "most dangerous," also favored a "volunteer" army! A volunteer army of "pros," void of "citizen" officers coming in out of the draft, would be "dangerous." As Peter Barnes recently put it:[25]

> . . . an end to the draft would shield the army from the influx of citizen-soldiers who are the yeast of internal change. The army needs Yosarians, Ronald Ridenhours, independent-minded ROTC junior officers and J.A.G. lawyers --soldiers who do their jobs but who are not committed to the cover-your-ass system, whose loyalties are to civilian, not careerist values.

Critics of ROTC, ironically, the Army needs you!

University of Pittsburgh

Ed Berger
Larry Flatley
John Frisch
Mayda Gottlieb
Judy Haisley
Peter Karsten
Larry Pexton
William Worrest

TABLE 8

	Willing to Obey Order Morally Repugnant	Willing to Respond Physically to Insult to Girl	Willing to Use Nuclear Weapons	Military Take-over Might Be Justified Some Day
Humanities (29)	14%	14%	37%	14%
Social Science (100)	30%	33%	65%	23%
Natural Science (102)	37%	40%	75%	26%
Engineering (117)	42.5%	30.5%	76%	22%

	Agreed with "My Country, Right or Wrong"	Disagreed with "My Country, Right or Wrong"	Felt Military Budget Too High	Felt Military Budget Too Low	Feel Military "Most Dangerous to U.S.Govt.
Humanities (29)	14%	72.5%	72.5%	6.7%	55%
Social Science (100)	39%	46.0%	51.0%	16.0%	14%
Natural Science (102)	37%	43.0%	41.0%	19%	8%
Engineering (117)	48%	38.5%	24.0%	17%	2%

NOTES

*We wish to thank Professor Laurence Glasco of the University of Pittsburgh, History Department, for his aid in enabling us to analyze our data with the IBM 360 computer (SPSS Program). Our errors in research design, presentation of findings, and conclusions, as well as our biases, are entirely our own.

[1]"Violence Strikes 26 ROTC Units," Air Force Times, XXX

(May 20, 1970), 4; Lyons and Masland, Education and Military Leadership: A Study of ROTC (Princeton, 1959), 21.

[2]I.e., R. W. Gage, "Patriotism and Military Discipline as a Function of the Degree of Military Training," Journal of Social Psychology, LXIV (1964), 101-111; E. G. French and R. R. Ernst, "The Relationship between Authoritarianism and the Acceptance of Military Ideology," Journal of Personality, XXIV (1955), 181-191; William A. Lucas, "The American Lieutenant: An Empirical Investigation of Normative Theories of Civil-Military Relations," unpublished Ph.D., University of North Carolina, 1967, p. 43.

[3]Cited in Harvard Bulletin (May 25, 1970), 26. See also "ROTC--Yes or No?" Defense Supply Association Review (January-February 1969), 111.

[4]Gage, loc. cit.; Lucas, loc. cit.

[5]Harvard Bulletin (May 25, 1970), 29.

[6]We asked the Military Academy and the Air Force Academy for permission to survey random samples of their cadets, but neither academy authorized the study. We recognize that Annapolis students may differ from their peers at the other two academies on some scores, but we have discovered virtually no statistically significant differences among the three ROTC groups; we feel that the "service academy" label is appropriate. (In any event, we do not claim that our analysis is any more than suggestive. None of us has any special training in social psychology or statistics. But we suspect that we are on to something significant. We would be pleased if our study were to provoke a more thorough and sophisticated analysis.)

[7]Lyons and Masland, op. cit., 169. Major Gilbert L. Whiteman has engaged in such research. Whiteman hypothesizes that "civilian college-trained officers [do not] retain their liberal views for very long after entering active duty...they sooner-or-later adopt the philosophies of power, influence, and authority which those not trained on college campuses might display." (From enclosure by Whiteman to Peter Karsten, October 1, 1970.) He may be right, Arthur Niederhoffer argues that "police authoritarianism does not come into the force along with the recruits, but rather is inculcated in the men through strenuous socialization." (Behind the Shield [New York., 1967], 160). But Whiteman's "sooner-or-later" will have to be precise; if it takes two or three years to sour the "liberalism" of college graduate officers, then many may function in an unsocialized fashion during that important first (and, for many, only) tour of duty. Moreover, Whiteman may be wrong.

[8]C. J. Lammers, "Midshipmen and Candidate Reserve Officers at The Royal Netherlands Naval College: A Comparative Study of a Socialization Process," Sociologia Neerlandica, II (1965),98-112;

John Lovell, "The Professional Socialization of the West Point Cadet," in Morris Janowitz, ed., The New Military (New York, 1946); Gage, op. cit., Lucas, op. cit.; Isabella Williams, "The Other West Points," unpublished term paper, August 1969, copy in the possession of Professor Peter Karsten, Department of History, University of Pittsburgh. See also Milton Holmen and Robert Kalter, Attitudes and Information Patterns of OCS Eligibles (HUMRRO, George Washington.University, October, 1953).

[9]Gage, 101-111.

[10]Charles Coates and R. Pellegrin, Military Sociology (College Park, Maryland, 1965), 80-82. Since many Naval Academy midshipmen expect to be assigned to men-of-war, comparison of the percentage of those preferring "combat" service at the Academy with those preferring "combat" service in ROTC (only a third of whom are Navy-bound) may be unfair to the Academy, since the options are somewhat different. Shipboard "combat" service is, of late, considerably safer than airborne or ground "combat" duty. On the other hand, many Annapolis graduates will serve on river gunboats, in combat-area aircraft, or in Marine infantry units-- that is, in posts equally perilous to those preferred by our "combat" ROTC sample.

[10a]Lovell, op. cit., 129.

[11]Many officer candidate respondents may have had in mind the use of low yield, "clean" tactical nuclear weapons, but "first-strike" use of "tac nukes" could easily provoke Armaggedon.

[11a]Cited in Ward Just, "Soldiers," Atlantic Monthly (Oct. 1970), 66.

[11b]Lieutenant Williams Calley says that he went to Vietnam "with the absolute philosophy that the U.S.A.'s right. And there was no grey . . . there was just black or white." He told John Sack: "I'll do as I'm told to do. I won't revolt. I'll put the will of America above my own conscience, always." (Calley, interviewed by Sack, "The Confessions of Lieutenant Calley," Esquire, November, 1970), 229.

[12]Janowitz, The Professional Soldier (Glencoe, Illinois, 1960); "Changing Patterns of Organizational Authority: The Military Establishment," Administrative Science Quarterly, III (March, 1959), 473-493.

[13]Lovell, op. cit.

[13a]Of that total universe of respondents who regarded the military budget to be too small, 76 per cent felt war a science best left to the "pros," 70.5 per cent felt that war was the inevitable fruit of human nature, and 69 per cent preferred

combat assignments, percentages much higher than the figures from
all respondents to these questions.

[14]Lucas, op. cit., 53; Lammers, op. cit., 109.

[15]Lammers, 106.

[16]Lammers, op. cit., 119; Lucas, op. cit., 75-77; 120-127.

[17]Lovell, op. cit., 129; Kenneth Feldman and Theodore Newcomb,
The Impact of College on Students (San Francisco, 1969), I, 31;
Donald Campbell and Thelma McCormack, "Military Experience and
Attitudes Toward Authority," American Journal of Sociology, LXII
(1957), 482-290.

[18]New York Times, November 25, 1969, p. 16, and March 18,
1970, pp. 1ff; U.S. Department of the Army, U.S. Army Register,
Vol. II (Government Printing Office, 1969), 157, 742.

[19]New York Times, March 18, 1970, p. 17.

[20]New York Times, May 29, 1970, 1.

[21]New York Times, May 8, 1968, p. 12; May 10, 1968, p. 1ff;
U.S. Department of the Navy, Register of Commissioned Officers
(Navy Personnel, 1966); Neil Sheehan, "The 99 Days of Captain
Arnheiter," New York Times Magazine, August 11, 1968, pp. 7-9,
69-75. Generous is presently a graduate student in American
History at Stanford University.

[22]Muhlenfeld, "Our Embattled ROTC," Army (February 1969), 28;
Atlantic Monthly(November 1970), 83.

[23]There was no statistically significant difference among
choice of major in our universe of respondents on grounds of
family income, father's level of education, or any other criteria.

[24]Cf. Feldman and Newcomb, Impact, I, 167; and Williams, op. cit.

[25]Barnes, "All-Volunteer Army?" New Republic (May 9, 1970), 23.
See also Peter Karsten, "The American Citizen Soldier: Triumph or
Disaster?" Military Affairs, XXX (1966), 34-40.

THE ROTC: MILITARY SERVICE ON THE COLLEGE CAMPUS

Nona Glazer-Malbin

In the 1960's ROTC became one major focus of student protest
against the growth of power of military institutions in American
society, and against continued United States military involvement
in Southeast Asia.[1] The removal of ROTC from university curriculum, or the change of the ROTC course from "required" to "optional"
was considered by many students to be a major blow to the armed
forces, and a victory for anti-militarism.[2] The demise of the
ROTC probably causes more immediate trouble for college administrators, the local police, the faculty, and the students than for
the armed forces. The ROTC is more a symbol of the military
problems of the United States than it is relevant to the continued
adequate functioning of the military. The ROTC is an immediately
available symbol of the influence of the military on American
foreign policy; the ROTC is symbolic of the military service which
is required of all young men. The attack on the ROTC is symbolic
of the use of violence to gain political ends. The changing position of ROTC is a blow to the prestige of the services on the
campuses, but not clearly relevant to changing the influence which
military advisors have on shaping foreign policy, keeping tabs on
dissenters in American society, requiring young men to perform
military duties, or obtaining control over a sizeable proportion
of national resources.

Moreover, if we consider the varying functions which have been attributed to military training on college campuses, it appears that the instrumental functions of the corps are obtained with relatively little success. In terms of what both the supporters and critics of ROTC see to be the explicit goals of the training, the success of the corps is limited, or at best, unclear.

This paper shall examine, primarily, the multiplicity of functions attributed to the ROTC (by founders, supporters, detractors) and consider how the functions have been redefined over time. Second, the social context in which these changes occurred will be discussed. The specific areas of our concern are as follows:

    I.   The social context. The function of locating ROTC on college campuses (rather than making military service a community located institution) will be examined. How is locating ROTC on college campuses related to the problem of legitimatizing military training in a society which is ambivalent about this social institution? How does the location serve to link military training to youth, to coerce commitment to military training?

    II.   The functioning of the corps. Varying functions of the ROTC have included a) the development of a socially desirable character among college men; b) socialization of cadets into an acceptance of military organization; c) the learning of military skills by cadets; d) recruitment of youth into a military career.

    III. The social context. The demands made of college men to participate in military training during college attendance has gone from expansion to contraction. While "militarism" may have diminished on the college campuses, the role of military institutions in the total society has increased. What can be concluded about the relative importance of ROTC to the prominence of military institutions in the political, social, and economic life of American society?

Most of the paper will actually be concerned with the functions of the Corps as outlined in II above. An adequate understanding of the functions of the corps rests on understanding the other problems outlined in the above list, so that we will also be considering these aspects of the social context of the development of the corps.

The Reserve Officers' Training Corps developed from the military

drill obligation placed upon the land-grant colleges by the
federal government in the Morrill Land Grant Act of 1862. The
War Department was given the obligation to supervise drill, and to
provide the military science departments with personnel, funds,
and materials. The Reserve Officers' Training Corps was not established until the National Defense Act of 1916.[3] The requirement
of a course in military tactics specified in the Morrill Act
applied only to the land-grant colleges, while the 1916 Act extended the right of the War Department to contract training arrangements with other colleges. The Department interpreted its directions from Congress to agree to establish ROTC training units only
when the colleges agreed to make military training compulsory for
the first two years of college. (Some of the discussion in this
paper applies only to the land-grant colleges while some applies
to other colleges as well.)

THE SOCIAL CONTEXT OF COLLEGE LOCATION: LINKAGE, LEGITIMACY AND COERCION

In examining the social functions of locating military training on the college campuses, two separate functions have to be
considered: (a) linkage; and (b) the legitimatization. First,
military training organizations on the college campus provide a
structure which is an overt linkage between the federal government
and higher education. The corps is a symbolic means by which the
federal government affirms that absolute power which it has to
demand that young men give their lives, if need be, for the protection of the government. Without pushing the analogy too far,
we consider the ROTC to be not unlike Youth Pioneer in Soviet
society. The link between youth and government that each of these
youth organizations provides includes a formal setting; written
materials; adult authority; supervision on the part of representatives of the government (army officers in the United States, Communist party members in the USSR); leisure activities which provide for informal social interaction among the youth (e.g,, Scab-
bard and Blade, and military balls in the United States); symbols
of membership embodied in such objects as uniforms and medals, and

other recognitions of compliance with standards set by the government. Certainly, there are important differences in the degree
to which youth can be coerced in each society to join, in the sex
of the members, the social stratum from which members are recruited,
and the importance of membership for the adult years. But a basic
similarity remains. The ROTC is an organization which formalizes
the contacts between civilian youth and the government, and is just
about the only day-by-day representative of the government in the
typical activities of American college students.

The second function of locating military training on college
campuses is to legitimatize such training. The university is perceived by most Americans as a social institution which transmits
knowledge necessary for adult functioning in the society: training is given to produce doctors, lawyers, ministers, business
executives, teachers, and accountants. Training men to be soldiers
may be easily accepted as an extension of the training function.
The activities in which the colleges train students are considered
ipso facto to be legal, moral, and of high status. Hence, teaching soldiers-to-be in a civilian college further validates the
military profession.

Moreover, locating military training on college campuses
legitimatizes requiring young men to participate in such training without seriously invalidating the American belief that the
country--in contrast to European nations--is anti-military. By
attending college, men essentially extend the period of youth,
during which it is proper for adults to continue supervisory roles.
Youth are defined as essentially irresponsible members of society,
who can be relied upon to make wise decisions only after acquiring
final certification by an institution of education. The notion
that youth status is inconsistent to some important degree with
adult decision-making rights pervades American attitudes toward
college students in particular, and youth in general. Legal rights,
political rights, sexual rights, and other matters of choice
including ones having to do with schooling are age-regulated.
The college requirement that young men take ROTC courses is only

an extension of the college requirements of grammar, foreign language, art, and physical education. (The attack on these kinds of requirements includes the academic courses as well as ROTC.) Insofar as military training for youth has acquired legitimacy which is society-wide, the function of locating ROTC on the campus becomes relatively insignificant for the coercive force of the services. If our analysis is correct, it would be expected that any significant change in recruitment policy from Selective Service to a volunteer army (the draft would be on a "standby" basis) would be followed by federal efforts to reinstate ROTC on the campuses. (The plans to expand the _Junior_ ROTC--that is, military training on the high school level--is probably an attempt to lay a base for a volunteer army which bypasses the colleges as a major recruitment ground.)

In summary, locating the ROTC on the college campuses has several social functions: (1) the ROTC serves as a structural link between the federal government and youth; (2) the ROTC obtains legitimacy as a teaching unit by virtue of its location in a setting devoted to teaching; (3) the course can be required of youth by an extension of the usual collegiate custom of requiring courses of its enrollees, without initiating a serious challenge of the right of the federal government to require military training in time of peace.

THE FUNCTIONING OF RESERVE OFFICERS'
TRAINING CORPS

The second major aspect of the ROTC which has to be considered is the changing goals of the organization, and the degree of success with which the varying goals have been reached. An examination of the writings of members of the armed services, their supporters, and sometimes their critics, suggest that the Reserve Officers' Training Corps, and the preceding "military drill" have had a variety of goals. The goals have altered considerably since the requirement of military drill was first established in 1862 in the modification of the Morrill Land Grant Act. The significant functions of ROTC include that of symbolizing the power which the federal government has over youth--but ROTC developed quite a different set of explicit goals. For the most part, the goals are broad in scope, and somewhat pretentious sounding--a not uncommon characteristic of goals which must be so worded that they do not offend public opinion. Each of the goals which will be considered in this section of the paper appears to provide a rationale for the continuation of a program rather than being functions with empirical documentation which demonstrates the success of the program. The ostensible functions end up sounding somewhat hollow because they cannot clearly be considered as critical functions of the training corps, and perhaps skirt the more pertinent goals of control of youth. In analyzing the goal attainment of the corps a variety of materials will be used: documents, statistical materials, discussion by military personnel, studies by social scientists including studies of the attitudes, opinions, and plans of ROTC cadets.

The purported functions of ROTC as perceived by the armed services, their supporters, and sometimes, their critics are:

Socialization into Military Ideology. Service in ROTC (and pre-1916, military drill) socializes youth into the norms, values, and ideology of military institutions. This has been a continually stated goal, and probably the only one of the four on this list which has been markedly obtained.

Character Development. The development of discipline, self-control, and other character traits are left undeveloped by the disorganization of the civilian groups--the family, the church, the schools, including the colleges. The training which young men receive in close order drill, theory, and demonstration in the classroom, and other military activities develop in youth the social character which is lacking. This theme has characterized discussions of both ROTC and military drill.

Socialization into Occupational Skills. ROTC (and earlier, military drill) provides a way of training young men in the administrative and technical skills required in military service. This training makes available an officer corps which can be called to

arms in time of national emergency. This perhaps has been the
single most important purpose of military training on the college
campuses. The various components of the reserves have continuously argued that a corps of citizen-soldiers, who regularly
take part in some exercises which keep the training up-to-date is
absolutely necessary for the continued strength of American military forces. This argument has been discarded by the military in
preference for the argument in the next statement.

Career Recruitment. The ROTC is a method by which young men
are recruited to lifetime careers in the armed services. The
post-World War II incentive plans were instituted to commit early
in the college career, youth who would hopefully decide after the
initial obligation of military service was over, to continue in
the military. (The military drill program which pre-dated ROTC
was not considered to have this particular function.)

Socialization into Military Ideology. American anti-militaristic traditions have been difficult for the professional military
men to encounter. Americans have traditionally seen themselves
as anti-militaristic (even though certain business interests and
the government have supported innumerable military adventures
abroad).[4] Conscription did not become institutionalized until
1950 as the armed services have experienced continuous difficulty
in recruiting men. The military was never supported strongly by
Congress or the public after the end of a war until after World
War II with the beginning of the so-called Cold War. Since that
time, of course, the armed forces have experienced an extraordinary growth in their power to influence foreign policy and in
the size of their budget. In spite of these recent changes, we
must recognize a tradition of anti-militarism in the United States,
though perhaps the tradition is most accurately called one of
"ambivalence."

The roots of anti-militarism are in the protestant ethic which
contends that work must be productive. To be sure, in the South
(the economically underdeveloped section of the country), military
service was an attractive career.[5] The distrust of highly cen-

tralized government, the immigrant pasts which included fleeing the conscript armies of Europe, the belief in reason, and the constantly expanding frontier which offered economic independence, each support anti-militarism.

It was not until well after the Civil War, under the guidance of Elihu Root, that the military began to develop into a "profession."[6] As Riesman and Jencks have noted, the military began to try to develop a sense of profession, even though there is little in the way of skills or knowledges that are peculiar to the military.[7] The professionalism served, perhaps, as a method by which the military could be accepted in a civilian setting relatively hostile to military institutions, and to nonproductive aspects of military duties.

Many American attitudes toward the military are ambivalent. In many ways, destruction and violence, if not military men and military activities, are respected, admired, and an absorbing preoccupation in American folklore, serious literature, and mass entertainment.[8] American war movies are rarely anti-war, and portrayals of military men are rarely critical, except for the stock comic sergeant or the Captain Quigg types. For every Major Major in a Catch 22, there are many more General MacArthurs, and for every "What Price Glory?" many more "The Longest Day."[9] The political scene shows Presidents Washington, Jackson, Grant, Theodore Roosevelt, and Eisenhower entering office on the basis of recent military accomplishments. The ROTC clearly has had to cope with a dual attitude toward the military: distrust, ridicule, and disgust have vied with respect, awe, and dependence.

Conclusion about the efficacy of the ROTC in accomplishing the goal of socializing youth to accept a military approach to solving national and international problems has to be tentative. No designed study has been conducted on the effects of ROTC training was available to the author. A number of different materials are available, and we shall present the findings of these in an effort to reach some conclusion about the extent to which ROTC has been able to accomplish the goal of making youth accept military training, and to look favorably at the military officer.

An early study which military officers frequently cite as evidence for success of ROTC was conducted by the U.S. Office of Education in 1932, some fifteen years after the founding of the corps.[10] Questionnaires were sent to 16,416 graduates of ROTC (classes of 1920 to 1930) from 54 land-grant colleges. Unfortunately, replies were received from only 10,166 (60 per cent), and while this is a considerable number, there is no way to know if the men who chose to answer were more or less favorable than the 6,500 (40 per cent) who did not reply. Among the men who did reply, the majority were favorable toward the course, and had a favorable attitude toward the continuation of the course, the skills learned in the course, and favored compulsory ROTC courses during the first two years of college.

In 1964, the writer conducted a study of ROTC cadets.[11] Graduating senior ROTC cadets at Ivy League University (ILU) where ROTC is voluntary, a small sample of non-cadets at ILU, and graduating senior ROTC cadets at a well-known southern military academy (SMA) provided information (see Table 1 for percentage of replies). The questionnaire deals with career choices, career characteristics, social background, intergenerational mobility, with only a small number of the questions being about the military. The questionnaire was specifically presented as one which was gathering information on the plans of college men, not about ROTC.[12]

Essentially, the students in the study have the same ambivalence toward the military that other Americans have. Students and other Americans seem, at least in the past, to support the military by according them fairly high social standing,[13] by supporting American military adventures abroad, by listening seriously to military statements about foreign policy, and by allowing military men to make a variety of decisions which effect foreign relations. Students have a fairly flattering picture of military men even though they themselves are not particularly interested in being professional soldiers.

TABLE 1

PER CENT REPLIES TO QUESTIONNAIRES IN THE STUDY
OF ROTC CADETS AND NON-CADETS

Institutions	Number and Per Cent Replying	Total N and Per Cent Asked to Reply
Ivy League University ROTC Cadets, graduating seniors	146 (83%)*	176 (100%)
Ivy League University Non-cadets, graduating seniors	80 (33%)	257**(25%)
Southern Military Academy ROTC Cadets, graduating seniors	198 (93%)	214***(100%)

*Most of the cadets who did not fill out questionnaires were the "completed" cadets who were not currently enrolled in ROTC since they had already finished the course work. Questionnaires at the ILU were administered when possible by the writer, but in some cases by a member of the armed services.

**There were 1,041 graduating seniors at ILU who were residents of the United States but who were not enrolled in ROTC. We considered these to be eligible to be included in the study as a comparison group.

***According to the academy officials, fifteen of the students who did not fill out questionnaires were in the infirmary or out of town when the questionnaires were administered. Incidentally, the questionnaires were administered by a civilian professor of social science at the academy to lessen the possible influence of men in military uniform.

Cadets and non-cadets both, as Table 2 shows, see the military man as basically a responsible, able person with high social standing, and relatively high political influence. While there are some variations among the three sub-samples, these are not merely between the cadets and non-cadets. ILU students (cadet and non-cadet) both reject the notion that the career military officer is untalented. The SMA cadets are least favorable with half of the weighted sample, and 40 per cent of the unweighted sample either agreeing, or being undecided about the talents of career officers.

TABLE 2

ATTITUDES TOWARD SELECTED ASPECT OF MILITARY SERVICE

Statement in Questionnaire and Response Considered Favorable to the Military Services	Per Cent Favorable Responses Sample		
	ILU Non-Cadets %	ILU Cadets %	SMA Cadets %
Career military officers do Not have talents and aptitudes for good civilian jobs.(disagree)	69	77	51
Social standing of career military officer is "high". (Agree)	93	85	85
Military service has good opportunity for my field. (Agree)	21	27	21
Political influence of career military officer is "high". (Agree)	47	22	23
Political influence is "okay" as is. (Agree)	63	72	83

On the question of political influence, the non-cadets are much more likely than the cadets to think that the officer is "high" in political influence (perhaps here is where we see the result of exposure to sources in Military Science departments in American politics), but the overwhelming majority of all the students think that the military have a just amount of political power. Only small proportions of students in any of the samples say that their own fields are provided with good opportunities in the military. Interestingly, there is no difference between the three types of men in the view of what the service has to offer in their own fields.

Similarly, when the attitudes which students have toward military service are considered, little evidence points to the ROTC having much positive influence. Nearly twenty years ago (1952), when supposedly students were less critical of American foreign policy and less "radical" than in the 1960's, and shortly after

Selective Service was established, student attitudes reveal an
unfavorable view of military service. Opinions about the military
establishment are available from 2,975 men who in the early 1950's
were at Fisk, the University of Texas, the University of North
Carolina, Wayne State University, the University of Michigan,
Wesleyan, Cornell, UCLA, Yale, Harvard and Dartmouth.[14] Among
these men, the majority (89 per cent) preferred to stay out rather
than go in the military forces; 84 per cent said that if it were
up to them, they would not go in the service after college graduation; 72 per cent said that if they had an opportunity to stay
out of the service, they would certainly take advantage of it;
67 per cent disliked the idea of being called to fulltime service;
63 per cent said that the disadvantages of going into the military
service full time outweighed the advantages; and 60 per cent wanted
to be deferred from military service as long as possible.

A survey conducted among third term male freshmen at Michigan
State University who were the first to complete a year of ROTC
after the program became voluntary shows differences between Air
Force ROTC cadets, Army ROTC cadets, and non-ROTC men in attitudes toward military service.[15] Nearly one-half of the non-ROTC
men compared to a quarter or less of the ROTC cadets considered
the length of the required tour of duty to be an important consideration about the military service obligation. This could be taken
to indicate a more favorable attitude toward the military institution among men exposed to ROTC training than among the unexposed.
However, neither the Air Force ROTC cadets nor the non-ROTC men
indicated that "prestige and patriotism" was an important consideration: 10 per cent of the AFROTC and 8 per cent of the non-ROTC
men compared to 21 per cent of the Army ROTC cadets selected these
as their prime concern. In contrast, one-quarter of AFROTC cadets,
and 14 per cent of the non-cadets compared to only 7 per cent of
the Army cadets selected personal considerations—travel, adventure,
flying—as the prime concern in considering the military obligation. Sizeable proportions of each (31 per cent AFROTC; 32 per
cent, AROTC; and 24 per cent non-cadets) indicated another per-

sonal concern as the primary one: the "desire to use university training."

Among the men in our study of ROTC cadets, a confusing picture about obligatory military service emerges. Table 3 below shows the distribution of cadets and non-cadets among the four scale types of the Military Obligation Scale. Scale Type IV includes the men who are favorable toward fulfilling their service obligation while the men who are not favorable are in Scale Type I. The data presented in Table III show that men who are in the ROTC are more frequently favorable rather than unfavorable toward fulfilling the military service obligation compared to men who are not in ROTC. Sixty-nine per cent of the ILU cadets and 67 per cent of the SMA cadets are in the two scale types most favorable to fulfilling the service obligation compared to 23 per cent of the non-cadets from ILU. However, among the scale type representing the most favorable attitude toward the military service obligation, we find about the same proportion of men from each of the sub-samples: 15 per cent of the non-cadets from ILU, 10 per cent of the cadets at ILU and 12 per cent of the cadets from the military academy fall in Scale Type IV. This suggests that ROTC does have a possible positive effect on at least maintaining a somewhat favorable attitude toward military service, but that a most favorable attitude exists independent of the ROTC experience. We emphasize that the effect is more likely one of attitude maintenance rather than attitude change since we assume that men who stay in the ROTC for the four year college training period already have somewhat favorable attitudes toward military service.

Student opinion about whether or not military service ought to be continued varied among cadets and non-cadets. As Table IV shows, cadets from the military academy were most likely to agree with the statement that universal military training ought to be continued: 67 per cent of the SMA cadets compared to 49 per cent of the ILU cadets and only 37 per cent of the non-cadets at ILU were clearly favorable toward universal military training.

Now, to summarize the discussion thus far about the function

TABLE 3

MILITARY OBLIGATION SCALE*

Attitudes toward Military Service Obligation Scale Type	Non–ROTC ILU %	ROTC Cadets ILU %	ROTC Cadets SMA %
IV Most Favorable	15	10	12
III	8	59	55
II	42	25	16
I Least Favorable	34	7	16
	(71)	(142)	(213)

*The items which compose this scale are: "Military service helps a young man to mature." Agree (87) favorable; "Every man has a responsibility to help his country by serving some time in the military." Agree (68 per cent favorable); "Most of my friends would like to avoid military service." Disagree and undecided (18 per cent favorable). $R = 1 - \frac{46}{3(497)} = .95$

TABLE 4

STUDENT OPINION AT IVY LEAGUE UNIVERSITY AND SOUTHERN MILITARY ACADEMY TOWARD UNIVERSAL MILITARY TRAINING

Statement	ILU, Non–cadets	Per Cent "Agree" ILU Cadets	SMA Cadets
"Universal Military Training (UMT) ought to be continued." (Agree)	37%	49%	67%
	(71)	(142)	(123)

of the ROTC as an agent of socialization for youth into the norms, values and ideology of the military institutions. The conclusions must be tentative. Data on the attitudes of college men indicate that students who have served in ROTC are more likely than those who did not to have a favorable attitude toward serving some time in the military forces. Overall, however, students are not particularly favorable toward fulfilling a military obligation on college campuses where ROTC is required. This suggests that students in voluntary ROTC programs may initially have been favorable towards the military services compared to students who have had to take part in compulsory programs. Finally, students like

other Americans view the military with a fair amount of respect
rather than seeing military men in the stereotyped version of the
untalented man who could not succeed in civilian life, who is
power hungry, and the like. In order to draw more soundly-based
conclusions about the results of the ROTC experience on the attitudes of youth toward the military, it is necessary to conduct
longitudinal studies so comparisons can be made between attitudes
before and after the ROTC experience.

Character Development. The second function with which military drill, and then, ROTC have been charged is to develop sound
social character in college youth. The myth of dissipated youth
is a pervasive one in Western society. Some presumed special
problems of youth and their supposedly recent "degeneracy" have
been connected with a variety of phenomena. The change in social
organization from feudalism to capitalism,[16] particular social
structural, psychological, and cultural problems which characterize modern America,[17] the general level of permissiveness in the
home,[18] and universal psycho-social developmental problems have
all been considered responsible.[19] Opinions from the days of
Socrates to the present have compared youth unfavorably with their
elders and have attributed the deficiencies of youth to laxity in
the home, the schools, and religious institutions.[20] Kenneth
Keniston gives us a portrait of dissenting youth which is a
slightly more extreme portrait of youth than the one used in
arguing for college ROTC or military training, but very much part
of the same traditional American perspective. The youth is
"[b]earded, be-Levi-ed, long-haired, dirty and unkempt, . . .
profoundly disaffected from his society, often influenced by
'radical' ideas, an experimenter in sex and drugs, unconventional
in his daily behavior . . . a 'failure' . . . [T]he sources . . .
are to be found in the loss of certain traditional American
virtues. The 'breakdown' of American family life, high rates of
divorce, the 'softness' of American living, inadequate parents,
and above all, overindulgence and 'spoiling'."[21]

Supporters of military training have made use of this per-

spective in arguing for ROTC on the college campuses. The Assistant Secretary of Defense for Manpower, Charles Finaucane, made
the following statement before the Mershon National Security Conference in 1960:

> An officer must accept responsibility. At the moment it
> appears that great numbers of young men do not want to accept
> the self-discipline that is inherent in responsibility. It
> seems to me that we in the Department are somewhere lacking
> in our approach to parents, to yough of college caliber,
> and to the college educators who exercise such great
> influence in this matter . . . We must succeed in point-
> ing out if possible, that apart from the personal and
> financial advantages of officership as compared to enlisted
> status, it is incumbent upon each youth to serve his country
> and himself in the highest capacity which his mental, moral
> and physical stature will allow.[22]

A former assistant professor of military science in 1949
writes:

> . . . disciplinary training is now neglected in the
> home . . . ROTC training tends to exert a stabilizing
> influence upon undergraduate students at a time in life
> when it will do the most good.[23]

He goes on to note that "a majority of ROTC graduates, class of

1920 to 1930 at the land-grant colleges, argued that disciplinary
training is now neglected in the home, and that the ROTC exerts a
stabilizing influence . . ."[24] In 1939 the report prepared for
the Regents of the University of California, Berkeley, in rebuttal
to a critical Peace Committee study prepared by Student Government, praised the virtue of preparing young men who had the
"ability to perform activities other than those associated with
the term 'bookworm'."[25]

A comparison by Willard Nash of stated aims and goals of the
land-grant colleges and their department of military science and
tactics at the college in the early 1930's is interesting. The
colleges have generally more diffuse goals than do departments of
military science and tactics as far as developing social character is concerned. The study indicates that the military training department found more acceptable than did the colleges the
view that youth were in special need of character training.

Table 5 shows the stated aims and goals of the colleges and the
departments of military science. The military science departments
and the colleges both show some interest in social character
traits: leadership, loyalty, citizenship training are included
among the stated aims of both. But there are some differences.
The colleges but not the military science departments state the
following aims: training in research skills, efficiency, character,
and democracy. Sizeable numbers of military training departments
but not the colleges state that discipline, leadership training,
loyalty, mental and moral training and initiative are aims.

TABLE 5

STATED AIMS AND GOALS IN 1934 AMONG LAND-GRANT COLLEGES*

Aims Listed in Catalogues	Dept. of Military Science	College
Physical training	34	---
Reserve officers produced	31	29 (com-
Leadership training	31	2 pliance
Preparation for national emergency	26	-- with
Discipline	24	-- Morril
Use in industrial and professional careers	19	13 Act)
Respect for authority	14	---
Loyalty	10	1
Citizenship training	10	11
Mental and moral training	10	--
Initiative	9	--
Devotion to duty	3	---
Neatness	3	---
Horsemanship	3	---
Educational value	3	---
Research	--	14
Efficiency	--	11
Character	--	8
Democracy	--	5
	N=52	N=52

*Based on Willard L. Nash, "A Study of the Stated Aims and
Purposes of the Departments of Military Science and Tactics, and
Physical Education in the Land-Grant Colleges of the United States,"
Contributions to Education, No. 415, Teachers' College, Columbia
University, 1934, Table IX, p. 51.

This author concluded that the War Department "distributes material

that is propaganda in the sense that it strongly advocates the
defense of a particular type of society--that is in existence
today."[26]

The same concern with discipline of youth is exemplified in
the comments of Secretary of the War Department, Newton D. Baker,
in an introduction to a book favoring military training. Baker
says:

> The only danger one hears urged against (military)
> education . . . is that expressed by those who fear that
> the habit of obedience is destructive of initiative, and
> is in some obscure way un-American. But I wonder whether
> the truth is not that we have so little of the habit of
> obedience in America that our danger really lies in the
> other direction . . .[27]

The author of the book, a colonel in the United States Army, refers
to "the slack, self-indulgence and unregulated impulses of which
we see so much in this land and generation." The high delinquency
rate of 1913, and the decrease in the delinquency rate in Wyoming
(where military training was started in 1911) are interpreted to
support the virtue of military training.[28] Earlier in 1904, the
land-grant colleges debated the place of ROTC in the curriculum,
and considered a motion to restrict military drill to two hours
a week for the first two years of college. But military drill was
also defended as "being good for men."[29]

In spite of the notion not being carefully worked out, or
presented in a sophisticated manner, it appears that training
young men in civic virtues was considered as important a goal as
military tactical training for the military on college campuses.
This argument was developed partially from the perspective that
views the military as being capable of making a genuine contribution to the character training of young men in response to the
character defects of "contemporary" youth. In 1916, Alexander
Meikeljohn, then President of Amherst College, gave a sociological
answer to such an argument when he noted that military training
cannot discipline the young when the problem of lack of discipline
is presumably an unwillingness of the young to obey elders. Why
will they obey drillmasters? Either, he went on to argue, the

military virtues of discipline, obedience and the like are present in other subjects such as mathematics, or it is useless to
expect that two to four hours a week drill will create them.[30]
But the problem was never resolved.

Former ROTC cadets tend to evaluate positively their college
military experience, and to see themselves as having benefited by
developing such character traits as "discipline" and "good citizenship" as a result of the training.[31] Such self-reporting is of
limited utility since it gives us no information about behavior
which might reasonably be considered evidence of good character.
Two kinds of information were gathered from the students in our
study at Ivy League University and Southern Military Academy which
may be considered more directly possible outcomes of the cadet
experience. First, there are data on cumulative grade point
averages (GPA) (see Table 6). The reported GPA of cadets averaged
somewhat lower than that of the non-cadets at ILU. Two fifths of

TABLE 6

CUMULATIVE GRADE POINT AVERAGE OF STUDENTS AT ILU

Cumulative Grade Point Average*	ROTC Cadets	Non-cadets
	%	%
High (79 or more)	27	30
High Pass (76 to 79)	19	34
Passing or below (76 or less)	53	36
	100%	100%
	(142)	(71)

*No student reported a grade point average over 87. The grad-
ing system at the university was based on figures running 55, 60,
65 and so on to 95 and 100. Grading was considered 'tough' so that
a cumulative average in the low 80's was considered to be quite
good.

the cadets compared to three-fifths of the non-cadets had the
higher grade averages. Second, students were asked to indicate
whether or not they considered a number of values to be an important ideal in a life-time career. Table 7 shows the per cent of
students in each of the sub-samples selecting items which suggest
a broader concern than personal kinds of satisfactions. There

TABLE 7

PER CENT OF STUDENTS SELECTING SOCIAL BETTERMENT
ITEMS AS AN IDEAL IN A CHOSEN LIFE-TIME CAREER

Ideal in a Chosen Career	ILU Non-cadets %	ILU ROTC Cadets %	SMA ROTC Cadets%
Have political influence	11	20	7
Help people	63	51	64
Important and worthwhile to the world	65	65	74
Leave world better place	51	47	50
N =	(71)	(142)	(213)

are no consistent differences between cadets and non-cadets which
would show a better social character insofar as character is relevant to a concern with society. About the same per cent of non-
cadets (51 per cent), ILU cadets (47 per cent), and SMA cadets
(50 per cent) say they want to leave the world a better place.
Virtually identical percentages of ILU non-cadets (63 per cent)
and SMA cadets (64 per cent) want to help people. A somewhat
smaller percentage of ILU cadets (51 per cent) select this ideal
in a career. ILU students (65 per cent of non-cadets and cadets)
are somewhat less likely than SMA cadets (74 per cent) to have as
an ideal in a career the wish to do something important and worthwhile to the world. Small percentages of ILU students (11 per
cent of non-cadets and 20 per cent of cadets) and 7 per cent of
SMA cadets want political influence. Clearly ROTC membership does
not distinguish among students in their concern for social betterment.

To summarize the discussion of the development of social
character as a function of the ROTC, it appears that the concern
about a deficient social character among youth is indeed an ancient
one. Whether or not the ROTC, or any other kind of military training, can overcome such a perceived weakness is at best highly
arguable. Furthermore, examination of what can at least tentatively
be considered indicators of social character shows no difference

among students who have and have not had an ROTC experience. The
whole "problem" of the deficiency of youth acts as a rationale
for the development of any number of programs ranging from military
training to the study of Latin, Greek, and mathematics to training in physical education programs to participation in team sports,
all in attempts to deal with the skeptical perception on the part
of adults of the world of youth.

Socialization into Occupational Skills. Some members of the
armed forces have argued regularly, and strongly, for the continuation of compulsory ROTC on the grounds that the analysis of the
officers who served in both World Wars shows a sizeable number of
men who graduated from ROTC. At the height of mobilization during
World War II, some 11 per cent of the officers were graduates of
ROTC.[32] The impressive figures of 150,838 men and women who
served in World War II is given as "trained on campuses" of the
land grant institutions but many of these were obviously trained
during rather than before the war.[33] In 1963, one officer observed
that only 6 per cent of freshmen who entered ROTC later graduated
as commissioned officers and that at some institutions the man-
years expended by active duty personnel in training ROTC cadets
exceeded the man-years of military duty performed by the commissioned graduates.[34] A high proportion of officers on active
duty are graduates of ROTC but it must be noted that these
officers are among the lower rather than the upper ranks, and are
not a permanent source of upper level officers.[35]

ROTC graduates, furthermore, are not exempt from the initial
training required of all newly commissioned officers, or would-be
officers, nor does the Department of Defense think that ROTC basic
training is even necessary for the contemporary officers.[36] Whatever the virtues of ROTC may be for the army, it does not seem to
be that of substituting for any training which the armed services
normally carry out. The idea of a citizen army has long been
given up, and the ROTC is no longer thought to have the purpose
of creating any facsimile of the early American ideal of each
man-a-soldier.

What ROTC has been in the past is a mechanism by which college graduates have been recruited into reserve components of the armed service. Commitment to service in a Guard unit means a commitment to the practice of military skills, and further training. The ROTC graduate, however, has not traditionally made a commitment to the Guard beyond the required period of military service.[37]

Recently, the content of ROTC courses--that is, the materials which constitute part of the content of socialization into military skills--has come under scrutiny. Universities have set up commissions to study the materials, and the results on the campuses which still continue to offer ROTC programs have varied. For example, a 1970 report by the University of Oregon concluded that the ROTC curriculum met academic standards. A similar report prepared by a commission at Cornell University (which evaluated curricula at Dartmouth, Stanford, Yale, Cornell, and six other private and public universities) recommended that regular university personnel rather than military officers teach ROTC courses with historical, political, and policy content, courses which fall in technical areas such as engineering, and courses in applied social science.[38]

The armed forces themselves have been ambivalent about the utility of ROTC as a means of socialization into occupational military skills. As far back as 1960, it was suggested that the corps change its name from Reserve Officers' Training Corps to "Officers Education Program" while the emphasis of the corps also be changed from the preparation of reserve officers to the recruitment of career officers. How the ROTC has functioned to recruit career officers will be considered in the next section.

To summarize the discussion of the ROTC as a method of socializing men into military skills, it appears that the ROTC does not carry out a task which excludes officers training of ROTC graduates by the regular army itself after the commissioning of graduates as junior officers. Perhaps the regular army may find the job of training the junior officers somewhat easier than the training of new candidates for officer rank. This is by no means clear.

Furthermore, socialization during the college career does not
appear to produce a particularly large proportion of men from
ROTC who commit themselves to long term service in the National
Guard units.

Career Recruitment. Career recruitment into the armed forces,
as we mentioned above, has become an increasing concern of the
ROTC. In a profession which is seen by many to have undeservedly
low social standing and which presents extreme hazards to life,
the problem of recruitment is indeed a difficult one. A variety
of inducements have been used to recruit officers and enlisted
men. Free medical care and maternity benefits, housing allowances,
travel benefits for the immediate family, pensions, early retirement, higher education, and foreign travel have all been used as
means of luring men to the occupation. In spite of these, recruitment continues to be a chronic concern of the armed services. The
military services are a more likely career for the black man who
faces somewhat less discrimination in government service than
elsewhere than for men with many civilian opportunities open to
them. In popular opinion, a career in the military is sometimes
seen as an easy escape from the rigors of competition for the
untalented.

The ROTC is a means by which conceivably young men can be
recruited to careers in the armed services. Lyons and Masland,
sympathetic observers of the military services, have recommended
that the services develop some special position if they wish to
attract young men. They note that the services by no means secure
a fair share of talent, and that even among the contract students
(a part of the Navy's program to insure career officers), continued service after completion of the military obligation is low.

A large number of young men enroll in the ROTC programs in the
colleges and universities in the United States. A recent book on
the ROTC notes, with pride, that in 1963 there were 175,000 young
men enrolled in the Army ROTC programs, 10,083 in Naval ROTC, and
99,955 in Air Force ROTC.[40] These figures can hardly be interpreted to mean that young men are favorable toward serving in the

military, or toward a life-time career in the military: over 285
thousand men were in ROTC among two million 18-24 year olds in
higher education.[41]

The Selective Service System, as established in 1950, has been
a major reason for enrollment in ROTC since this is a means by which
young men could be deferred from military service. Studies of
college students clearly support the conclusion that enlistment in
the ROTC is largely because the course is compulsory. Interviews
with several hundred students at eight institutions enrolled in
compulsory ROTC in the late 1950's showed that the majority of
students would not have enrolled if the choice had been voluntary.
Those who enlisted for the advanced course did so to avoid the
draft, for scholarship programs, or to be an officer when they did
have to serve an active duty tour.[42] A study of ROTC at Arizona
State University in 1964 shows that among students taking the two-
year basic course, the overwhelming majority of freshmen (70 per
cent) and sophomores (77 per cent) said they were taking it because
it was compulsory.[43] During the 1960's several events acted to
make ROTC a less likely choice for a young man who did not want to
do military service. First, the growth of the peace movement and
the serious criticisms which have been made of American military
policy abroad have led young men, in increasing numbers, to apply
for conscientious objector status, to refuse draft induction, or
to leave the United States to avoid induction into the military.
Secondly, ROTC was increasingly made optional between 1961-1964
(22 major campuses changed from compulsory to optional among 227
schools which offered ROTC) and by 1970 most programs were optional.
Four schools--Harvard, Dartmouth, Columbia and Colgate--have
dropped ROTC entirely. Finally, the possibility of the draft
lottery and a volunteer army have further decreased the number of
young men enrolling in ROTC. In 1969, a special report from the
Pentagon noted a decrease of 25 per cent between 1968 and 1969
enrollment. The Pentagon itself noted that the decrease could be
attributed, partly, to a "wait-and-see attitude" among young men

who feel that there are increasingly better prospects that they will not be drafted.[44]

The ROTC's original plan of giving men who enrolled fairly long term deferments was changed very shortly after the initiation of the program since most young men chose not to go on active duty. The Navy's Holloway Plan, which offered sizeable financial inducements to young men, succeeded in producing almost 1,000 ensign in the first full class of graduates. But ten years later, only 100 were still on active duty. By the late 1950's, the Navy had altered the contract with enlistees to one which required a four-year tour of active duty to increase the likelihood of a naval career as well as to meet the immediate need for officers. For the same reasons, the Air Force ROTC began to require its graduates to agree to a five-year tour of active duty. The Army ROTC requires a two-year tour of active duty, followed by four years in one of the other components of the Reserves.[45]

While ROTC graduates constitute the single largest source of new officers, they usually leave the service after finishing their required active duty period.[45] The Air Force, for example, conducted a nationwide survey of AFROTC cadets in 1952 which illustrates the small proportion of cadets who are planning on a career in the military services. The proportion of cadets who planned on a career in the Air Force was small in each class, decreasing from a high of 11 per cent among freshman cadets to a low of 7 per cent among senior cadets. Moreover, the seniors more frequently than other cadets agreed with the statement that people who remained in the service after completing the required tour of duty did so because they could not get a good civilian job.[47]

The military was not a frequently chosen occupation among the students we studied at Ivy League University and Southern Military Academy. A majority of men had decided on a life-time occupation by the middle of the senior year: 81 per cent of the non-cadets and 65 per cent of the cadets from ILU said they had tentatively or definitely decided on a life-time occupation, as did 75 per

cent of the Southern Military Academy students. Table 8 shows
that the overwhelming majority of students who had occupational
plans selected civilian occupations.

Men who attended SMA are the most likely to indicate plans
for a military career, followed by men from the cadet corps at
ILU. Among those who select a civilian career, the choice of
ROTC cadets but not among the non-cadets is heavily in engineering. Among the other occupational choices there are no consistent
differences between cadets and non-cadets.

The military was the third, rather than the first or second,
occupational choice among the ILU cadets who had not decided on a
career. Many wanted a career in business (24 per cent), in teaching (18 per cent), and in the military (14 per cent). Among the
undecided military academy students, the first choices were
engineering (25 per cent) and business (25 per cent), then the
military (18 per cent). Considering both occupational plans, and
occupational possibilities, 35 among 198, or 17 per cent of the
Military Academy students, and 11 among 132, or 8 per cent of the
Ivy League cadets thought about a military career. Neither setting
seems particularly conducive to intentions to enter a career in
the military. This phenomenon is something which the armed services have long recognized, but have been unable to change.

Even among West Point cadets, the number of years spent in
military training is positively related to thinking about careers
which are not in the military. According to Lovell, the list of
careers which are seriously considered as alternatives to the
military increase with increasing time in training so that the
only choice of sizeable proportions of freshmen is in Engineering
and Scientific Research.[48] Among West Point seniors, however, the
list of possible careers is a good deal longer. A third or more
senior cadets indicate they are considering seriously careers in
Engineering, Scientific Research, Business Management, Foreign
Service, College Teaching, and Law. If the military experience
does socialize men into the ethic of the career soldier, the
reverse relationship would have to be the case.

TABLE 8

THE CHOSEN LIFE-TIME OCCUPATIONS OF
SENIORS AT TWO INSTITUTIONS UNWEIGHTED

Profession, Occupation or Field	Non-ROTC ILU	ROTC ILU	SMA
Per cent who say they have a chosen career	74%	62%	64%
TOTAL N	(80)	(132)	(198)
Military service	--%	5%	11%
Engineering	15	24	32
Law	14	11	10
Social Science	15	8	1
Natural Science & Medicine	19	9	25
Business (hotel, bank, P.R., personnel, etc.)	18	22	10
Other (agricultural, architecture, art, government) and all others	18	19	10
Total	99%	98%	99%
N=	(59)	(81)	(126)

According to our 1965 study of students at ILU and SMA, plans
to enter the military service as a life-time career appears to
be related to what kind of career is considered desirable rather
than simply to having or not having the ROTC experience.[49] Three
distinct career styles emerged among the occupational preferences
of the cadets and non-cadets. Some students viewed a career
mainly in terms of the personal satisfaction which would come
from a feeling of being able to use skills and abilities on the
job. Some viewed a career in terms of a desire to be upwardly
socially mobile, and were concerned with the organizational
setting of the career. Finally, some had a commitment to improving the society, and saw their career as one which ought to be
relevant to social and political events.

The Personal Satisfaction ideal was a career aspect which was
connected to university affiliation rather than cadet status.
Ivy League students, cadets and non-cadets alike, were more likely

than Military Academy students to want to maximize personal skills
in their careers.

ROTC cadets are more frequently quite concerned than non-cadets
with Assured Advancement in the chosen occupation. Thirty-eight
per cent of the non-cadets compared to 48 per cent of the ILU
cadets and 66 per cent of the MA cadets scored high on a measure
of concern with organizational aspects of a career which would be
conducive to a good deal of assurance that careerists would
regularly advance.

TABLE 9

ROTC MEMBERSHIP AND ASSURED ADVANCEMENT SCALE TYPE

| Characteristic | Per Cent "High" on Scale | | |
	ILU	ILU Cadet	SMA Cadet
Scale Types III and IV Assured Advancement*	38% (71)	48% (142)	66% (213)

*Assured Advancer Scale: My ideal in a job or occupation must:
"Enable me to look forward to a stable, secure future." (Yes--
85 per cent) "Advancement is for merit rather than politicking."
(Yes--63 per cent) "Allow me to get further ahead in life than
my parents did." (Yes--32 per cent) R=59/3(497), or .96.

A career as a professional soldier--aside from any attitudes
about military activities--may be most attractive to men who not
only want to be assured of career advancement, but who also see
the organizational structure of the military as compatible to that
type of career. Cadets who are considering a military career are
more likely to be "high" rather than "low" on the "Assured
Advancement" measure. The military careerists are similar in their
interest in advancement to men who are thinking about a career in
medicine, natural science, banking, finance, and accounting. The
military careerists are unlike men who intend a career in public
relations or social sciences. (Would-be lawyers fall in between
these two contrasting types.)

On the third aspect of career style, Social Betterment, there
were no marked differences between cadets and non-cadets. Would-
be soldiers were right in the middle between the least concerned

TABLE 10

CAREER CHOICE AND SCALE TYPE

Occupational Choice is	Assured Advance* Scale Type III & IV HIGH Per Cent HIGH	Social Betterment** Scale Type III & IV HIGH Per Cent HIGH
Public Relations	4% (24)	88% (24)
Social Science	23% (13)	75% (13)
Law	60% (57)	34% (57)
Medicine and Natural Science	66% (41)	48% (42)
Engineering	67% (70)	33% (70)
MILITARY SERVICE	78% (27)	50% (24)
Banking, Finance, Accounting	90% (40)	10% (40)
All Others	56% (78)	21% (47)

*See footnote on preceding table for items in this scale.

**The Social Betterment Scale was composed of the following items: My ideal job or career must: "Give me a feeling of participating in something important and worthwhile to the world." (Yes—71 per cent), "Make me feel I am leaving the world a little better place than when I came in." (Yes—48 per cent), and "Give me a chance to have a good deal of political influence on political affairs in the United States." (Yes—14 per cent). 45/3(497) or .97.

with social betterment, such as men entering banking and finance (10 per cent were in the low types), and those most concerned, and social science and public relations (75 per cent and 88 per cent scored "high"). Fifty per cent of the military careerists were "high" and 50 per cent were "low" on interest in social betterment as a career style, similar to would-be physicians, natural scientists, and somewhat more concerned with social betterment than engineers (34 per cent) or lawyers (34 per cent).

To summarize, the ROTC as a means of recruiting professional

career officers for the military services has been of limited
success. ROTC cadets are more likely than non-cadets to consider
a career in the military services, but the overwhelming majoring
of the cadets do not, in fact, indicate this as a likely career
(see Table 8). Our study of cadets indicates that selection of
the military forces as a career is related to a concern with
career stability.

Let us summarize our discussion of the four functions of
(1) socialization into military ideology; (2) character development; (3) socialization into occupational skills; and (4) career
recruitment. Either these functions have not been fulfilled to
any great extent by the corps, or the function is such that the
corps can not actually be expected to fulfill the function. We
suggest that attributing these four functions to the corps serves
as a rationale for continuing to have the organization on the
college campuses, in a civilian setting. Here, the armed services
is presumably less isolated from civilian society than in the
usual setting in which young men are trained for military service.
If the sociological base of the continuation of the corps on the
college campuses rested on the fulfillment of the four functions
just discussed, the corps would be in a tenuous position.

NOTES

[1]Obviously, many other reasons than United States involvement
in Indo-China account for student dislike of the ROTC: the amount
of time the course takes from other activities, an alleged trivial
or watered down curriculum, and the appropriateness of military
training in an institution devoted to knowledge and broad humanistic goals are other such problems. While this paper was being
typed the President expanded the Vietnam war into Cambodia.

[2]Neil H. Jacoby, Chairman, President's Task Force on Economic
Growth, argues that the lessening influence of ROTC is evidence
of growing anti-militarism in the United States, and rejects the
assertion that the country is becoming (or is) a militaristic
society. "Anti-militarism Is Strong and Growing," The Center
Magazine, Vol. 3, No. 1, January, 1970, p. 35.

[3]The National Defense Act of June 3, 1916, authorized the
establishment of senior divisions in colleges, military schools,

and junior divisions in the high schools. The purpose of this
section of the Act was to provide a reservoir of reserve officers
from which could be drawn men for military service during periods
of emergency. See William F. Levantrosser, Congress and the
Citizen-Soldier, Ohio State University Press, 1967, pp. 13-14.

[4]See the Congressional Record, Vol. 115, No. 103, 91st Congress,
First Session, for a listing inserted by the late Senator Everett
M. Dirksen, (R-Ill.) According to Dirksen, the United States used
military force abroad 153 times prior to 1945 excluding formally
declared wars. Fifty-eight military actions occurred before 1860,
26 between 1863 and 1898, 35 between 1898 and 1917, 24 between
1918 and 1941. An additional four have occurred since 1945; Cuba,
Lebanon, Vietnam, and the Korean action are the citations in the
list. This listing excludes all actions against American Indians.

[5]Morris Janowitz, The Professional Soldier,(Glencoe: The Free
Press, 1960), pp. 88-89 gives materials on regional background of
officers. Studies of stratificational rankings by sample populations from George Counts (1920) to Hatt and Goode NORC list show
slightly higher rankings for "captain in regular army" in South
than elsewhere. See Albert J. Reiss, Jr., and others. Occupations and Social Status (New York: The Free Press of Glencoe,
1961).

[6]See Samuel P. Huntington, The Soldier and the State (New York:
Vintage, 1957), pp. 241-254, for a discussion of the development
of military training.

[7]Christopher Jencks and David Riesman, The Academic Revolution
(New York: Doubleday, 1968),p.p. 202; 220.

[8]C. Wright Mills has an interesting discussion of this
ambivalence in his chapter on the "warlords" in The Power Elite
(New York: Oxford University Press, 1959), pp. 176-179.

[9]See Robert Hughes, ed., Film: Book 2, Films of War and Peace
(New York: Grove Press, 1962) for an interesting international
comparison of films.

[10]R. C. Bishop, A Study of the Educational Value of Military
Instruction in Universities and Colleges, 1932.

[11]Nona Glazer, Which Men March? A Pilot Study of Factors
Affecting Membership in ROTC, Ph.D. thesis, 1965, Cornell University. Appreciation is extended to Professor Robin M. Williams, Jr.
who supervised the study, and to the National Institutes of Health
for financial support, N.I.M.H. Grant No. MH 07761-01.

[12]The social background of the men who answered the questionnaire varied among the three sub-samples. There were many men

of the Jewish background at ILU among non-cadets, and few in the
other two sub-samples. There were more professional men among the
fathers of cadets and non-cadets at ILU than among the fathers of
the cadets at SMA. In order to control for this, the data were
standardized following Morris Rosenberg, "Test Factor Standardiza-
tion As a Method of Interpretation," Social Forces, Vol. 41, 1963,
pp. 41-53. The data must now be read, unless stated to be
"unweighted," with the proviso that since religious background and
father's occupation are now being held constant, generalizations
cannot be made about the ILU, or SMA student bodies. The generalizations are as if the student bodies were the same on these two
background characteristics.

[13]Military officers have ranked in about the top third or
better in the national opinion studies of attributed social stand-
ing. See Robert W. Hodge, Paul M. Siegel, and Peter H. Rossi,
"Occupational Prestige in the United States: 1925-1963," in
Reinhard Bendix and Seymour Martin Lipset, Class, Status and Power
(New York: The Free Press, 1966), p. 324.

[14]Rose K. Goldsen, Morris Rosenberg, Robin M. Williams, Jr.,
and Edward A. Suchman, What College Students Think (Princeton;
N.J.: D. Van Nostrand Co., Inc., 1960), pp. 140-142; 223-224.

[15]John M. Engebretsen, Gordon W. Paul, and Edward D. Ozybko,
Who Takes ROTC at Michigan State? Michigan State University, May
1963 (unpublished manuscript).

[16]See S. N. Eisenstadt, Essays on Comparative Institutions
(New York: John Wiley and Sons, 1965), pp. 146-173.

[17]Arthur L. Stinchcombe, Rebellion in a High School (Chicago,
Illinois: Quadrangle Books, Inc., 1964).

[18]Bruno Bettleheim

[19]Lewis Feurer, The Conflict of Generations (New York: Basic
Books, Inc., 1969).

[20]See David Gottlieb and Charles Ramsey, The American Adolescent
(Homewood, Illinois: The Dorsey Press, Inc., 1964), pp. 1-26.

[21]Kenneth Keniston, "The Sources of Student Dissent," Journal
of Social Issues, Vol. XXIII, No. 3, July, 1967, p. 110.

[22]Charles C. Finaucane, "Statements of Department of Defense
Representatives," Role of Colleges in ROTC Programs. The Ohio
State University Mershon National Security Program, 1960, pp. 49-
50.

[23]Cited in George H. Rankin, Major, U.S. Army, The Administration of Army Reserve Officers' Training Corps (ROTC) Units.
M.S. thesis, Political Science, Syracuse University, June, 1949,
p. 57.

[24]Ibid., p. 213.

[25]Bruce F. Allen, ROTC: Elective or Required? Answer to the
Report of the ASUC Peace Committee, University of California
Archives, n.d., c. 1939, p. 25.

[26]Willard L. Nash, "A study of the stated aims and purposes of
the departments of military science and tactics, and physical
education in the Land-Grant Colleges of the United States,"
Contributions to Education, No. 614, Teachers' College, Columbia
University, 1934, p. 106.

[27]Colonel L. R. Gignilliat, Arms and the Boy (Indianapolis:
Bobbs-Merrill Company, 1916), Introduction, n.p.

[28]Ibid., p. 114.

[29]U.S. Department of Agriculture, Proceedings of the 18th
Annual Convention of the Association of American Agricultural
Colleges and Experiment Stations, Des Moines, Iowa, November 1-3,
1904, U.S. Government Printing Office.

[30]Alexander Meikeljohn, "The Schoolmaster and Military Train-
ing," pp. 171-178, William L. Ransom, ed., Military Training,
Compulsory or Voluntary, Proceedings of the Academy of Political
Science, Vol. VI, No. 4, July 1916.

[31]See J. W. Bowles and Donald V. Torr, "An Attitude Survey of
AFROTC Cadets," Air Force Personnel and Training Center, Lackland
Air Force Base, Texas, Project No. 7701, Task No. 77040, 1952
(unpublished), p. 16; R. C. Bishop, A Study of the Educational
Value of Military Instruction in Universities and Colleges, U.S.
Office of Education, Government Printing Office, 1932; Lt. Col.
Theodore Wyckoff, USA, "Required ROTC: The New Look," Military
Review, November, 1964, p. 28.

[32]Based on materials presented in Captain V. Gondos, Reserve
Officers' Association, "The Reserves of the Armed Forces: A
Historical Symposium," Military Affairs, V. 17, Spring, 1953, p. 5.
Gondos states that the Reserves had 191,698 men in the services as
officers, or about 25 per cent of all officers were from the
Reserves. Among these, 95,000, or 11 per cent of all officers in
the services were graduates of ROTC.

[33]James E. Pollard, Military Training in the Land-Grant Colleges
and Universities, Ohio State University, no. pu., n.d. (c. 1962),
pp. 32-33.

[34]Lt. Col. Allan R. Scholin, Air National Guard, "The Guard Needs ROTC!" The National Guardsman, April, 1963, p. 7.

[35]About 45 per cent of the officers currently on active duty in 1964, for example, were ROTC graduates. These ROTC men were 65 per cent of 1st. lieutenants, 85 per cent of 2nd lieutenants, but only 10 per cent (N=90) of general officers. See "Reserve Officers Training Corps—The Nation's Largest Academy," no author, Army Information Digest, December, 1964, p. 12.

[36]Russell I. Thackrey, "Financing ROTC Programs," Role of Colleges in ROTC Programs. Ohio State University, 1960, p. 38.

[37]Lt. Col. Allan R. Scholin, "The Guard Needs ROTC," The National Guardsman, April, 1963, pp. 6-7; William V. Kennedy, "ROTC Officers for the National Guard," Army, July, 1963, p. 34.

[38]For a summary of the Cornell report see School and Society April, 1969, pp. 235-239.

[39]Gene M. Lyons and John W. Masland, Education and Military Leadership,(Princeton, New Jersey: Princeton University Press, 1965), p. 11.

[40]Monro MacCloskey, Brig. Gen. USAF (ret.), Reserve Officers Training Corps (New York: Richard Rosen Press, Inc., 1965), p.11.

[41]U.S. Department of Commerce, Bureau of the Census, Current Population Reports, 1965, p. 9.

[42]Raymond Fink, The College Student and the ROTC: A Study of Eight Colleges, cited in Joseph W. Scott, "ROTC Retreat," Trans-action, Vol. 6, September, 1969, p. 49.

[43]Op. cit., Wyckoff, p. 26.

[44]Associated Press Release, March 8, 1970. "ROTC Drops 25 per cent in 1969," The Oregonian, Portland, Oregon.

[45]MacCloskey, 1965: 71-72; 11-112; 69.

[46]Gene M. Lyons, "Officer Recruitment on the College Campuses," Role of Colleges in ROTC Programs, Ohio State University, Mershon National Security Program, 1960, p. 23.

[47]J. W. Bowles and Donald V. Torr, "An Attitude Survey of AFROTC Cadets," Air Force Personnel and Training Research Center, Lackland Air Force Base, Texas, Project No. 7701, Task No. 77040, 1952, unpublished. Cited percentages computed from data presented in Table 1, p. 6 and Table 15, Appendix B, p. 38. The data here cited are derived from the questionnaire which was administered

by civilians, and on which the cadets did not sign their names. These data were considered by Bowles and Torr to be the most reliably representative of the total population (see pp. 3-4).

[48]John P. Lovell, The Cadet Phase of the Professional Socialization of the West Pointer, Ph.D. thesis, University of Wisconsin, 1962, pp. 144-145.

[49]Glazer, op. cit.

ANTICIPATORY SOCIALIZATION AND THE ROTC*

William A. Lucas

A central subject of the growing literature on comparative
civil-military relations has been military professionalism. In
this paper we report on a study of cadets and midshipmen enrolled
in Reserve Officer Training Corps programs in order to identify
some of the factors that determine how and when professional
values are transmitted to new members of the officer corps.

Someone choosing a profession generally has a relatively
positive orientation towards it and the expectation that he would
fit into the chosen group. But as a career decision begins to be
made, there are further psychological forces at work, which we
might call anticipatory professional socialization. The concept
is anticipatory socialization as discussed by Robert Merton. The
individual, through a complex process of mediating social images,
changes his values to make them consistent with the norms of the
group he anticipates joining. "For the individual who aspires but
does not belong, this orientation may serve the twin functions of
aiding his rise into that group and of easing his adjustment after
he has become a part of it."[1]

It would seem as if this phenomena is particularly applicable
to admission into a profession. In today's society, boys begin to
develop occupation orientations quite early. Douvan and Adelson
found strong support for the view that our culture pushes the male

99

into considering his vocation even before he reaches high school.
In their national study of adolescents, the boys were asked about
the decisions they would make in the future, and 66 per cent mentioned a vocational decision.[2] "The fact that boys select a
broad variety of jobs, that no one or two jobs dominate the scene
for them, and that the jobs they choose are highly specified, all
lead us to conclude that they have a degree of sensitivity that
implies active involvement."[3] The future orientation of boys in
grades seven through twelve is in terms of an occupational identity, with concrete plans and active aspiration towards that
identity.[4]

For many professions, the period of professional anticipatory
socialization can extend from adolescence into the college years.
Serious consideration of law, medicine and other vocations with
advanced professional schools has begun. In three separate studies,
over 80 per cent of medical students had begun considering a
medical career by age 16 or 17; one reported that 44 per cent had
reached a final decision by that age.[5] For these budding professionals, a career decision is followed by a period of prolonged,
advanced education with little direct contact with the chosen
professions. The student who enters college in order to become
a doctor has four years to wait before he can enter medical school.
In that period, many will have no inter-action with doctors, and
organic chemistry will be as close as they will get to medicine.
They will nonetheless be anticipating their future career. The
future doctor may well begin to change his values to make them
consistent with his perceptions of what will be expected of him as
a doctor, and his expectations need not involve direct contact
with the medical profession. As a consequence, a key distinction
between anticipatory professional socialization and other forms is
that anticipatory socialization can be predominantly psychological,
requiring little to none of the face-to-face interaction   the
other forms used to transmit professional values.

All professions do not have this phase between occupational
choice and entry into professional instruction. In a comparative

study of the development of work identities of graduate students
in different fields, Becker and Carper found a great variation.
The engineering graduate students had already established work
identities as undergraduates; physiology students had strong preferences in other fields and only began to develop work identities
after starting graduate school.[6] Thus one must consider both the
age of the future professional when he makes a career choice and
his age when he enters a profession. If the difference is on the
average very brief for a particular profession, then there is
little likelihood that anticipatory socialization is important in
that case. Whether professional socialization is anticipatory or
direct also varies in degree from profession to profession. Most
children know their doctor, and have often encountered more than
one through the chicken pox and tonsilitis years. When medical
students at one university were asked whether they could think of
a doctor who comes close to being an ideal doctor, 68 per cent
could name one. By contrast, 43 per cent of the law students at
that university could name a comparable lawyer.[7] Prospective
teachers, dentists and clergymen generally have an opportunity to
interact with and learn from practicing professionals in addition
to those among their own relatives;[8] the prospective architect,
journalist, or physicist must rely on more indirect sources for
role-models. The less this direct professional contact is available, the more likely the theory of anticipatory socialization
might apply.

The military profession meets the conditions that would be
required for anticipatory socialization to have an impact. The
potential officer has access to considerable information about the
style and content of the officer role, and can recognize it as a
distinct occupation at an early age. The legal obligation to
register for the draft compels the individual to think about his
future relationship with the military. There is opportunity for
early career decisions, and there is consequently an extended
period of time for the individual to anticipate his entry into the
profession.

Many prospective officers have had contact with veterans, but, except for the sons of military men, few have contact with practicing professionals. The physical separation of the military from civilian life may be less than it was before the Second World War, but the military remains as one of the more isolated professions. Consequently, anticipation based on social images could be playing a role equal to or greater than conventional learning through direct contact.

The potential impact varies, of course, from one type of commissioning program to another. The officer who entered Officer Candidate School because, at age 22, he had no other occupational choice is quite different from the one who resolved to enter West Point at the age of twelve. This study examines the utility of the concept of anticipatory socialization for only one source of active duty officers, the Reserve Officer Training Corps. But the factors of commitment and clarity, which prove to be important explanatory variables, have relevance beyond the ROTC.

If the theory of anticipatory professional socialization applies to the development of attitudes among ROTC cadets and midshipmen, we would expect two facts to be true: (1) there should be a strong sense of occupational or professional commitment among a significant proportion of the ROTC students that develops before they "enter" the profession; and (2) commitment should in turn lead to the development or change of values congruent with those held by the military profession. To measure that learning, we must study the congruency between the attitudes of ROTC cadets and midshipmen and the attitudes of professional military officers. To test this perspective, we employ data on two thousand ROTC students and 145 officers in the National War College.

PROFESSIONAL COMMITMENT

The first task becomes the measurement of professional commitment, and showing its relationship to other types of pro-military attachments that might not involve any commitment to the military career.

Measurement

The respondents were over two thousand ROTC cadets and midshipmen at four universities. The specific universities and ROTC
detachments were selected according to criteria that blended availability with the need to have different types of academic institutions represented. The University of North Carolina, The Ohio
State University, and the University of California at Los Angeles
were accessible and representative of diverse regions. Duke
University was added in order to include a private institution.

Eight different ROTC programs were included in the study.
Both the Navy and the Air Force ROTC at the University of North
Carolina were surveyed, although the sophomores--who did not meet
ROTC classes that semester--were not contacted. All three service
programs are represented at Ohio State University. About one-half
of the Army and Air Force ROTC freshmen and sophomores were given
questionnaires, but due to an adminstrative misunderstanding the
results from the Army lower classmen were lost. A sample of the
advanced Air Force classes, virtually all the Army upperclassmen,
and all four years of the Navy midshipmen took the questionnaire
without complication. At Duke and UCLA the Air Force ROTC units
could not be included, despite efforts to do so. Since there is
no Army ROTC program at Duke, the final result is that data on the
Army (juniors and seniors only) and Navy ROTC at UCLA and on the
Navy ROTC at Duke were obtained.

To demonstrate the strength of the positive orientations of
the ROTC cadets and midshipmen, we extended the study to include
two comparison groups. That same spring, after the ROTC data had
been collected, random samples of non-ROTC male undergraduates
were drawn and then interviewed both at the University of North
Carolina and at Ohio State University.[9] At Ohio State, many cadets
and midshipmen in the Army and Air Force Basic program--the freshmen and sophomores--took ROTC only to satisfy certain university
requirements.[10] Consequently, the first two years of the non-
ROTC population has self-selected out of the ROTC. Any differences

between all the ROTC and all the non-ROTC could thus be interpreted as an artifact of the semi-compulsory nature of the programs
and the liberal views of the lower classmen who actively avoided
the ROTC. Comparisons at Ohio State will therefore be limited to
upperclassmen.

The key question on the interview schedule was to measure
commitment, but commitment to what? Most of those in the ROTC
were either already obligated or intent on serving a period of
active duty. Those planning to leave military life after their
first tours are likely to be influenced more by the civilian
occupational roles they had begun to think about beyond their
military service than by a temporary military role.[11] Expectations
about the nature of that short period did not seem to be central
to professional socialization. Rather, we were interested in
judgments related to a long-term professional identity or role.

In short, the notion of professional socialization seemed to
imply commitment to a career, so the respondents were asked to
indicate the likelihood that they would choose a military career.
The results, when we compare the ROTC students at North Carolina
and Ohio with the appropriate non-ROTC comparison groups, reveal
striking differences (Table 1). At the University of North Carolina, we did find three non-ROTC students who thought they would
probably make a career of the military, but about half the Navy
midshipmen and 40 per cent of the Air Force cadets had definite or
probable career intent.[12] Less than a third of the ROTC were
either probably not or definitely not in the ROTC going on for a
career. At Ohio State, two of the random samples would probably
elect a military career, while a sixth of the Army, over 40 per
cent of the Navy, and almost half of the Air Force ROTC juniors
and seniors planned a career. Clearly, career intent is present
for a substantial proportion of the ROTC.

TABLE 1

NON-ROTC AND ROTC COMMITMENT

TO A MILITARY CAREER

University of North Carolina

Likelihood of Choosing A Military Career	Non-ROTC N=113	Navy ROTC N=101	Air Force ROTC N=125
Definitely Will	0.0%	11.9%	10.4%
Probably Will	2.7%	37.6%	28.0%
Uncertain	6.2%	20.8%	30.4%
Probably Will Not	31.9%	22.8%	28.0%
Definitely Will Not	59.2%	6.9%	3.2%
	100.0%	100.0%	100.0%

Chi Square Significant at the .001 level.

Ohio State University
Upperclassmen

Likelihood of Choosing A Military Career	Non-ROTC N=49	Army ROTC N=374	Navy ROTC N=78	Air Force ROTC N=128
Definitely Will	0.0%	1.9%	6.4%	9.4%
Probably Will	4.1%	14.2%	35.9%	39.8%
Uncertain	12.2%	26.5%	24.4%	29.7%
Probably Will Not	38.8%	44.3%	29.5%	19.5%
Definitely Will Not	44.9%	13.1%	3.8%	1.6%
	100.0%	100.0%	100.0%	100.0%

Chi Square Significant at the .001 level.

Commitment and Attachment

Although most of the concepts on the questionnaire were opera-
tionalized in straightforward questions, steps were taken to
obtain a second type of measurement. There is the persistent
problem that structured opinion questions might crystallize or
create opinions that were either non-existent or weakly held. In
the case of commitment, there was the further problem that the
cadets and midshipmen might have strong attachments to the military
that are unrelated to the idea of career. The individual could

simply think it would be great to be an officer, or he could feel a moral obligation to serve in uniform that stemmed from a strong, pro-military ideology. What was needed was a measure of attachment in the sense of strong positive affect for the military that, based on an independent methodological framework, could be tested for its relationship to career intent.

As a technique to deal with this problem, we employed a simplified version of the semantic differential developed by Charles E. Osgood. Our purpose was to move to the level of psychological affect, thereby obtaining responses and less colored by current politics and casual opinions. Testing of the differential led to the conclusion that a shortened, two-scale version was an adequate and valid method to test for affect respondents hold for objects.[13]

The objects for these scales that seemed to test directly the positive affect the respondent has towards being a military officer seem to be military and officer. In this instance, we are measuring a reaction at a "gut" level of psychological affect that could come from a conservative ideology, a childhood experience, or one of many idiosyncratic factors.

The results again revealed striking differences between the ROTC and non-ROTC groups. On a scale ranging from +6 to-6, at the University of North Carolina, the average responses of the non-ROTC student sample to the concepts military and officer were mildly positive (+2.30 and+2.34). By contrast, the Navy and the Air Force ROTC were moderately positive both towards the military (+3.49 and +3.82) and towards officer (+4.43 and +4.03). The juniors and seniors in the Ohio State random sample are even less favorable to officer (+1.31), and the military (+1.37) than were the North Carolina group, but the upperclassmen in the Army, Navy and Air Force ROTC had average rsponses that were quite positive towards both symbols (Table 2). Strong positive orientations are clearly present; the further question is what is the inter-relationship between attachment of this sort and commitment more specifically focused on a career?

Career commitment strongly co-varies with affect for the

military as measured by the semantic differential. Because of the very small number of respondents who reported that they "definitely were" or "definitely were not," going to make a career of the military, those two categories were merged with the "probably" and "probably not" responses respectively. This step reduced considerably the interpretation problem caused by unstable means. The only exception to the rule that as career commitment rises, positive attitudes towards military objects increase as well, is found for the UCLA Army ROTC. The groupings for that program are small enough to cause unstable means through sampling error even after the categories are collapsed (Table 3), and there is a marked difference between those who definitely or probably will not make a career in the military and those who are more committed. When we tested these differences using analysis of variance, the variation due to all five levels of career commitment were statistically significant at the 0.1 level or higher for all the ROTC programs we studied except two. Differences in the small (N=72) UCLA Army ROTC group and the North Carolina Navy ROTC midshipmen illustrated the same patterns but each achieved statistically significant differences on only one of the two concepts. In all, there are large and quite consistent trends across the eight ROTC programs.

It seems evident that career commitment is accompanied by a strong positive attachment to the military, but the data reveals another point as well. When we compare the non-ROTC with those cadets and midshipmen who are probably or definitely not going on for a military career (Tables 2 and 3), we find both at North Carolina and Ohio State that there is still a substantial residual not explained by career intent. Although members of the ROTC frequently can be heard to explain their participation by suggesting that it was draft motivated, even those without career commitment are still significantly more positive towards the concept officer than are their non-ROTC peers. The fact of ROTC participation alone is very likely to be accompanied by a positive orientation towards the idea of being an officer.

TABLE 2

ROTC AND NON-ROTC AFFECT

FOR MILITARY CONCEPTS*

	University of North Carolina				
	Non-ROTC N=110	Navy ROTC N=99		Air Force ROTC N=128	
Concept	Mean	Mean	Sig.Level**	Mean	Sig.Level
Military	+2.30	+3.49	.001	+3.82	.001
Officer	+2.34	+4.43	.001	+4.03	.001

	Ohio State University Juniors and Seniors Only						
	Non-ROTC N=49	Army ROTC N=379		Navy ROTC N=79		Air Force ROTC N=133	
Concept	Mean	Mean	Sig. Level	Mean	Sig. Level	Mean	Sig.Level
Military	+1.37	+3.16	.001	+3.33	.001	+3.58	.001
Officer	+1.31	+3.83	.001	+4.09	.001	+4.22	.001

*The maximum possible range is from +6.0 to-6.0. A score of +4.0 is "moderately" positive, +2.0 is "slightly" positive, and zero is neutral. Because of the lack of a better means of reporting and evaluating the data, we shall assume that the semantic differential meets the interval assumption.

**This figure is obtained by testing the difference between the means of the ROTC group in question and the appropriate random sample.

Our concern is with the careerist, however. Affect alone is an ambiguous index of his professionalism, but the intent and affect together give us a measure of the broad factor of commitment. It remains to demonstrate at what point this factor develops.

Commitment and Professional Education:

For anticipatory professional socialization to apply to the ROTC, career commitment must be present before "entry" into the profession. If commitment were to develop during ROTC education, we would be faced with the ambiguity of whether or not being in the

ROTC constitutes membership in the military profession. As it happens, commitment does not increase in ROTC and therefore, by inference, commitment emerges before college.

Critics of the ROTC have charged that the ROTC "militarizes" the student who takes it. The implicit empirical theory is that the ROTC program influences the cadet or midshipman by intensifying his attachment to military institutions. By contrast, a liberal arts education is sometimes held to be a liberalizing influence, and part of the liberalism is a skeptical evaluation of military men and action. Both views assume something about the nature and direction of attitude change in the college years.

To identify changes brought about during college, we must in large measure rely on the pseudo-longitudinal or cross-sectional approach. By comparing one academic year with another, we should be able to identify systematic change that might be occurring during the college experience. Error can be introduced with this approach, however, because entering classes might be gradually changing due to historical factors. Fortunately, few factors in 1966 could have influenced one ROTC entering class without similarly affecting the other. All enrolled in the ROTC before the war in Vietnam had become the issue tearing at society that it became. The freshmen had started after the major United States involvement of February 1965, but the draft calls had not begun to disrupt college life. The issue of the ROTC as the "military on campus" was not yet salient.

The most complete data, and the most useful for the pseudo-longitudinal approach, is found for three of the Navy ROTC programs. The respondents at Duke, UCLA, and Ohio State included midshipmen of all four academic classes, allowing us to compute the class means and infer change from four points in "time." More care must be taken with results based on only three classes, so less weight should be placed on the responses by academic year of the Navy and Air Force ROTC at North Carolina.

In general the data on all five programs support the same conclusion: there is no consistent rise in positive orientation to

TABLE 3

ROTC AFFECT FOR MILITARY CONCEPTS BY CAREER COMMITMENT

Program	Concept	High Career Intent	Uncertain Career Intent	Low Career Intent	Level of Significance*
University of North Carolina:					
Navy ROTC	Military	N=48 +4.15	N=21 +3.67	N=30 +2.33	.05
	Officer	+4.69	+4.57	+3.93	ns
Air Force ROTC	Military	N=48 +4.65	N=38 +3.84	N=39 +2.69	.001
	Officer	+4.63	+3.95	+3.36	.01
Duke University:					
Navy ROTC	Military	N=26 +3.96	N=41 +3.00	N=35 +2.20	.001
	Officer	+4.77	+3.98	+3.40	.001
Ohio State University:					
Army ROTC (Upperclassmen only)	Military	N=59 +4.46	N=99 +3.42	N=215 +2.71	.001
	Officer	+4.95	+4.03	+3.46	.001
Navy ROTC	Military	N=107 +4.26	N=64 +3.53	N=61 +2.57	.001
	Officer	+4.66	+4.22	+3.33	.001
Air Force ROTC	Military	N=222 +4.07	N=268 +3.20	N=398 +2.34	.001
	Officer	+4.26	+3.67	+2.72	.001

TABLE 3
(continued)

ROTC AFFECT FOR MILITARY CONCEPTS BY CAREER COMMITMENT

Program	Concept	High Career Intent	Mean Responses for ROTC with: Uncertain Career Intent	Low Career Intent	Level of Significance*
University of California at Los Angeles:					
Army ROTC (Upperclassmen only)		N=10	N=15	N=44	
	Military	+4.10	+4.33	+3.05	.05
	Officer	+5.30	+4.67	+4.07	ns
Navy ROTC		N=49	N=45	N=33	
	Military	+4.14	+3.53	+2.33	.001
	Officer	+4.67	+3.84	+3.82	.01

*This statistic was computed using all five levels of career commitment.

TABLE 4

AFFECT FOR MILITARY CONCEPTS BY ACADEMIC YEAR

Program and Concept	Freshman	Sophomore	Junior	Senior	Sig. Level
Duke Navy ROTC:	N=30	N=22	N=21	N=20	
Military	+3.10	+2.73	+2.67	+3.35	ns
Officer	+4.03	+3.73	+4.00	+4.25	ns
Ohio State					
Navy ROTC:	N=83	N=71	N=34	N=45	
Military	+3.75	+3.80	+3.18	+3.44	ns
Officer	+4.40	+4.10	+4.03	+4.13	ns
UCLA Navy ROTC:	N=44	N=33	N=24	N=22	
Military	+3.80	+3.09	+3.88	+3.18	ns
Officer	+4.45	+4.03	+4.17	+3.91	ns
No. Carolina					
Navy ROTC	N=51	N=0	N=12*	N=35	
Military	+3.76	–	+3.25	+3.23	ns
Officer	+4.55	–	+5.00	+4.09	ns
No. Carolina					
Air Force ROTC:	N=51	N=0	N=38	N=39	
Military	+4.29	–	+3.84	+3.18	.05
Officer	+4.12	–	+3.97	+3.97	ns

*See Footnote 12.

TABLE 5

CHANGE IN ROTC AFFECT FOR THE CONCEPT "OFFICER":
NORTH CAROLINA PANEL DATA

	N	1965 Mean*	1966 Mean	Average Change
Navy ROTC	33	+2.30	+2.33	+0.03
Air Force ROTC	36	+2.17	+2.25	+0.08
Total	69	+2.23	+2.29	+0.06

*The means are based only on the good-bad scale, with scores ranging only from +3 to -3.

the military concepts over the four classes. When tested by analysis of variance, all differences in group means are readily attributable to chance except one (Table 4). Responses to one of the concepts by the Air Force ROTC provide the single inconsistency. Examination of the group means, however, shows the difference is attributable to a trend that is the reverse of that expected. Positive sentiment for the military actually appears to decline. Whatever interpretation one might choose, there is no exception to the view that there is no change during the college and ROTC period that could account for the pro-military attitudes of the ROTC cadets and the midshipmen reported above.

As an additional source of data, we have the responses of sixty-nine Navy and Air Force ROTC students who were surveyed both in the 1965 pre-test and in 1966. Although the questionnaires were quite different, both included one semantic differential scale with the symbol officer. These data serve as a limited check on the pseudo-longitudinal method, for with this panel we are measuring change directly not inferring it. Furthermore, the panel bridges the period that includes the six weeks of required ROTC summer duty, the most intensive and direct exposure to the military profession the cadet or midshipmen receives until he is commissioned. Because the second wave was conducted in the late spring, the year of the test period also includes the time when the reality of military service is fully upon the individual. Commissioning is only weeks away, and first assignments are being discussed with the ROTC cadre. If there is any influence by the ROTC program upon the individual, it certainly should be present here. There was, however, no indication of any influence by the ROTC program that would account for the basic differences between the ROTC and the nonROTC comparison groups.. Sentiment towards the symbol as measured by mean values in 1965 and 1966 on the semantic differential showed virtually no change at all in either the Air Force or the Navy panels (Table 5). Again there is no evidence that the positive sentiment the average ROTC student feels for the military develops during college. When we move to the career intentions of the ROTC, we also find no evidence that career motivation increased in the college years. The closest case to an increase was found in the Air Force ROTC program at the University of North Carolina. There a slight upward shift in the career commitment of the senior cadets was evident, but it was neither a

strong relationship nor statistically significant (Table VI).
There was little change in the Navy ROTC at Duke or at North Carolina. By contrast, there was a slight but not significant decline
in the commitment of the Navy midshipmen at Ohio State and a
stronger downward trend among the midshipmen at UCLA. The evidence
suggests that the period of professional education has no impact
on the likelihood that the average ROTC student will go on to a
career after his first tour of active duty. If any change is present, it is that the probability is lessened rather than increased
over the four years.

One additional influence might be at work here. Remembering
that there are some resignations from the ROTC programs, one might
surmise that a basic positive orientation is essential to the
individual's continuance in the ROTC. The college environment
could be having a mild negative impact on the pro-military attitude of the ROTC cadets and midshipmen. But the negative trend
that could result from this liberal, anti-military influence might
not appear because the few individuals who lose their positive
orientations drop out of the ROTC. We have no evidence to deal
with this problem of attrition, but it does not alter the view
that the basic positive orientations and career commitment must
have been largely determined in the pre-college period of the
individual's life.

These findings taken together are strong evidence that the
commitment factor does not change during the period of college
and ROTC. Similarly, the ROTC does not "militarize" cadets and
midshipmen in the limited sense of creating greater attachment or
commitment to the military. Whether other attitudes are shaped
by the ROTC will be discussed below, but commitment is not inten-
sified. Indeed, at a more liberal university like UCLA, the net
effect of the combined ROTC and college experience is more likely
to be a weakening of the average cadet's commitment to the military.
And why should we expect anything else? We might note that the
few hours a week required by the ROTC must compete with a college
environment rich with other influences. When a cadet leaves the

TABLE 6

CAREER COMMITMENT AS A FUNCTION OF ACADEMIC YEAR

Air Force ROTC Cadets at the University of North Carolina

Likelihood of Choosing A Military Career	Freshmen	Sophomores	Juniors	Seniors
	N=51	N=0	N=36	N=38
Definitely Will	9.8%	—	13.9%	7.9%
Probably Will	23.5%	—	25.0%	36.8%
Uncertain	35.3%	—	19.4%	34.2%
Probably Will Not	25.5%	—	38.9%	21.1%
Definitely Will Not	5.9%	—	2.8%	0.0%
	100.0%		100.0%	100.0%

Gamma = -.117, Chi Square not significant

Navy ROTC Midshipmen at UCLA

Likelihood of Choosing A Military Career	Freshmen	Sophomores	Juniors	Seniors
	N=42	N=33	N=24	N=22
Definitely Will	19.0%	3.0%	8.3%	0.0%
Probably Will	35.8%	33.3%	29.2%	13.6%
Uncertain	26.2%	42.4%	33.3%	50.0%
Probably Will Not	19.0%	15.2%	25.0%	36.4%
Definitely Will Not	0.0%	6.1%	4.2%	0.0%
	100.0%	100.0%	100.0%	100.0%

Gamma = +.318, Chi Square significant only at the .10 level.

drill field, he returns to a peer group that is usually skeptical, if not actively hostile, towards the military. Courses on air power must compete with Shakespeare and Burke, and sometimes with Sartre and Russell. Commitment and positive orientations towards the military do well to hold their own.

If these attitudes do not change during college, and if the ROTC is much more committed to military career than the non-ROTC, then attachment must develop before the entering student puts on an ROTC uniform. A central test of the relevance of anticipatory professional socialization has been met: the future ROTC officer has a strong career orientation before he joins the military profession.

TABLE 7

ROTC AND NON-ROTC ORIENTATIONS TOWARDS
PROFESSIONAL CONCEPTS

	University of North Carolina				
	Non-ROTC N=110	Navy ROTC N=99		Air Force ROTC N=128	
Concept	Mean	Mean	Sig. Level	Mean	Sig. Level
Military	+2.30	+3.49	.001	+3.82	.001
Professional Soldier	+0.98	+2.90	.001	+3.23	.001

	Ohio State University (Juniors and Seniors Only)						
	Non- ROTC N=49	Army ROTC N=379		Navy ROTC N=79		Air Force ROTC N=133	
Concept	Mean	Mean	Sig. Level	Mean	Sig. Level	Mean	Sig. Level
Military	+1.37	+3.16	.001	+3.33	.001	+3.58	.001
Professional Soldier	+0.47	+2.65	.001	+2.94	.001	+2.90	.001

ANTICIPATORY PROFESSIONAL SOCIALIZATION

Since the ROTC student has begun to develop professional commitment before he comes into direct contact with the military profession, there is the possibility that this factor will lead in
turn to the development of other attitudes. The concept of anticipatory professional socialization suggests that there are alter-
rations in the individual's attitudes to help him fit into the
military profession. If this process is to be effective in expe-
diting the recruits' entry into the profession, attitude change
must bring about a set of beliefs which are similar to those held
by the practicing members of the military profession. Thus we are
not concerned with simple attitude change because the dependent
variable in a professional socialization study is the congruency

between the attitudes of the candidates and the professionals. Thus, unless there is data available on the attitudes of the military profession, the meaning of a trend found among cadet attitudes is difficult to evaluate.

To meet that need, data were also collected on the attitudes of professional military officers. In the two years following the ROTC study, self-administered questionnaires were completed by two classes of the United States National War College. These officers were mostly colonels in the Army, Air Force, and Marines and captains in the Navy. There were a few lieutenant colonels and commanders. If the past is any guide, well over half of these respondents will eventually achieve the rank of general or admiral. Congruency can thus be measured by the similarity between the officers and the ROTC cadets and midshipmen on a given attitude.

Clarity, Commitment and Congruency. We do not expect the students in the ROTC to mirror all the views held by these officers. Certainly we would not predict that an ROTC cadet would change his views in areas unrelated to the military profession, while we expect that he would learn values central to his anticipated professional role. Thus the relevance and centrality of an attitude to the professional identity of the cadet will help determine whether he will perceive it as appropriate for an officer and whether he will feel a need to accept it. Much turns on the individual's expectations of what military officers believe, and the more "obviously" a value is directly linked to the profession, the more likely he is to accept it.

One such concept central to military professionalism is the professional soldier. If the future officer looks beyond his first tour of obligated duty, he will be a professional, and we feel the implications of career intent are in this instance "obvious" to the future officer. Assuming that anticipatory socialization has any impact at all, positive affect for this concept should be strongly related to career commitment.

Affect for this concept is also valuable because it is not always related to conservative, non-career orientations the way

affect for many military symbols might be. The standing army and
the military professional have long been viewed in the United
States with more or less hostility, largely depending on the
society's perception of external threat. The virtues of the
citizen soldier, not the professional, have been extolled by
American politicans and political thinkers. This emphasis on
the citizen in arms has declined since the Second World War, but
the rhetoric of grammar school history books continues to focus
on the legitimacy of the militia. Because of this cultural tradition, those young men that are pro-military but not interested
in the military as a vocation can be much less positive to the
notion of the professional.

If anticipatory socialization is operative and accurate, committed ROTC students should also have attitudes congruent with
those of professional officers, similar in direction and intensity. Whether or not the cause is anticipatory socialization,
there is a strong mechanism at work, leading to distinct differences between the ROTC and non-ROTC groups at the University of
North Carolina and at Ohio State University. As was presumed,
the Anglo-American prejudice against the professional soldier
was evident for both the ROTC and non-ROTC groups in that they
all ranked the military higher than they did the professional
soldier (Table 7). The ROTC was, however, much more positive
towards the latter concept, and they tended to differentiate less
between the two than did the non-ROTC samples at North Carolina
and Ohio State.

Moreover, career commitment explains consistent and massive
differences in the positive sentiment held for the concept professional soldier. The differences were statistically significant even for the small Army ROTC program at UCLA (Table 8), and
the means consistently rise as one moves from low to high career
intent. If we probe deeper, using all five levels of career
intent, we find that an even wider variation can be accounted
for. Means based on only one or two individuals created problems, but the large Army and Navy ROTC programs at Ohio State

suggest the nature of the results. The seven Army cadets who
were definitely going to make a career in the military had a
strongly positive view (+5.43) of the professional soldier. Those
that felt they would probably choose a career were moderately
positive (+4.44), and the trend continued through those definitely
not choosing a career who were not very different from the non-
ROTC group (Table IX). The Navy pattern was equally clear if not
as strong.

The officers of the National War College were also positive
towards the concept. For 143 officers, the mean response to the
professional soldier based on the same semantic differential
scales was +4.10, a moderately positive orientation. This level
of affect is quite similar to that held by the ROTC students committed to a military career, suggesting a high degree of congruency between the professionals and the candidate members. The
mean attitude of those who are probably or definitely going on
to make a career in the military varies from a low of +3.00 to a
high of +4.56, approaching or right on the mean orientation of
the officers. The seven definitely committed Army cadets at Ohio
State probably reflect the over-zealousness of the neophyte, but
in general those going on for a career are not extremely positive,
nor are they just slightly positive--they have adopted the feel-
ings of the professional referent.

As another index of the degree of adaptation to the profession, we can move to the level of opinion rather than simple
affect. The respondents were quizzed about their concern with
the corporate military point of view. Samuel Huntington has
argued that a shared corporate identity is a central component
of military professionalism.[14] We took it one step further to
ask the individual how he felt about the attention given the
"military point of view." Doctors could be expected to pump for
more attention to medicine and businessmen would be more concerned
about policy that would help business. Similarly, we asked the
respondents to evaluate whether the national government gave the
military point of view too much attention, adequate attention, or

TABLE 8

ROTC AFFECT FOR PROFESSIONAL CONCEPTS
BY CAREER COMMITMENT

Program	Concepts	High Career Intent	Uncertain Career Intent	Low Career Intent	Level of Significance*
University of North Carolina:					
Navy ROTC	Professional Soldier	N=48 +3.77	N=21 +3.67	N=30 +1.43	.01
Air Force ROTC	Professional Soldier	N=48 +4.27	N=38 +3.13	N=39 +2.00	.001
Duke University					
Navy ROTC	Professional Soldier	N=26 +3.00	N=41 +2.63	N=35 +1.57	.01
Ohio State University					
Army ROTC (Upperclassmen)	Professional Soldier	N=59 +4.56	N=99 +2.86	N=215 +2.06	.001
Navy ROTC (ALL)	Professional Soldier	N=107 +3.69	N=64 +2.72	N=61 +1.64	.001
Air Force (Upperclassmen)	Professional Soldier	N=63 +3.51	N=38 +2.89	N=27 +1.59	.01
University of California at Los Angeles					
Army ROTC	Professional Soldier	N=10 +4.00	N=15 +4.33	N=44 +2.86	.05
Navy ROTC	Professional Soldier	N=49 +3.35	N=45 +2.60	N=33 +1.36	.01

*This statistic was computed using all five levels of commitment.

whether it was occasionally or dangerously neglected. If the future officer is committed to a career, if he has learned to think of the profession as a corporate body, then we might expect him to be concerned about the attention it receives. What profession does not want a "little more" respect or attention? Although this attitude is not as closely linked to commitment as affect for the professional soldier, it also should be related to career intent so as to produce responses congruent to those of the active duty officers.

At the two universities where we have random samples of non-ROTC male undergraduates, there was a clear difference between the ROTC and non-ROTC groups on the question of the attention given the military point of view. At North Carolina, 37 per cent of the Navy and 46 per cent of the Air Force ROTC felt that the military point of view was either "occasionally" or "dangerously" neglected. Only 14 per cent of the North Carolina comparison group was similarly dissatisfied. The differences between the Ohio State ROTC and non-ROTC upperclassmen fit the same pattern. Where a fifth of the non-ROTC were dissatisfied with the attention given by the national government, 40 per cent of the Army, 57 per cent of the Navy, and 42 per cent of the Air Force ROTC upperclassmen were dissatisfied (Table 10).

For all eight ROTC programs, higher career intent is also associated with greater dissatisfaction with the attention given the military point of view. The pattern was not as consistent as that found for the professional soldier, as the strength of the relationship varies considerably from program to program. For example, commitment explains substantial variation in the satisfaction of the advanced Air Force ROTC cadets at Ohio State and very little for the Air Force ROTC at North Carolina (Table 11). The lack of variation in the responses to the satisfaction question may artificially limit the relationship, however. The ROTC cadets and midshipmen who feel the military point of view is given adequate attention or occasional neglect constitute from 85 to 92 per cent of the various programs. Necessarily the variation is largely

TABLE 9

MEAN AFFECT FOR "PROFESSIONAL SOLDIER"
AT OHIO STATE BY LEVEL OF
CAREER INTENT

Likelihood of Choosing A military Career	Army ROTC		Navy ROTC	
	Mean	N	Mean	N
Definitely Will	+5.43	(7)	+4.00	(21)
Probably Will	+4.44	(52)	+3.62	(86)
Uncertain	+2.86	(99)	+2.72	(64)
Probably Will Not	+2.29	(168)	+1.69	(55)
Definitely Will Not	+1.21	(47)	+1.17	(6)
Significance Level:	.001		.001	

TABLE 10

NON-ROTC AND ROTC SATISFACTION WITH ATTENTION
GIVEN THE MILITARY POINT OF VIEW

Attention Given by The National Government	University of North Carolina		
	Non-ROTC	Navy ROTC	Air Force ROTC
	N=114	N=101	N=130
Too much attention	14.0%	6.9%	2.3%
Adequate attention	72.0%	56.5%	52.0%
Occasional neglect	10.5%	28.7%	40.3%
Dangerous neglect	3.5%	7.9%	5.4%
	100.0%	100.0%	100.0%

Chi Square significant at the .001 level.

Attention Given by The National Government	Ohio State University (Juniors and Seniors)			
	NON-ROTC	Army ROTC	Navy ROTC	Air Force ROTC
	N=50	N=375	N=79	N=133
Too much attention	18.0%	5.3%	6.3%	2.3%
Adequate attention	62.0%	55.2%	36.7%	55.6%
Occasional neglect	18.0%	33.9%	50.7%	34.6%
Dangerous neglect	2.0%	5.6%	6.3%	7.5%
	100.0%	100.0%	100.0%	100.0%

Chi Square significant at the .001 level.

TABLE 11

SATISFACTION WITH THE MILITARY POINT OF VIEW
AND CAREER COMMITMENT

Air Force ROTC at the University of North Carolina

Likelihood of Choosing a Military Career

Attention Given by National Government	Definitely Will	Probably Will	Uncer- tain	Probably Will Not	Definitely Will Not
	N=13	N=35	N=37	N=35	N=4
Too much attention	0.0%	0.0%	0.0%	8.6%	0.0$
Adequate attention	30.8%	57.1%	48.6%	57.1%	25.0%
Occasional neglect	53.8%	40.0%	48.6%	31.4%	50.0%
Dangerous neglect	15.4%	2.9%	2.8%	2.9%	25.0%
	100.0%	100.0%	100.0%	100.0%	100.0%

Gamma = -.179, Chi Square significant only at the .1 level

Air Force ROTC at Ohio State University
Upper classmen Only
Likelihood of Choosing a Military Career

	N=12	N=51	N=38	N=25	N=2
Too much attention	0.0%	2.0%	0.0%	8.0%	0.0%
Adequate attention	25.0%	45.1%	68.4%	72.0%	0.0%
Occasional neglect	41.7%	43.1%	31.6%	16.0%	100.0%
Dangerous neglect	33.3%	9.8%	0.0%	4.0%	0.0%
	100.0%	100.0%	100.0%	100.0%	100.0%

Gamma = -.456, Chi Square significant at the .01 level.

confined to a shift within these two categories. Career commitment is associated with a mild trend from a feeling that the military point of view is given adequate attention to the feeling that
it is occasionally neglected. Of the small numbers who did give
other answers, those who felt that the military is given too much
attention tend to be the uncommitted, while those that perceive a
dangerous neglect are generally among the committed.

When we set the committed ROTC students beside the professional officers, we find that there is indeed a similarity in the
distributions (Table 12). Among the officers of the National War
College, there was mild concern for the attention the national
government gives the military view. Only one officer thought the

TABLE 12

SATISFACTION WITH THE MILITARY POINT OF VIEW
FOR OFFICERS AND COMMITTED ROTC

	Attention Given by National Government			
	Too Much Attention	Adequate Attention	Occasional Neglect	Dangerous Neglect
North Carolina				
Navy ROTC(N=50)	4.0%	50.0%	30.0%	16.0%
Air Force ROTC (N=48)	0.0%	50.0%	43.8%	6.2%
Duke University				
Navy ROTC(N=26)	3.8%	34.6%	53.9%	7.7%
Ohio State				
Army ROTC (N=60)	3.3%	41.7%	40.0%	15.0%
Navy ROTC(N=109)	1.8%	35.8%	54.1%	8.3%
Air Force ROTC (N=27)	1.6%	41.3%	42.8%	14.3%
UCLA				
Army ROTC(N=10)	0.0%	40.0%	60.0%	0.0%
Navy ROTC(N=49)	2.0%	55.1%	38.8%	4.1%
National War College				
Officers(N=145)	0.7%	35.0%	51.7%	12.6%

military point of view got too much attention; 13 per cent felt
it was dangerously neglected. The vast majority thought it
received adequate attention (35 per cent) or was occasionally
neglected (52 per cent). The committed ROTC cadets and midshipmen also fall heavily into the "adequate" and "occasional neglect"
categories, and of the extremes, "dangerous neglect" is a more
likely choice. The evidence supports the view that commitment
leads to socialization of the ROTC in the direction of the attitudes held by the professional military referent, but that it
falls short of producing the same intensity. The difference
could easily be accounted for by the greater professional experience of the senior officers, by the off-setting environments of
the universities, by age and historical causes, or by a host of

other factors. Indeed, what is important is not that the committed cadets and midshipmen do fall short but that they come so close despite these other differences.

Professional Socialization and the ROTC. There is a process of anticipatory professional socialization at work, and career commitment contributes to attitudinal congruence between the future officers and their military referent. To what degree is this congruence produced in adolescence, and what change comes about in college while enrolled in the ROTC?

Whether professional socialization occurs before or after college enrollment seems to be largely determined not only by career intent but by the availability of information about professional roles as well. Career commitment, as reported above, appears to be relatively constant during the college years, so that the major difference between freshmen and seniors is the amount and clarity of cues about what a military officer is expected to be. If an expected value is already obvious to the adolescent and if he is already committed to the military profession, then the development of that value can precede college. Others cannot develop until more cues are offered.

Whether the socialization that continues during college is anticipatory in nature may be a definitional question. Is the "entry" into the profession when the potential officer enrolls in a four year program as an entering freshman, when he signs up for the advanced course at the end of his sophomore year, or when he goes on active duty? What one calls it is less important than the realization that socialization through the ROTC program still does not involve extensive contact with military professionals. In large programs, a cadet may not interact with an ROTC instructor for weeks at a time, and even in small programs the contact for the average ROTC student is limited. The condition is thus one of semi-membership in the reference group at best, and the variables of commitment and clarity play a key role.

Partly for convenience, we shall view the ROTC period as a moderately high informational phase of anticipatory socialization.

In the ROTC classroom, the cadet or midshipman encounters active
duty officers who become additional sources of professional values
to be learned or models to be copied. Textbooks may provide some
unfamiliar facts, and there is the experience of wearing the uniform and the reactions to it. When these sources provide new or
conflicting information, attitude development continues. If, however, the new input only supplements things the young student
already picked up as an adolescent, it will not affect the nature
of the belief except possibly the firmness with which it is held.

Such is certainly the case for affect for the professional
soldier and, less clearly, for satisfaction with the attention
given the military point of view. There was simply no change in
the level of affect (Table 13) held for the professional soldier.

TABLE 13

VALUE ORIENTATIONS TOWARD PROFESSIONAL CONCEPTS BY
ACADEMIC YEAR

(VOLUNTARY PROGRAMS WITH 3 OR 4 RESPONDING CLASSES)

Concept	Mean Response by Academic Class				
	Fresh-men	Sopho-more	Junior	Senior	Sig. Level
Duke Navy ROTC Professional Soldier	N=30 +2.47	N=22 +1.91	N=21 +2.05	N=20 +3.00	ns
Ohio State Navy ROTC Professional Soldier	N=83 +2.95	N=71 +2.75	N=34 +2.85	N=45 +3.00	ns
UCLA Navy ROTC Professional Soldier	N=44 +2.68	N=33 +2.33	N=24 +2.63	N=22 +2.55	ns
North Carolina Navy ROTC Professional Soldier	N=51 +2.73	N=0 −	N=12 +3.42	N=35 +3.00	ns
North Carolina Air Force ROTC Professional Soldier	N=51 +2.96	N=0 −	N=38 +3.58	N=39 +3.23	ns

The means for the various academic classes in the five ROTC programs we considered above again showed no change at all. The Air
Force and Navy ROTC panels at North Carolina provide data of real
change on the concept and they lead to the same conclusion. The
mean on the single scale for the thirty-three midshipmen only
shifted in one year from +1.70 to +1.79. The thirty-six Air Force
cadets were also basically constant, for the change was from a
mean of +1.97 to +1.83 in that important senior year.

The average level of affect is only part of the story, however.
If both career intent and additional cues are required for attitude development, then increasing information might only affect
the views of the more committed cadets and midshipmen. The uncommitted may perceive the cues, but not change because the cues are
about a highly professional referent that does not concern them.
Alternatively, the committed might be more sensitive to subtle
cues and nuances that escape the notice of those less intent on a
career. One possible consequence is that the lack of change
among the less committed might mask a trend among those who are
committed to a military career.

When we consider the average sentiment for the professional
soldier, however, we find that there is again no evidence of
change during college. The committed freshmen and sophomores are
not different from the committed juniors and seniors, nor does
academic year explain any significant differences with other
levels of career motivation. This result is consistent with the
view that no new information is provided the ROTC students about
how they should feel about the professional soldier, probably
because they already know when they arrive.

Similar but more ambiguous results were obtained on the satisfaction over the military point of view. The pseudo-longitudinal
data again suggests that dissatisfaction is not a product of
either ROTC training or of college education generally. There is
very little shift in the level of dissatisfaction (as measured by
the relationship between academic year and that attitude) for the
Navy ROTC at North Carolina (gamma = .190) and no change at all

at Ohio State (gamma = -.019). At Duke and USLA, the Navy ROTC
programs again show very little change (gamma = .131 and .158 respectively). All of these weak relationships could easily have
occurred by chance.

Only the results for Air Force ROTC suggest a change (Table 14).
Three-fourths of the freshmen felt that adequate or too much atten-

TABLE 14

SATISFACTION WITH THE MILITARY POINT OF VIEW
AND ACADEMIC YEAR

University of North Carolina Air Force ROTC

The Military Point of View Receives	Freshmen	Sophomores	Juniors	Seniors
	N=51	N=0	N=39	N=39
Too much attention	3.9%	–	2.6%	0.0%
Adequate attention	72.5%	–	35.8%	41.0%
Occasional neglect	21.6%	–	46.2%	59.0%
Dangerous neglect	2.0%	–	15.4%	0.0%
	100.0%		100.0%	100.0%

Gamma = .409, Chi Square significant at the .01 level.

tion is given the military point of view as opposed to around 40

per cent of the juniors and seniors. The relationship (gamma =

-.406) is based almost entirely on the remarkably high level

of freshmen satisfaction but it does suggest a strong shift of

increasing dissatisfaction among the Air Force cadets with the

attention the national government gives the military point of view.

Fortunately, however, we need not rely solely on the pseudo-longi-

tudinal format in reaching a conclusion. The reason is that the

panel data at North Carolina also included this question. Although

one of the answers was not presented as a possible choice in 1965

("too much attention"), the other three options and the structure

of the question were precisely the same in 1966 as they had been

in the 1965 pre-test. After the "adequate" and "too much" cate-

gories were collapsed, we could find out the direction of real

change over the intervening year. Of thirty-six Air Force seniors,

55 per cent had not changed, 17 per cent had become more dissatis-

fied and 28 per cent had become more satisfied. For the Navy ROTC, there was a parallel result: 63 per cent of the thirty-two North Carolina midshipmen were unchanged, 31 per cent were more satisfied, and only 6 per cent grew more dissatisfied. The change is not all that great, it could have happened by chance, and it is in the direction opposite to that which was by the isolated trend found in the Air Force pseudo-longitudinal data.

We have therefore a contradiction between the pseudo-longitudinal findings and the panel results. Although one cannot argue the point conclusively, the pseudo-longitudinal result should probably be disregarded because it is the weaker method, because it is created by the attitudes found among Air Force freshmen alone, and because it stands in contrast with the results for the four Navy programs. The freshmen must be different because of some anomally, perhaps what they were studying in class the week the questionnaire was administered. This difficulty should further sensitize the reader to the logical problems of the pseudo-longitudinal approach, however, and the limitations of the data discussed here.

When consideration was limited to just the ROTC groups committed to a career, there is also no apparent pattern that would suggest a change over time in their levels of satisfaction with the attention paid the military point of view. Nor does the relationship between career intent and satisfaction vary systematically from one academic class to another. While the data is weaker, it would again appear that differences between ROTC and non-ROTC on this question are a function of career commitment and that they develop before the cadets and midshipmen arrive on campus. They had already reached the level of mild dissatisfaction congruent with the opinion of their referent, and further information provided by the ROTC program did not contradict the position they had already reached.

DISCUSSION

The strength of the findings presented here varies. The validity of generalizations that can be developed from a patchwork quilt of eight ROTC programs at four universities is difficult to asses. On the positive side, we have dealt with four universities that are quite diverse geographically, culturally and politically. Ohio State had at that time a two-year basic program with thousands of male students enrolled in the ROTC, the others have small all-voluntary programs. Duke University is a private university with students from fairly well-to-do backgrounds, while many of the students at Ohio State and UCLA come from working class origins. This diversity, while limited, gives us some confidence that the findings are not peculiar to a particular region or program, but rather are likely to be characteristic of most ROTC programs.

Another weakness is the pseudo-longitudinal approach. The fact that there was no change on many of the attitudes considered gives us some confidence that one class did not vary from those preceding or following it for historical reason, an important assumption of the method. The panel also strengthens the arguments made. For these reasons, we feel that the lack of change found during the college years is persuasive. Except for a limited impact on the committed ROTC students, the ROTC does not influence, change, or "militarize" its students. The basic differences develop before college.

The second part of the argument is on very weak ground, however. We have in no way proven that the socialization is anticipatory in nature because there is an alternative explanation. Perhaps all the differences in the values and opinions emerge before career commitment, and career intent follows, rather than causes, the attitudinal differences observed. Our own view is that the configuration of attitudes is too rounded out to be totally the product of predispositions. An adolescent probably has values somewhat compatible with a military profession and develops commitment. Commitment in turn leads to a heightened congruency, which continues the cycle by leading to further commitment. But we cannot sort out the relative weighting that should be given to self-selection and subsequent anticipation without panel data on adolescents. For these reasons, this study provides hypotheses that were useful rather than propositions that were tested. The strength of the anticipatory socialization hypothesis is that for this study it ordered and integrated disparate findings when other plausible explanations were in one way or another inconsistent with one or another aspect of the results.

The data is also of limited value to an understanding of American civil-military relations because it deals with only the ROTC. Even if anticipatory socialization is an appropriate model for the ROTC, the weak nature of the psychological forces involved could be over-whelmed by other, more direct factors in the socialization of officers in flight training, Officer Candidate Schools, and other commissioning programs. The argument may not even apply to the ROTC in the environment of the military colleges such as the Virginia Military Institute or the Citadel.

Yet it is remarkable that John P. Lovell's study of the United States Military Academy led to the conclusion that, "Socialization at West Point produces only slight impact upon professional orientations and strategic perspectives of the cadet."[15] If our data on the ROTC is relevant to his study, it suggests that Lovell's basic conclusion is correct. The attitudinal differences of the ROTC are already evident among freshmen, suggesting that a major component of professional socialization must operate prior to the time the individual enters either ROTC or a military academy. Hence change in the Academy years would not be very evident because much of it has already occurred. Those shifts that Lovell did find are also consistent with the ROTC data. The professional orientations of cadets from military and civilian families collapsed in towards each other, but it is important to note that the cadets from non-military backgrounds changed in the direction of lessening their absolutism and that they changed considerably more than did the cadets from military backgrounds.[16] Conceivably, the civilian background group, in absence of cues, over-learned as adolescents through incorrect anticipation, and are learning through the cues provided at West Point that absolutism is not all that appropriate.

If the theory of anticipatory professional socialization is in fact applicable to the military profession generally, however, some other interesting lines of inquiry become evident. What if anticipatory socialization is frequently wrong? Not the least of the weaknesses of anticipatory professionalization is that it might well involve the adaption of the cadet or midshipmen to an inaccurate image. The Air Force cadet who has seen a lot of James Stewart playing the crusty pilot may be altogether unprepared for the reality of military service. Sanford Dornbusch discussed the problem of "reality shock" after graduation from the Coast Guard academy years ago,[17] and the probability of vague or incongruent anticipatory socialization might well contribute to the problem. Officer retention might well be related to the nature and clarity of the referents perceived by ROTC students. By making the referents both clear and accurate, one might lessen reality shock and avoid attracting cadets and midshipmen who will later drop out because they have the wrong view of what military life is like. An important consideration for the future is not only the way images, expectations, and commitment develop in professional education, but also their consistency with the realities of active service.

NOTES

*This research could not have been satisfactorily concluded without the aid and support provided by a Post-Doctoral Fellowship at the Mershon Center for Education in National Security, The Ohio State University in 1966-67.

[1] Robert K. Merton, Social Theory and Social Structures (The Free Press of Glencoe, 1957), p. 265.

[2] Elizabeth Douvan and Joseph Adelson, The Adolescent Experience (New York: John Wiley and Sons, Inc., 1966), p. 362.

[3]Ibid., p. 29.

[4]Ibid., p. 33.

[5]Natalie Rogoff, "The Decision to Study Medicine," in The Student-Physician, Robert K. Merton, George G. Reader, Patricia L. Kendall, eds. (Cambridge: Harvard University Press, 1957), pp. 111 and 115.

[6]Howard S. Becker and James W. Carper, "The Development of Identification with an Occupation," American Journal of Sociology LXI (1965), p. 209.

[7]Wagner Thielens, Jr., "Some Comparisons of Entrants to Medical and Law School," in The Student-Physician, p. 138.

[8]The availability of professional models within the family also varies from profession to profession. Ibid., p. 134. The relationships reported in this research hold up even when the sons of military men are dropped from consideration, so that factor does not affect the conclusions.

[9]The sample at Ohio State (N=181) had no evident bias, but freshmen were somewhat over-represented in the North Carolina sample (N=114). They tended to be more conservative than the upperclassmen, making it more difficult to demonstrate that differences exist between the non-ROTC and ROTC, but weighting the sample would not affect the basic results.

[10]The requirements and the nature of the selectivity varied, for a student had to take basic ROTC courses or alternative courses stipulated by the various colleges.

[11]This view is suggested by Merton's discussion of the individual's expected duration of membership in the group in Social Theory and Social Structure, p. 311.

[12]The response rate for the NROTC juniors at the University of North Carolina was quite low, due in part to allowing the mid-shipmen in that program to take their questionnaires home. The more motivated midshipmen, being more likely to turn in completed questionnaires, are probably over-represented.

[13]Osgood and his associates, have found that his evaluative dimension and standard Thurstone scales correlate 0.80 and higher. The Measurement of Meaning (Urbana: University of Illinois Press, 1957), pp. 193-194. Independent validity studies confirmed this fact, and discovered that the results of two scales correlated over 0.90 with the use of six. The use of the simpler two scale approach (good-bad and fair-unfair) was therefore adopted.

[14] Samuel P. Huntington, The Soldier and the State: The Theory and Practice of Civil-Military Relations (Cambridge: Harvard University Press, 1957), p. 10.

[15] "The Professional Socialization of the West Point Cadet," The New Military, p. 145.

[16] Ibid., p. 131.

[17] "The Military Academy as an Assimilating Institution," Social Forces, XXXI (1955), pp. 316-321.

Part II.

CIVILIAN RESPONSE TO MILITARY ROLES

THE MILITARY AS A WELFARE INSTITUTION

Bernard Beck

In recent years, military organizations have been defended
for reasons not traditionally associated with the "military
mission". These have included technical and organizational
sophistication, fostering of scientific research, and leadership in achieving racial justice. An additional rationale
mentioned by both the Secretary of Defense and the Secretary of
Labor is the unique success of the armed services as manpower
training and rehabilitation programs.[1] Such public statements
were made in response to public sentiment against the war in
Vietnam, the draft, and the neglect of internal social problems.
This appeal to the social benefits of military service reinforces
the interest of a comparison of military and welfare institutions. Accordingly, what light can be shed on the military by
viewing it from the perspective of welfare?

A standard approach to welfare sees the development of such
institutions in modern industrial societies as a counterpart of
the decline of traditional agencies which performed so-called
"welfare functions", such as the extended family. All societies
have institutions to deal with residual persons and populations:
the poor, widows, orphans, the disabled, and others. In modern
societies, these activities become formalized and invested in
specialized agencies.[2]

137

The suggestion that modern armies operate as large-scale manpower programs is matched by the traditional role of armies as outlets for residual populations which were not easily assimilable into the structure of civilian society. In both traditional and modern contexts, military organizations offer a possible social response to the presence of residuals in the population. Among the advantages of the army from this point of view is the fact that it removes residuals from the social scene (and even the physical scene) while conferring a legitimate status. Thus it makes an addition to the ordinary social structure which accommodates residuals without producing much dislocation of that structure.

These considerations lead me to some theoretical arguments about welfare which have an interesting extension to the military. Welfare is an increasingly important area in modern societies, but there are some difficulties in a definition of welfare which meaningfully distinguishes it from other institutional areas. I have suggested in an earlier paper[3] that there are no structural differentia associated with welfare, but rather that the distinction is a moral one, derived from the public theory of deservingness. To elaborate briefly, welfare is one kind of response to the problem posed by the presence in a population of persons residual to the institutionalized structure for maintaining and governing such residuals. A distinguishing feature of welfare is that roles are created for persons and structures are added to the basic structure in such a way as to discourage the construction of careers. In terms of the public definition of such additions, the roles are "roleless", the structures are deviant and the resulting careers are morally suspect and reputationally degraded. For if such roles and structures of welfare were legitimatized, the validty of folk-theories which define necessity and possibility for ordinary members would be compromised.

Most attempts at structural definitions of welfare are thus open to question, especially when it can be shown that they

theoretically include many institutions which no one wishes to
treat as welfare (such as tax concessions) and exclude many that
are commonly discussed as welfare (such as social insurance
schemes). More specifically, under virtually all proposed definitions, the military would be logically included, if all aspects
of public moral evaluation were left out of account. Among the
criteria which the military fulfill are: public subsidy of a
social need which is not or cannot be treated in the private
sector; provision of subsistence to persons who are not economically productive in a direct way; suspension of the ordinary rules
of earning a share in the allocation of rewards, justified by an
appeal to a higher social good. This higher social good is
characteristically phrased in terms of the well-being of the total
society and of all the members. The conceptual result is not that
the military is really some form of welfare, but rather that it
has such a divergent public reputation while being so similar
structurally.

These preliminaries now bring me to posing a basic question
about the military as compared with welfare. Since structures
which provide careers for residual persons can pose a moral threat
to the commitment of ordinary persons, as shown by the negative
moral reputation of welfare recipients, how does the military
create and maintain a high moral evaluation? Since military
careers, especially in the lower ranks are not justified by
ordinary civilian standards, the general answer must reside in a
special folk-theory of social honor. Thus the creation and maintenance of social honor can be seen as an important aspect of the
work to be done by military organizations. It has of course long
been recognized that the military has a high moral evaluation in
most societies, and in particular that there is a special kind of
social honor which attaches to the military.[4] Explanations which
have been offered for this fact, range from those which appeal to
the constitutional aggressiveness of the human animal [5] to Veblen's
argument about the maintenance of differential social prestige
based on pseudo-predatory activities in the formation of the

leisure class.[6] Sociologists of the military have focused on the importance of social honor in the recruitment of personnel and in combating the competition of civilian careers.[7] This analysis merely places military honor in the context of generating legitimate credentials for residuals.

Several dimensions of social honor available throughout the military are familiar. The first and most important centers on the physical danger and threat to life involved in being a soldier. Second is the notion of self-sacrifice in behalf of the communal good which is built on that threat to life. (The dangers of military activity are accepted because of the higher benefit accruing to society in terms of its defense and aggrandizement.) Furthermore, the military makes available to itself notions of masculinity, virility and excitement, so that the activities which are presented as the major part of military life are considered as ends to be pursued for their own sake. Whatever the source and content of the military theory of social honor, it is a prime factor which preserves the military in its relatively exalted position, and therefore the variations in the strength and legitimacy of the theory ought to be matched by variations in the actual social distance defined between participation in the military and participation in welfare. Some other sources of military prestige should also be mentioned. In contrast with welfare, the military represents a potentially autonomous concentration of power in its rawest form. Thus it can command a high position independent of any considerations of legitimacy under a reputational theory. Furthermore, under certain circumstances, military activities can be reputationally assimilated to ordinary careers. Two forms of this assimilation can be called professionalism and universalism, and they have their counterparts in the field of welfare as attempts to generate a non-invidious image of participation.

Professionalism is a complex term when applied to military careers and some uses of it are at odds with the standard meaning of "profession" in the sociology of occupations. Military professionalism includes such components as the elimination of

141

ascriptive bases of recruitment and advancement, the rationaliza-
tion of duties and activities, and assimilation of military organization and delegation of functions to prevailing patterns of
civilian bureaucracy.[8] This last component is of interest here.
By emphasizing the similarities of a military career with the
circumstances of an ordinary, legitimate civilian career,
especially through the notion of "transferability of skills",
legitimacy under the ordinary theory of social structure may be
won for military roles. This effect is a potential benefit of
the recent notion of convergence between military and civilian
organizations.[9] In welfare, correspondingly, people who participate under the rubric of professional or occupational roles (such
as welfare case workers) have access to ordinary legitimacy, even
though their utilization of welfare programs may be similar to the
recipients.[10] Thus professionalism maximizes the similarity of a
military career to an ordinary work career.

Universalism is a pattern under which the personnel, rather
than the activity, is made ordinary. In the military, it is
represented by Universal Military Training or the draft. All
appropriate members of the society have a military career at some
time in their lives, so that the distinction between those who are
soldiers and those who are ordinary people is blurred. In welfare,
likewise, universalism is a popular recent notion. Welfare benefits are made available and routinely dispensed to all appropriate
members of the society (e.g., family allowances, child-care programs, Medicare) so that the boundary between recipients and respectable people is blurred. Under universalism, however, a distinction may arise between those who participate but are not
dependent on the institution and those who make permanent
dependent careers through it.

If the military social honor is the source of the disparity
in the public reputations of military and welfare participants,
then that disparity can be used as a measure of the efficacy of
honor and can be associated with the conditions which affect the
acceptance of the theory. That is, under conditions which

inhibit popular acceptance of the folk-theory of social honor, the reputation of military participation should decline and come more to resemble the reputation of welfare participation. An empirical reflection of this relationship may be found in the appearance of the problems of military careers during peacetime.[11] Since virtually all military honor is derived from the actuality or possibility of war, a decline in the saliency of public involvement with war makes it harder to maintain the special theory of social honor. Thus during protracted periods of peace we find that characteristics usually attributed to welfare recipients are attributed to career soldiers: lack of ambition, suspect motivation, dependency, idleness, irresponsibility and even personal immorality. To construct a military career in peacetime or a welfare career in a period of affluence is to bring suspicion of moral and motivational inadequacy. The alternative, after all, would be to call into question the structural arrangements of society to which most people have become committed in constructing their ordinary careers.

An important concomitant of the military theory of social honor, which distinguishes the military from welfare, is military discipline. As institutions which provide alternative careers to residuals, both the military and welfare present problems of citizenship. The person who makes use of such an alternative career may in general have to accept an altered definition of participation in the society at large. The enjoyment of citizenship is contingent on acceptance of the dominant moral theory of deservingness. In the history of welfare institutions, the development of egalitarianism in the definition of citizenship has inhibited the imposition of a special status on welfare recipients. In earlier periods, a client of a welfare institution forfeited many rights and perquisites of ordinary citizenship and was subject to the special disciplines of total institutions, such as poor houses. He was constrained in where and how he could legally live, was required to perform certain kinds of onerous work, and was limited in his legal recourses. Progress

in the welfare field is usually measured in terms of removing the
burdens of degraded citizenship from the client. We take pride
in the fact that we no longer consign the poor to workhouses where
their entire round of existence was dictated and controlled by
overseers. The imposition of special disciplines on welfare
recipients is today perceived as an indignity and an abridgement
of inalienable rights of citizenship, especially by recipients
themselves as they become organized and vocal.[12]

In the military, however, the abridgement and alteration of
citizenship is still routine and statutory. Its legitimacy can
be connected with the speical theory concerning military activity.
As long as the rationales associated with the military are
accepted, military discipline and total institutional control
remain legitimate.[13] Thus while the folk-theory of honor allows
military institutions to escape the burden of the low reputation
accorded to welfare, it also makes it possible for the military to
maintain the altered citizenship which in the case of welfare has
been found inconsistent with the dominant political ideology.
From the point of view of ordinary members and their commitment
to the ordinary structure, military discipline can be seen as the
functional equivalent of the degraded reputation of welfare. Both
are defined as the price of career deviation. The ordinary
theories of career and deservingness remain intact, since variation is penalized.

A further effect we might expect is that as a military honor
loses efficacy and the reputation of a military career declines,
the legitimacy of military discipline should also decline and
resistance to alterations of citizenship should increase. In part
this effect might be attributed to the participants own state of
commitment to military value structure. But it is also related
to the negotiations he enters with outsiders. If his own commitment to military honor falls, he may be less willing to accept
discipline, but it is also true that as the public evaluation of
military honor declines, the acceptance of military discipline
becomes socially stigmatized. Thus the career military man finds

his reputation degraded for his subjection to discipline when ordinary persons treat autonomy as a valuable.

When the special status of military participation becomes problematic, as the status of welfare participation routinely is, the defensive responses of career participants and the conditions which permit such defenses are similar to those revealed by welfare. In the welfare field, when the distinction between residual and ordinary members coincides largely with a pre-existing category distinction, such as race or ethnicity, sub-cultural introversion and resistance to admonitory messages from respectable elements is fostered. The formation of welfare ghettos enhances this effect, so that the morally suspect recipient can reduce to a minimum encounters in which he (or, more likely, she) will be directly censured for participation in welfare.[14] Similarly, military personnel in periods of public indifference to theories of military honor can be expected to withdraw into the mutual sympathy of their fellows, to become sensitive and defensive to civilian attitudes and to define civilian values as irrelevant. We can also expect a shrinking of social participation within the confines of military bases, which then become, in effect, "military ghettos".

When military honor is devalued in ordinary society the process of re-entry into civilian life for veterans becomes problematic in much the same way as the process of "rehabilitation" of former welfare recipients.[15] In both cases, the lack of an adequate record of ordinary activities, such as an ordinary job history, puts one at a disadvantage in the conduct of a career from then on. In particular the absence of credentials which certify that a person has performed adequately under the ordinary structure renders him unreliable. This unreliability is not merely in specific areas of civilian job skills, training or intelligence, but in the diffuse area of socialization for general role performance as a stright, square or civilian, i.e., as an "ordinary". I suggest that this diffuse criterion is primarily a moral one.

It is now possible to make some comments on the success claimed for the services as latent manpower training and rehabilitation programs. There are several important factors which should be mentioned which are extrinsic to the type of argument presented here. To begin with, considering the military and civilian manpower programs as two alternative treatments, it should be clear that the level of investment of social resources and the level of compelled participation by "target populations" is lopsidedly in favor of greater effectiveness of the military, even if the actual content of its programs were in no way different. Furthermore, the military is allowed greater leeway, margin for error and autonomous control of its programs than any civilian manpower agency. That is, there is less supervisory control of military manpower procedures from outside. Finally, army rejects are not considered failures of army manpower procedures, as hard-core populations are considered failures of civilian manpower projects.

But for the present purposes the interesting source of differential effectiveness of these programs may arise from the differential social reputations usually found to characterize two types of activity which appear so similar in many respects. In an earlier paper,[16] I suggested the public welfare, which is regarded as a failure in its ultimate mission of rehabilitating recipients, also furnishes a striking model of success in rehabilitating welfare workers. Welfare workers often use welfare in much the same way as is intended for recipients, that is, as as hopefully temporary but indefinite backstopping alternative until people can return to suitable positions in the ordinary occupational or role structure. A major difference is the legitimacy for the welfare worker conferred by "holding a job", a quasi-professional job, at that. In examining the differences between the two kinds of participation in welfare, I concluded that the factors associated with a success model (welfare workers) were:

A) Placements must be respectable and reputable for the

worker on a possibly permanent basis. Even if labor market conditions never alter to the point of being able to absorb him, his
persistence in the "interim" position must not damage his social
definition.

B) If opportunities arise to enter positions generated by
the labor market, the record of participation in an interim
position must not damage his chance. His interim activities
must create a respectable history for him.[17]
And, in addition:

It follows that manpower projects might profitably be
planned to reflect some of the naturally occurring features of
welfare work careers, such as high demand for personnel, tolerance
for high personnel turnover, public reputation for social contribution, concentration on a defensible organizational goal as
opposed to emphasis on the organization as a means of helping the
needy.[18]

It should be apparent that these prescriptions, produced in
another context of analysis, apply in virtually every particular
to the military, especially to the U.S. Army. Note that this
analysis is based solely on processes of public reputation,
rather than any internal details of the programs themselves. The
effectiveness of the military in this respect is based on the
social honor of the military which differentiates its reputational
consequences from those of welfare. Furthermore, we have seen
that this folk-theory of honor may be vulnerable, and that as its
acceptance declines, the reputational consequences come increasingly to resemble the public reputation of welfare. Consequently,
in such circumstances, we might expect the effectiveness of the
military as a manpower program to decline accordingly. If we
concentrate for a moment on the last two prescriptions, "public
reputation for social contribution, concentration on a defensible
organizational goal as opposed to emphasis on the organization as
a means of helping the needy", the relevance of the theory of
honor emerges in the terms "social contribution" and "defensible
organizational goal".

A final word is in order about the recent attention to the military as a manpower program in the public eye. The Cold War which began soon after the end of World War II has made possible a protracted public consciousness and high evaluation of the military mission which has been fostered by the public relations work of the services themselves. The pattern contrasts markedly with the period between the First and Second World Wars, when many of the processes I have attributed in general to peacetime military reputations appeared.[19] The Cold War has acted as a support to the military honor, altering the expected fluctuation in terms of the cycle of war and peace. (I am deliberately invoking the image of business cycle fluctuations and public intervention to prop up the economy.) Statements about the manpower role of the military appear at a point in time when some public disaffection with the military theory of honor appears and they are, in fact, responses to it. This is an anomalous situation, for if manpower effectiveness is based on the acceptance of the theory, then that effectiveness is being invoked at the very time when its foundation appears to be weakening (compare "reputation for social contribution"). Furthermore, the invocation of that effectiveness in public might further weaken that basis (compare "emphasis on a defensible organizational goal as opposed to emphasis on the organization as a means of helping the needy"). In other words, the army can be effective as a manpower program because it does not have the reputation of being one, but instead has an accepted theory of social honor. To emphasize it as a manpower program is to jeopardize that effectiveness and to further undermine the folk-theory of social honor which is necessary to make it effective in the first place.

NOTES

[1] Reference to newspaper accounts.

[2] Walter A. Friedlander, Introduction to Social Welfare (Englewood Cliffs, New Jersey: Prentice-Hall, 1955 [2nd ed. 1968]).

[3] Bernard Beck, "Welfare as a Moral Category," Social Problems, 14 (Winter, 1967), pp. 258-277.

[4] Morris Janowitz, "The Military Establishment: Organization and Disorganization," in Merton and Nisbet, eds., Contemporary Social Problems (New York: Harcourt, Brace and World, 1961 1st ed.) p. 522.

[5] Robert Ardrey, African Genesis and The Territorial Imperative.

[6] Thorstein Veblen, The Theory of the Leisure Class.

[7] Janowitz, op. cit., pp. 526-527.

[8] Ibid., p. 521 ff.

[9] Albert D. Biderman and Laura M. Sharp, "Convergence of Military and Civilian Occupational Structures: Evidence from Studies of Military Retired Employment," American Journal of Sociology, 73 (January, 1968), pp. 381-399.

[10] This point will be explained more fully below. See Bernard Beck, "Welfare Careers and Manpower Programs," paper read at meetings of the Society for the Study of Social Problems, San Francisco, August, 1967.

[11] Janowitz, op. cit., pp. 526 ff.

[12] Friedlander, op. cit., Chapters 1 and 2.

[13] Janowitz, op. cit., pp. 523-525.

[14] Beck, "Welfare as a Moral Category," pp. 275-276.

[15] See Dixon Wecter, When Johnny Comes Marching Home.

[16] Beck, "Welfare Careers and Manpower Programs."

[17] Ibid., p. 4.

[18] Ibid.

[19] Janowitz, op. cit., pp. 515-517.

THE MILITARY MISSION AGAINST

OFF-BASE DISCRIMINATION

David Sutton

On July 26, 1963, Robert McNamara, the Secretary of Defense, launched a new mission for the military in American society, designed to combat racial discrimination against black servicemen in civilian communities adjacent to military installations. In a directive to the military departments, McNamara charged military commanders with the responsibility of opposing discriminatory practices affecting their men and dependents and of fostering equal opportunity for them, not only on base, but also in nearby communities where many lived or gathered in off-duty hours.[1]

SUBJECT AND APPROACH

The purpose of this study is to: (1) describe the change in the official racial policy of the military from that of accommodation to off-base discrimination and segregation to one of confrontation; (2) explore how the military has attempted to fulfill its mission of reducing social injustice in nearby civilian communities; (3) explain why the results of the new function have been less sweeping than the memos and directives promulgated by the Defense Department might indicate; and (4) examine the ramifications of the mission on traditional civil-military relations.

The observations presented in this paper are based on information obtained by the writer from a wide variety of sources. In the spring of 1968, the author undertook a field trip to seven

Air Force installations in six Southern states. In each base-
community situation, semi-focused interviews were conducted with
top military and civilian leaders.[2] Local military officers knew
the Air Force did not sponsor or control the study, but the fact
that the writer had obtained prior approval from the Air Force
and that the Air Force recommended they cooperate, indicated to
them that they were not acting indiscreetly by talking with him.
All respondents, military and civilian, were assured anonymity.

Prior to the field trip, the writer had several preliminary
discussions with officials in the Civil Rights Office of the
Defense Department and the Community Relations Division of the
Air Force for background on the civil rights mission and the base-
community relationships. Finally, the reports of local base commanders to the Civil Rights Office of the Defense Department provided valuable information. After McNamara's 1963 directive, the
military departments began requiring annual reports from installation commanders. The commanders were to note off-base conditions
adversely affecting equal opportunity and their progress in eliminating or reducing racial discrimination.

Military Accommodation to Local Racial Customs. Until the
McNamara directive, the traditional policy of the military had
been one of accommodation to the discriminatory practices of local
communities. During World War I an incident occurred which
attracted much attention and illustrated military policy. A Negro
medical corps sergeant, stationed at Camp Funston, Kansas, attempted
to enter a movie theater in nearby Manhattan, Kansas, and was barred
by the white manager. In response to the occurrence, the commanding officer of the division at Camp Funston issued a bulletin
which stated:

> To avoid such conflicts the Division Commander has
> repeatedly urged that all colored members of his command,
> and especially the officers and noncommissioned officers,
> should refrain from going where their presence will be
> resented.
> . . . good will depends on the public. The public
> is nine-tenths white. White men made the Division and
> they can break it just as easy if it becomes a trouble
> maker. . . .[3]

Secretary of War Henry Stimson in a 1944 letter to a Louisiana Congressman expressed the official attitude of the military establishment toward off-base discrimination and segregation:

> I reiterate that the War Department is not an appropriate medium for affecting social readjustments. It has never been so employed nor will it be. . . .
> As stated in your letter, the War Department has no right to seek to effect changes in the life of the people of the Southland, or for that matter, in any other part of the country. This it has not attempted to do. The fact is, military personnel are carefully informed, in all sections of the United States, that without the confines of the military establishment they are subject to state law. . . .[4]

After President Truman on July 26, 1948, issued an executive order declaring his policy of equality of treatment and opportunity for all persons in the armed forces, most of the racial barriers to the participation of blacks in the military were eventually dismantled.[5] The remaining impediments to integration both on and off base stemmed primarily from the civilian society adjoining the military post.

Two reports issued in 1963, one by the United States Commission on Civil Rights and the other by the President's Committee on Equal Opportunity in the Armed Forces, documented how host community racial attitudes and policies impinged on the operation of military bases and tainted their atmosphere of equality. The reports cited instances of Negro members of military bands, choral groups, demonstration teams, and honor details being excluded in off-base performances in deference to the wishes of local white populations. For the same reason, at some installations black military police were not stationed at the base gate or used for off-base assignments in white areas. Some commanders discouraged their men from interracial association off-base.[6]

The commander of an Air Force base in Mississippi in his 1963 report to superiors detailed the conditions confronting his black servicemen in the nearby host community:

> Negroes sit in the rear of buses. No difference is made for military members—they are likewise segregated. The bus terminal has separate waiting rooms.

TABLE 1

SEGREGATION OF PUBLIC FACILITIES IN COMMUNITIES ADJACENT TO MILITARY INSTALLATIONS

Types of Segregated Public Facility	Number of Surveyed Installations and Activities with Such Segregated Facilities*		Number of Personnel Stationed Where Facilities are Segregated		Percentage of Surveyed Installations and Activities with Segregated Facilities	
	Army	Navy	Army	Navy	Army	Navy
Public Schools	48	143	178,109	58,500	24%	25%
Restaurants and Bars	68	238	257,893	110,000	34	43
Theaters	63	223	232,301	105,000	31	40
Swimming Pools	19	226	178,201	102,000	9	40
Golf Courses	38	164	190,931	82,000	19	29
Beaches	10	203	123,502	90,000	5	36
Bowling Alleys	32	194	205,901	103,000	16	35
Libraries	10	49	130,179	28,000	5	9
Public Transportation	4	47	41,091	22,000	2	8
Hotels, Motels	12	252	205,618	141,000	6	45
Churches	23	163	127,402	70,000	11	29

*The Army survey for this table covered 201 installations and activities, while the Navy survey covered 559. Each installation and activity surveyed had 100 or more military personnel assigned to it.

Sources: President's Committee on Equal Opportunity in the Armed Forces, Initial Report: Equality of Treatment and Opportunity for Negro Military Personnel Stationed Within the United States, June 13, 1963, p. 45.

There is complete segregation in public schools
attended by dependent children.

All restaurants, motels, and hotels are segregated.
The two Negro hotels have only one restroom for the entire
hotel.

There are two libraries (one for each race). The
one bowling alley is segregated. There are three city
parks (two for white and one for colored). The tennis
courts are in the white public parks. The golf driving
range is segregated.

There are two theaters (one for white only and one
with a separate section for colored). The theater with
a separate section for colored closes the section after
1600 when a first rate movie is playing and there is a
possibility of needing those seats for white customers.
There is a separate section for Negroes in the Drive-In
Theater.

Negro personnel do not have equal opportunity in
housing off-base. Landlords and realtors maintain
separate listings for each race. Housing available
to Negroes is below standard available for whites.

Studies undertaken by the Army and Navy in 1962 of 201 Army
and 559 Navy installations documented the extent of the segregation encountered in the communities neighboring to the bases: 24
per cent of the Army posts and 25 per cent of the Navy stations
had segregated schools nearby; 34 per cent of Army installations
and 43 per cent of the Navy units were adjacent to communities in
which the bars and restaurants were not integrated; 31 per cent of
the Army posts and 40 per cent of the Navy stations were next to
segregated theaters (see Table 1).[7] In 1967 base commanders conducted a nationwide survey of housing opportunities within normal
commuting distance of their installations. The survey found that
Negro servicemen were denied access to housing in at least one-
third of the rental units surveyed.[8]

Unable to obtain redress from his military superior, the
Negro serviceman, for the most part, had patiently endured the
traditional pattern of discrimination and segregation. In the
early 1960's, however, there were black men in uniform who, like
their civilian counterparts, were no longer willing to acquiesce
to racial indignities. In an era of growing protest and social
activism, black servicemen began engaging in public demonstrations
and sit-ins which sometimes resulted in their arrest by local

law officers or military police.[9] As an organization that must
maintain its members in a maximum state of readiness, the Defense
Department reacted to the problem by prohibiting military participation in civil rights demonstrations not only during duty hours
or while in uniform but also when their activities could be a
breach of law and order or when violence was reasonably likely to
occur.[10]

Although convinced that they were not sitting on a racial
powderkeg, Defense Department decision-makers were receiving new
demands, some generated within and others outside the military
organization, to redefine their policies and responsibilities in
the civil rights field. First, Defense officials recognized that,
having severely restricted the civil rights activity of servicemen,
the organization needed to provide a functional alternative by
which black soldiers could register grievances. Second, reports
of base commanders and opinion surveys of black servicemen generally indicated that off-base discriminatory practices were sapping
morale, undermining efficiency, and interfering with the performance of the military mission.[11] Third, military statistics showed
that blacks, attracted to the military as an avenue of social
mobility, had become an important source of manpower for the armed
forces.[12]

In addition to these factors, Defense Secretary McNamara was
receptive to suggestions for redefining the military mission in
American society. While he considered the military's primary
responsibility to be protecting the nation from foreign aggression, he believed that domestic poverty and social injustice could
endanger the national security as much as any external military
threat. McNamara wanted to use the vast resources of the Defense
Department to help alleviate the social ills he saw confronting
the nation.[13]

The strongest demand for change in military policy, however,
originated outside the military organization. Having been elected
by a narrow margin with strong black support, President Kennedy
faced pressure from civil rights groups to fulfill his campaign

pledges to them. Yet, he did not wish to alienate key Southern congressmen by sending a dramatic civil rights program to Congress. As a compromise, Kennedy sought to act against discrimination in federal programs and activities which could be corrected by executive action. At the urging of the Leadership Conference on Civil Rights, Kennedy reactivated in June 1962, the President's Committee on Equal Opportunity in the Armed Forces, first established by President Truman in 1948. He directed the Committee to consider what measures should be employed to improve equal opportunity off-base.[14] After a year of fact-finding visits to military bases, the Committee recommended that the Defense Department take aggressive action against off-base discrimination. The President forwarded the report to McNamara and noted that the recommendations were in the spirit he believed should characterize the administration's approach.

In response to the President, the Secretary of Defense issued his 1963 directive, placing responsibility squarely on military commanders for opposing discriminatory practices against their men in nearby communities. The directive also vested in the Assistant Secretary of Defense for Manpower the authority and responsibility for promoting equal opportunity and authorized him to create the Office of Deputy Assistant Secretary of Defense for Civil Rights. To the military departments, the directive assigned the task of providing instructions and guidance materials to installation commanders so that the policy could be carried out and progress measured.

The service instructions urged commanders to use persuasion and discussion in enlisting community support for equal opportunity and treatment. The commanders could utilize their command-community relations committee (or an equivalent group) whose members include representatives of both base and community. Such committees could provide the commander with an organizational framework for discussion of racial problems. Another approach suggested to commanders involved using informal, private contacts with community leaders and officials. Where the local

commander found his persuasive efforts to be unsuccessful, he
could with the permission of the service's civilian secretary
declare a business or area "off-limits" to military personnel.[15]

Four years later on April 11, 1967, the Defense Department
issued another memorandum in its war on racial discrimination.
This time the Department focused its attention on discrimination
in family housing. The memorandum instructed base commanders to
undertake a census of off-base rental housing facilities and determine the availability for rental without racial discrimination to
military personnel. Wherever housing discrimination was found,
commanders were once again to mobilize community support to eliminate it. An earlier housing memorandum on March 8, 1963, had provided that listings maintained by base housing offices of available private housing should include only those units which are
available without regard to race, color, creed, or national origin.
However, the 1963 directive gave no further advice to the services
on how this policy could be implemented so as to improve the
housing opportunities for all military personnel.[16]

COMBATING OFF-BASE DISCRIMINATION

The second part of the study explores how base commanders
have attempted to implement the equal opportunity directives. It
also examines the influence of a military base on the racial attitudes and policies of nearby civilian communities. A perusal of
the annual equal opportunity reports from 1963 to 1967 reveals
only a few reported attempts by commanders to reduce discrimination off-base. While all of the military and most of the community leaders interviewed said that the local military installation had had an impact on the host community's racial attitudes
or policies, few attributed the influence to any direct action
initiated by the base commander.

Those steps commanders have taken to halt discrimination have
generally involved situations over which they have some measure of
control. For example, base commanders frequently allow local
civilian groups to use base facilities for meetings. In one
Alabama community, the local chamber of commerce had held its

annual banquet at the nearby base for several years. However, the
chamber had a policy of excluding Negroes from its membership.
After McNamara's directive, the commander denied the use of base
facilities to the group until they accepted their first Negro
member.

The 1966 report of a naval air station commander in Florida
illustrates another type of practice which commanders generally
act to halt:

> One man complained that a local church refused to
> admit his child to its weekday nursery and kindergarten.
> The pastor stated that his church's by-laws prohibited
> their integrating their privately operated nursery and
> kindergarten. In view of the church's position, this
> commander revoked the privilege of the church bus to
> enter the Naval Air Station to pick up children who
> attended the nursery and kindergarten. The bus now
> picks these children up at the gate.

Other examples frequently reported by commanders of actions
taken to discharge equal opportunity responsibilities include:
refusing to permit groups from the base to participate in segregated community events; denying speakers to local organizations
which request a "white only" speaker; inviting local black leaders
to base affairs; employing integrated police patrols off-base; and
dispatching integrated honor guards for ceremonial occasions in
the community.

While most of the activity of commanders has occurred in
areas under their jurisdiction, a few commanders cited racial
incidents off-base in which they personally and directly intervened.
In his 1964 report to the Air Force, the commander of a Louisiana
base related how he had desegregated the public buses through his
direct involvement and use of economic pressure. The commander
wrote:

> A Negro airman failed to observe the local laws on
> seating on public buses. When he refused to comply with
> the directions of the bus driver, he was charged with
> disturbing the peace under Louisiana statutes. This
> incident was resolved after meetings of the bus company
> owner and the base commander. There neither is nor will
> be a segregated seating arrangement while the bus company is
> exercising its Air Force granted license to traverse on

on the AFB. The complaint by the transit company was
withdrawn. The majority of the transit line patrons
embark or disembark on federal property. To an overwhelming extent, its customers are military and
civilian personnel at the base and the bus line is
dependent upon this traffic for its existence.

Since the resports of installation commanders and the interviews of military and community leaders reveal few actions initiated by local commanders against off-base discrimination, how do
local officials perceive the installation influencing the host
community's racial order?

Military and civilian respondents suggested four ways a local
base may influence the racial situation. First, a base may promote
desegregation in the civilian community, not as a result of any
activity of local military officers, but through national laws or
administrative orders pertaining to federal installations and
employees. A North Carolina congressman, whose district includes
one of the bases visited, gave an example:

> I do believe that the presence of military installations
> in the South has accelerated school desegregation. This is
> so because the school administrative units adjacent to mili-
> tary installations receive large sums of money under the so-
> called "impacted area" legislation (Public Law 874). There-
> fore, when the Civil Rights Act of 1964 was passed giving
> the Secretary of HEW authority to cut off federal funds
> from school districts not in compliance with the desegrega-
> tion provisions of Title IV of the Civil Rights Act, these
> communities moved more quickly to satisfy the Office of
> Education on the matter of compliance than the average
> southern school districts, because they had more to lose
> by failure to comply, and in many instances had become so
> heavily dependent upon the PL 874 funds that to lose them
> would have created a major fiscal crisis.

Another community respondent, the president of the local
chamber of commerce and one of the directors of the United Fund in
a Georgia town, credited military participation in the United Fund
for eliminating discrimination in the activities of the member
agencies. The Civil Service Commission which conducts the combined federal campaign among federal employees requires charities
to certify that they do not discriminate in service or employment.
Local agencies generally comply. They are reluctant to lose

military participation, particularly since the military frequently oversubscribes its goal.[17]

Second, many of the respondents attributed the influence of a base on the local racial order as stemming from the power of the military example: the base experience demonstrates that black and white can live, work, and play together. A newspaper editor in South Carolina observed: "The military seems to have adjusted to integration. It may suggest we could also adapt to it." An equal opportunity officer at a Georgia base pointed out that black and white civilian employees eat together at the PX cafeteria and that a black may be in charge of white employees. He concluded that such experiences improve the racial attitudes of civilian employees and that the employees carry back to their communities the new attitudes.[18]

Most community leaders indicated that they believe integration is working on base and creating little or no trouble. However, many did not consider the military experience applicable to their local situation. The president of a local real estate board in North Carolina reported the following exchange:

> The proponents of racial change in the community point out to the racial die-hards that integration is working on base without any difficulty. The die-hards respond by arguing that the experience of the military is not applicable because the base is fewer than ten per cent Negro while Negroes comprise over forty per cent of the community's population.

Another respondent, the president of the local chamber of commerce in a Louisiana town, agreed that integration was working on base but that it was not desirable. He contended that military personnel had had integration forced on them by Washington and that they would prefer racial segregation if they were free to choose.

Negro airmen were sometimes singled out by military and civilian respondents as a third way the military influenced the host community. The judge advocate at a South Carolina base noted that the first school integration in the local community resulted from a federal court order initiated by Negro military personnel. Most respondents, however, saw the influence of the Negro serviceman as more indirect and intangible. They reported that the black airman is perceived by the local citizenry as possessing several desirable traits missing among most local Negroes—clean, well-dressed, high school-educated, and skilled. Because of the favorable image he generates, the Negro airman, so the reasoning goes, enhances the image of blacks generally and thus disposes whites toward adopting more favorable racial attitudes.

Finally, military and civilian respondents cited a more moderate community atmosphere as a primary contribution of a military installation. Respondents noted that the social and racial atmosphere in a host community is more tolerant and less traditional than in communities without installations. The more moderate environment appears to stem from several factors. First, the interaction between local people and military personnel who come from all parts of the country and who have been exposed to different attitudes and customs engenders an atmosphere that is more cosmopolitan and less provincial than that of comparable towns of the area.

Diversity of opinion in the civilian community may also be enhanced by retired military personnel who settle permanently and by the wives of servicemen who teach in the local schools. The superintendant of a South Carolina school district reported that he had 53 wives of military personnel who taught in his district in a total staff of 380. [19] The teachers may expose local children to differing socio-economic views. Of course, changes in attitude can operate both ways. The judge advocate at one base lamented that his children had acquired racial prejudices at school.

An information officer at an Alabama base told how his attitudes had changed after living in the local community:

> I'm from California and I came here with a neutral position on the racial situation. I wondered what or which way I would go. I have come to sympathize more with the white southerner. The Negroes here have a

horrible lack of desire. They have a long way to go.
They need some more civilizing.

Finally, some respondents attributed the more moderate
environment, particularly in racial matters, to the efforts of
host community leaders who recognize the economic importance of
the base to the community and their own livelihood. The civilian
leaders foster moderation and tolerance because they know that if
their community is plagued by racial strife, the military will be
less likely to consider the base in any deployment of forces.[20]

THE FATE OF EQUAL OPPORTUNITY
DIRECTIVES IN THE FIELD

The reports of the base commanders and the interviews with
local military and civilian leaders indicate that a base does
have some impact on the racial attitudes and policies of nearby
communities but that the change does not generally stem from any
direct activity by installation commanders. In 1967 Defense
Secretary McNamara sent teams to a dozen bases to look into every
aspect of equal opportunity since his 1963 directive. McNamara
reported that one fact emerged: the Department's voluntary program of obtaining equal opportunity off-base, especially in
housing had failed.[21] According to one writer, the Defense
Department, despite all its directives and memos, has had little
influence outside the confines of the military installation.[22]

Why have base commanders seldom taken aggressive action in
the off-base equal opportunity area? Why have the directives
and memos promulgated by the senior echelon of the military
establishment had only limited influence in the field? The focal
point for attempting to answer these questions is the local base
commander who is primarily responsible for translating the broad
pronouncements at the top levels into tangible accomplishments
in the field.

As in any large organization there are centrifugal tendencies
operating in the military establishment that serve to divert base
commanders from carrying out faithfully the directives or official
policy of the Defense Department. The writer proposes to examine
what he believes are three key factors accounting for field

behavior inconsistent with the Department of Defense's equal opportunity directives: (1) the personal preferences of local military
commanders; (2) "capture" of the commander by the local population; and (3) problems of internal communication between commanders and their superiors.[23]

Personal Preferences. First, the personal preferences, attitudes, or values of a local commander are among the determinants
of his behavior and they can slow or modify his field behavior
as compared with the behavior mandated from the Defense Department. He may harbor racial prejudices or espouse racial equality;
he may narrowly or loosely construe the military mission; he may
be enthusiastic or indifferent or reluctant in his efforts to
implement the civil rights directives.

The way in which commanders personally interpret the military
mission explains largely why the equal opportunity directives
have not been aggressively implemented off-base. Many commanders
see the issue of equal opportunity off-base as outside the military mission. While they recognize that all servicemen must be
accorded equal treatment on the installation, commanders believe
that military responsibility ends at the base gate. As the
captain of a naval activity in Maryland put it: "The command takes
no aggressive interest in trying to insist upon equal treatment
off of the federal property." Beyond the confines of the installation, commanders say, the Justice Department and the Department
of Health, Education and Welfare should assume responsibility.

Military men generally resent the impulse of political and
civilian leaders to "cram new and unrelated roles and missions
into the soldier's knapsack."[24] At some bases the senior officers
who had conducted the off-base housing survey to determine the
extent of open housing expressed vehement opposition to being
used for such a task. As professional soldiers, they questioned
whether it was wise for the military to be asled to wrestle with
internal social problems, diverting its energies from its primary
mission of combat readiness.

Local military commanders conceive of their job as over-

whelmingly military in character. They look upon their assignment as an opportunity to exercise military command on a substantial scale and to demonstrate their abilities, thus providing
grounds for promotion and career advancement. Moreover, they see
the strictly military aspects of their job on the basis on which
headquarters grades them.

Most installation commanders feel they are overburdened in
discharging their assigned duties. They say that they have
neither the time nor the inclination to seek out or encourage
additional problems, particularly if they are not strictly military. The base commanders indicated that if a Negro airman
registered a complaint concerning off-base discimination or segregation, they would have the complaint objectively investigated.
If it were found to have merit, they would bring it to the attention of the appropriate community leaders and seek to enlist their
support in solving it. However, most of the commanders believed
that the Negro airman must exercise the initiative and bring the
complaint to the attention of the command.

In other words, commanders see their responsibility not to
ferret out discriminatory practices off-base or to aggressively
foster equal opportunity, but to remedy racial problems after
they are brought to their attention by others. As the commander
of a naval station in Louisiana expressed it in his equal opportunity report to the Navy Department: "The command has had no
reports of off-base discrimination and therefore no action has
been required."

In the past, Negro servicemen have failed to act as a stimulus to commanders. Base officers, who have been assigned to
handle off-base equal opportunity affairs, report that they
average only one or two complaints a year from Negro airmen.[25]
In assessing the small volume of complaints, one may offer several
explanations. First, one may accept the explanation of some base
officials that few complaints reflect the morale of black personnel and the state of equality existing in the civilian communities. Second, it may indicate that black servicemen choose

to suffer the humiliation of discrimination rather than be considered chronic complainers. Third, black personnel may fear some reprisal if they enter a grievance, or they may have little faith in the efficacy of registering a complaint.

Finally, the small volume of complaints may reflect the fact that black military personnel avoid racial incidents by minimizing contact with white civilian groups. The black soldiers endure a self-imposed segregation, shunning places in which they or their friends may be embarrassed. Of course, they may be simply showing a preference to maintain primary group ties and informal associations with their own racial group.

Many community leaders insisted repeatedly that local restaurants are open to Negroes but that they do not patronize them. Some off-base housing referral officers contended that Negro airmen do not seek to live in white neighborhoods. Under the Defense Department's housing policy, the only housing units which may be listed on base are those whose owners have signed open-housing pledges. When a Negro serviceman seeks off-base housing, he is given a list of potential sites. According to housing officers, he either asks other black airmen or drives around town checking the addresses to discover which are in the Negro sections of the community.

At a base in Georgia which has reported 100 per cent open housing in off-base housing facilities, the housing officer said that, although the housing program had been in effect about a year, he did not know of any Negro airmen who had moved into a previously all-white housing area or facility. In the adjacent host community, a major real estate dealer told the writer he would not rent or sell a place in a white neighborhood to a Negro even though he had signed the open housing pledges. As Negro servicemen become militant in pursuit of their rights and put more and more open housing pledges to the test, local commanders may be forced to play a more active role in achieving open housing.

In the past, one factor which has helped commanders to avoid difficult racial problems with community leaders has been the

small number of black officers stationed at their installations
(see Table 2). Social contacts between local civilian and military elite frequently take place at local Country Clubs which
maintain "white only" policies. In the past, invitations to
social affairs were generally sent only to white officers. Most
bases now expect invitations to be issued by rank regardless of
race. However, since the invitations are commonly extended only
to those officers with the rank of lieutenant colonel or higher
(and only one of the seven bases had Negro officers of that rank),
social gatherings remain white.

TABLE 2

NUMBER AND PERCENT OF BASE OFFICERS NEGRO, 1968

Base	Total Number of Base Officers	Number of Base Officers Negro	Per Cent of Base Officers Negro
A	815	4	0.49
B	1,859	186	10.00
C	419	2	0.47
D	357	1	0.28
E	856	6	0.70
F	680	13	1.90
G	813	8	0.98

Source: Information obtained from Civil Rights Office,
Department of Defense.

Negroes are generally absent not only from social, but also
from working relationships between the base and host community.
One of the most frequently employed means for community and base
officials to resolve their mutual problems is a base-community
council. However, because of the method of selecting the council's membership, Negroes are usually absent from it. The
civilian members of the committee are either appointed by the city
government or earn a seat by virtue of community positions they
occupy, such as mayor, president of the local chamber of commerce,
police chief, and so forth. Military membership on the council
is likewise generally determined by reason of position—commander,
judge advocate, fire and security chiefs, and information officer.
Civilian members of some councils have threatened to resign if a
Negro is appointed. Few base-community committees report having

a black member. As the number and rank of black officers advance, formidable strains will probably be placed on relations, both social and working, between the civilian elite and base commanders. The commanders may be faced with appointing a black information officer to the base-community council or declining a social invitation to the Country Club because a black colonel was not invited.

Localized Influence. The "capture" of base commanders by local populations is a second way national policy may become a fiction in the field. The danger of capture is twofold: (1) too close an identification by local commanders with community leaders rather than the Department of Defense; and (2) the considerable pressures brought to bear on commanders by powerful local interests. The first aspect of the danger arises because the armed services stress harmonious base-community relations and urge military personnel to cultivate the relationship by participating in the activities of local schools, churches, fraternal, social and civic organizations. Generally the local military commander is a member of Rotary and the Country Club; an ex-officio member of the Board of Directors of the Chamber of Commerce and the United Fund; and an active participant in his church, the Salvation Army, and the Boy Scouts.

As friendships with local leaders develop through contacts made in community organizations, the commander's discussion with them tend to deal with matters on which they agree and to omit examination of issues which might adversely affect rapport. The meetings of the command-community relations committees become social affairs as the minutes of a council meeting at a base in South Carolina in 1968 illustrate:

1. The coordinator of the council officially opened the meeting.
2. The base chaplain gave the invocation.
3. The coordinator called on the base commander for a welcome.
4. The base commander welcomed those present, expressed his appreciation for council activities, and introduced the new military members of the council.
5. The coordinator called on the mayor for response.
6. The mayor expressed his pleasure at the colonel's remarks on the value of the council, thanked the commander for

the warm welcome, and noted how civilian members look forward to attending council meetings.
7. An excellent dinner was served and a tribute was passed
   to the Officers' Mess.
8. The coordinator called for committee reports from the four
   functional committees (Police-Health-Safety, Religion-
   Welfare, Recreation-Education, and Housing-Commercial
   Services-Public Relations). Each committee chairman
   responded, "No report."
9. There being no other business before the council, the
   coordinator adjourned the meeting.

The command-community councils were, of course, designed as a
tool by which local military organizations could resolve problems
with their environment. When local military organizations approxi-
mated closed communities with their members working and residing
on base, they were relatively isolated from their environment.
However, as the military became unable to accommodate all their
personnel and were forced to rely on nearby civilian communities
for housing, mutual problems arose between the civilian and military communities. Through command-community councils, the military
co-opted prominent civilian leaders to help identify and solve the
difficulties.

The civilian members of the council generally include the
owners of local industries and department stores, the presidents
of all the banks, local government officials, and prominent
attorneys. Most of the members have links with public officials
at all levels of government. A base commander knows that he has
to work with and through these men if he is to achieve his
objectives whether they be new housing off-base, fair law enforce-
ment in the community, or a better highway adjacent to the base.

Since the success of a base commander hinges partly upon his
ability to work with these leaders, he may become, as the chairman of a history department in a state college in one host community observed, a "captive" of the local chamber of commerce
crowd. If he will "play ball" with these local leaders, they will,
in turn, do their best to further his interests.

While the practice of transferring field men rapidly is a
technique employed by organizations to prevent capture by local

populations, the rapidity of military transfer of commanders may enable local leaders with deep roots in the community to absorb a disproportionate amount of influence in the military–civilian relationship. In contrast to the military commander whose tour on base is about twenty months, the composition of the civilian leaders on the base–community council or the military affairs committee of the chamber of commerce rarely changes. For example, the chairman and members of the executive council of the military affairs committee in a Louisiana city adjacent to one base had served on the committee continuously since World War II when the installation was an Army Air Force station.

Because of their long tenure on, and familiarity with, the operation of the command–community councils, civilian leaders often control the way the committees will function. Suggestions by base commanders, for instance, to change the composition of the councils by adding Negro representatives or new and younger blood generally go unheeded or bring threats of resignation. When commanders plan social affairs on the base, it is common practice for the chairman of the military affairs committee or the manager of the chamber of commerce to provide the commander with the list of civilians whom he should invite to base affairs.

The civilian leaders may also channel the course of the commander in the community. The civilian chairman of the base–community committee or the manager of the chamber of commerce often plays an important part in determining which local social organization the base commander will join. In one host community the commander may traditionally join the Rotary, in another the Kiwanis. The president of a local Kiwanis Club related how such a tradition emerges:

> The chairman of the Chamber of Commerce's Committee on Military Affairs is a Kiwanian and he is among the first to meet the new commander. The present commander is a Kiwanian, and he is asked to bring the new wing commander in as a guest. He is promptly asked to join Kiwanis by the few people he knows in the new town.

If the local commander cooperates and follows the course chartered by civilian leaders, they will work to advance his

career. In almost every host community, local civilians boasted
of how they had schemed to get a promotion for a local commander.
Sometimes their efforts had been limited to writing warm letters
of commendation for the commander's folder. In one situation, a
prominent local leader worked through the headquarters of the particular air command to achieve a star for the base commander.
According to the local leader, he was an old friend of the head of
the command. He noted that the General was a good man to know
because he has the power to say how many pilots will go to each
training base. The community respondent went on to relate how
their friendship can benefit a local commander:

> Whenever the General comes here, we go fishing. If the
> commander's good and is easy to get along with, I build him
> up with the General. If we've had trouble with him, I just
> don't mention him and the General knows what that means.

A county judge in another community cited a third way of helping the local commander advance. The judge related how he and
other community officials worked with the state's congressional
delegation to win a promotion for a commander. Members of the
state's delegation hold important positions on the House and
Senate Armed Services Committees. The judge noted that the last
four wing commanders had moved from colonel to brigadier general
while at the base.

The furtherance of the interests of a local commander by community leaders may extend beyond his military career. Some officers, for example, are approaching retirement when they are
assigned to the position of base commander. They are seeking a
community in which to retire and are investigating the opportunities
for a second career. Of course, any new job must be of comparable
status to that of base commander. Local economic or political
elites can generally offer such jobs.

The president of a local real estate board indicated the
effect that job hunting may have on a commander's behavior. In
response to a question of how actively the commander had pushed
the open housing program in the local community, the realtor said:

> The commander recently retired from the base and we

offered him the job of city manager and he accepted. We
wouldn't have done that if he had pushed us very hard. I
think the military men are winking at this issue.

The comments of the chairman of the military affairs committee
in a Georgia community illustrate again how local leaders may
assist a retiring commander who had identified with them.

We were extremely pleased with him. He was born and
raised in Alabama and he understood our way of life, our
food, our talk. We had a party at the Country Club for him
when he retired. It cost us $2,800. It was probably the
biggest social affair we had ever had. . . . He is a vice-
president now in the bank across the street.

Retiring after his next tour of duty, the commander of an
installation adjacent to a resort area in Florida purchased a
home in the host community. From all indications, the commander
desired to carry out the open-housing program in a manner not
likely to disturb his future neighbors. The off-base housing
referral officer noted that the commander had refused to permit
him to use a staff car while discussing open housing with apart-
ment owners. According to the housing officer, the commander did
not want people to see a staff car being employed for such a purpose.

The second aspect of the danger of base commanders being
captured by local populations comes about through the pressures
community leaders may exert on them. While local leaders may
assist a commander in receiving a promotion or a job after retirement, they may also cost him his position or adversely affect his
career if he upsets them. Since a harmonious base-community relationship is often taken as a sign of an effective and successful
local commander, base commanders attempt to complete their limited
tour of duty without "disturbances." Further, they know that complaints by local people to their congressional representatives may
cause reverberations throughout the command and possibly result in
their being sacrificed even though the trouble arose because they
were carrying out official policy. A retired base commander in
South Carolina commented:

I don't believe you get the backing of superiors if
trouble develops. They want you to push the program (open

housing off-base) but not to create any ill will. If
trouble does develop, you don't change community leaders.
You change the base commander.

A similar argument was advanced by a commander in Alabama:

The wives of a couple of colored airmen complained
that they hadn't been able to use a local laundromat. I
contacted some chamber of commerce people about it. I
don't know whether it is open now and I'm not going to
test it to find out. If I got the community upset about
such a matter, I'd be shipped to Alaska or Greenland
pretty quickly.

Complaints by local power leaders to their congressman con-

cerning a commander's activity in the civil rights mission might

possibly jeopardize his career. Senator Stennis, chairman of the

Senate Armed Services Committee, hinted how such a promotion could

be refused:

In any event, the executive department does not have
the final say as to what shall be considered "fitness and
efficiency" entitling an officer to promotion. The final
power rests with the Senate and only those are promoted who
are confirmed by the Senate. Those who might be ranked
high by the President's Commission when it comes to "measuring progress" (in the civil rights field) might not be
ranked quite so high by those who finally act on the proposed
promotion. I emphasize this point to show that this directive
(1963 McNamara order) clearly proposes to throw the military
directly into political activities of the most sensitive
nature and to introduce a strictly nonmilitary factor into
the promotion system.[26]

Internal Communication. The third major factor accounting for

the gap between official policy pertaining to equal opportunity

and actual behavior in the field is the problem of internal com-

munication between commanders and headquarters. As the President's

Committee on Equal Opportunity in the Armed Forces noted: "There

has been a great failure of communications to bases of the atti-

tudes and policies of the Department of Defense concerning dis-

crimination."[27] The earlier comments of local commanders who did

not believe they would receive the support of higher command if

their programs were attacked by local interests demonstrate one

aspect of the communications failure.

Of course, if local commanders are correct in their assumption

that they will not be reinforced, then it is not necessarily a communications failure but rather evidence of the Defense Department's less than total commitment to the program. Some of the cues emanating from the Pentagon do suggest the latter interpretation. In September 1963, for example, an article appeared in the Army Times saying: "Defense has said that actions of local commanders on the integration front will not be made a part of efficiency reports. . . ."[28]

When the Defense Department launched its pilot program for open housing in the Washington-Maryland area, Secretary McNamara chose a brigadier general to be the field commander. A month later a story appeared in the Army Times reporting that the General had put down a $100 deposit for an apartment in a segregated apartment complex.[29] When McNamara ordered that housing advertised on the big concourse bulletin board of the Pentagon be available to persons of any race, the number of housing notices diminished about one third.[30]

Finally, the reluctance of the Department of Defense to use the "off-limits" sanction in its equal opportunity campaign may have provided another cue to local commanders. The only use of the sanction occurred in the open-housing drive in the Washington, D.C. and Maryland areas. Noting that proposals to consider housing bans in Georgia and Louisiana had been put aside by the Defense Department, the Army Times concluded: "Congressional delegations from Georgia and Louisiana are far more influential than Maryland's."[31]

In checking through the reports of base commanders from 1963 to 1967, the writer found only two requests submitted by commanders to their civilian service chief for the use of the sanction. Both were either ignored or denied. The following is an excerpt from a commander's report concerning his request for the sanction:

> On July 24, 1965, a Negro staff sergeant had entered a local coin-operated laundry to launder his clothing. The manager of the business asked him if he intended to use the facility and he indicated that he did. She told him the business was limited to white patrons and asked that he leave. In a short time, the owner of the establishment arrived and asked the sergeant to leave the premises. The owner

was accompanied by a police detective who affirmed to the
sergeant the owner's right to demand that he leave. When
the sergeant protested, the owner stopped the machine in
mid-cycle and the sergeant was required to remove his wet
clothing,wring them dry, and carry them from the store in a
cardboard container provided by the owner. Upon receipt of
the complaint, the owner was contacted by the staff judge
advocate at the request of the base commander to seek voluntary integration. The owner refused. The establishment was
not covered by the provisions of the 1964 Civil Rights Act.
The only remedy remaining would be to seek an "off-limits"
sanction which would have to be approved by the Secretary
of the Air Force. The sergeant requested this be done. A
file was prepared to this effect including a request for
suit by the Attorney General in an effort to obtain review
of certain points of the Civil Rights Act. The request
was forwarded with no positive result. The facility continues as a segregated business establishment.

In addition to the weak cues commanders have received from
headquarters, they believe they are called upon to execute directives which are not easily reconciled. Because of the inconsistent
directives, the commanders believe that they must attempt to
resolve conflicts in their own ways. First, commanders have the
obligation to house all of their people, white and black. Yet,
they may place on the base housing list only those housing units
which have pledged open housing. If the local housing market is
tight, the commander may find it necessary to make certain compro-
mises in carrying out directives concerning open housing. Otherwise, the rental agencies and landlords could thumb their noses at
the military and rent only to civilians.[32]

Second, to the extent that commanders deal with the community
beyond the base gate, they are expected to foster friendly and
cooperative relations. Yet, commanders know that attempts to alter
local customs and mores, especially in race relations, could
rupture a seemingly harmonious base-community relationship.
Finally, a commander in his annual report to the Civil Rights
Office presented still another dilemma. He pointed out that the
state legislature was considering a Model Housing Law. He wanted
to know if he could give public support to the principle of fair
housing legislation or help get such a law enacted. The commander
spelled out his problem:

It is the policy of the Air Force to encourage and assist community officials in eliminating any discriminatory treatment of any military personnel and their dependents. This policy is expressed in AFR 35-78, which is the Air Force implementation of DOD directive 5120.36.

It is also the policy of the Air Force, as set forth in AFR 190-6, that each member of the Air Force has a reponsibility to "refrain from public pronouncement on political, diplomatic, and legislative matters."

The judge advocate at the commander's base said that in his opinion the latter regulation prohibited the commander from giving public support to the Model Housing Law since it was being deliberated in the state legislature. Such dilemmas arising from inconsistent directives and weak cues from headquarters coupled with a commander's interpretation of his role and pressures exerted by the local population help explain why military commanders have handled gingerly and reluctantly the equal opportunity mission off-base.

RAMIFICATIONS OF CIVIL RIGHTS MISSION

The final objective of this paper is to examine the ramifications of the civil rights mission on traditional civil-military relations. Several congressmen and newspapers, primarily Southern, had predicted dire consequences emanating from the new military mission. They argued that the military in a democratic society is justified only to defend the society against external and, in extremity, internal aggression. The new mission proposed to utilize the military for implementing social patterns not only alien to the habits and traditions of the local people but, in many cases, contrary to local and state laws. Moreover, when McNamara issued his first directive, Congress was still debating the legislation later to become the 1964 Civil Rights Act. Critics contended that the military was being required to enforce a position which had no legal basis.[33]

Senator Stennis of Mississippi called the new mission a grave challenge to the long-established and traditional concept of complete separation of the military from all political matters and activities.[34] Arizona Senator Barry Goldwater warned that the action carried the seeds of a possible military takeover because commanders might get accustomed to running politics and the social life of the communities in which they are stationed.[35]

From most indications, the tradition of noninvolvement by military commanders in local political matters has been unimpaired by the new mission. For one thing, commanders have not waged an aggressive campaign in their host communities against discriminatory practices but have confined their activity to remedying specific problems brought to their attention by black servicemen. Moreover, as service instructions emphasize, the commander's concern is only with the morale of his black servicemen and their families, not with black civilian members of the community. If the proprietor of a bowling alley, for instance, is willing to allow black servicemen to use his facility, even though he is unwilling to permit local blacks to enter, the base commander has achieved his objective.

Further, when commanders deal with racial problems affecting their men, they handle them in the same manner as they would problems concerning rent gouging or bawdy houses. They seek to cajole the local power structure, the prominent businessmen and government officials on the command-community committee, to "carry the ball" for them. They shun involvement with local black activists and civil rights groups who want them to participate in ways they consider unacceptable. By taking their problems to the local leaders, allowing them to manage the solution, and avoiding contact with those outside the power structure, commanders allay the fear or apprehension of community leaders of military intervention in local political issues.

One year after the McNamara directive, Alfred Fitt, then Assistant Secretary of Defense for Civil Rights, reported that "affirmative anti-discrimination efforts by commanders have nowhere generated hostility or controversy in military-civilian relationships."[36] To learn if the more recent off-base open housing drive had damaged relationships, the writer asked base and community leaders if the campaign had improved, hurt, or had no effect on base-community relations. Not one respondent said that relations

had been injured. Most believed the open housing program had had
no effect. A few military respondents even maintained that the
program had improved base-community ties.

There seem to be three major reasons why respondents believe
the open housing drive has not damaged the local military-civilian
relationship. First, some respondents were either unaware that
the military was even attempting to get open housing or believed
that the military was not vigorously pushing it. As some of the
respondents put it:

> (South Carolina minister): The program would hurt base-
> community relations if the base ever tried to do anything
> of this sort.

> (North Carolina newspaper publisher): If the program
> were really pushed, it would hurt base-community relations.

Second, many respondents contended the open housing drive had
not affected the local relationship because everyone knew that the
directive originated in Washington and not in the local commander's
office.

> (City manager in North Carolina): The Community under-
> stands this wasn't the commander's idea. He must comply with
> orders.

> (City manager in South Carolina): Any negative
> reaction has been directed more to the national government,
> not to the local base.

> (President of a local chamber of commerce in Louisiana):
> It's a situation the military had no control over. It was
> something passed down from higher officials.

Finally, the open housing drive has apparently not disturbed
some community leaders because, while they would prefer that the
local commander not be involved in the civil rights mission, they
conceded the legitimacy of his efforts if off-base housing discrimination has resulted in a morale problem among his Negro personnel.

> (Realtor in Georgia): If I were a base commander, I
> would be concerned if housing was a morale problem. Whether
> a commander should be concerned with open housing depends on
> whether he is having a morale problem.

> (Newspaper publisher in North Carolina): The military
> should be concerned only with military affairs--that's enough.

Of course, we understand that a base commander must look
after the morale of his men. An executive must look after
his people. I look after my newspaper employees who are
colored.

While most respondents believed the open housing program has
had no effect on relations, a handful of military officials saw it
as having improved base-community relations. Representative of
their responses is that of a base-commander in North Carolina:

The good majority of the people are smiling but some
think we are treading on their toes. There has been some
strain but I think it has affected base-community relations
somewhat on the favorable side. The efforts have brought
people together to explain the program. It has given us a
problem to work together to solve.

Although some base commanders noted that civilian members of
their command-community committee listened in "stony silence" as
they outlined their plans for the off-base housing survey or that
some doors were slammed in the faces of their officers during the
survey, none said that the local relationship had been hurt. The
annual reports of commanders reveal only one base-community situation that has been badly damaged since the military was handed the
equal opportunity mission.

Immediately after the 1963 directive, the late Leander Perez,
archsegregationist and political boss of Plaquemines Parish,
Louisiana, declared he was going to beat the military to the draw.
Perez announced that the United States Naval Air Station at Belle
Chasse was "off-limits" to civilian residents of his southeast
Louisiana parish and that all parish-licensed bars and lounges
were "off-limits" to uniformed military personnel.

Perez notified the Navy that the children of Navy personnel
were no longer welcome in the public schools. He gave the Navy a
year to find or build classrooms for children at the station but
warned that if the Navy attempted to implement equal opportunity
measures in his parish, the children would be turned out at once.[37]
Four years later with the Perez edicts still standing in the parish,
an insulted and humiliated commander of the naval air station concluded his 1967 report to superiors: "I, a captain in the U.S.

Navy, cannot buy a beer in his area in uniform. This man is destroying the image of the U.S. serviceman."

Although the Plaquemines Parish episode is exceptional, the civil rights mission does appear to have lessened somewhat the ties between the civilian and military communities. In an Alabama community, for instance, base officials planned to honor the anniversary of the WAF's by inviting six women members, including one black, to be honored guests at a luncheon of the military affairs committee. The information officer said it was the worst attendance for such a meeting he had ever encountered. Civilian members reported they were sick or going out of town that day. Earlier, the community had discontinued its support of the USO center rather than integrate; the local chamber of commerce had halted its welcome tour of the area for newly arriving military personnel rather than integrate the tour bus; and member agencies of the United Fund denied the base the opportunity to participate in the campaign by refusing to comply with federal equal opportunity requirements.

Other examples may be cited of how the Defense Department's equal opportunity policy has resulted in reduced base-community contacts: the withdrawal of the base team from the community's Little League when colored children of the team were denied playing privileges; the construction of an on-base school when the local educational system refused to integrate; the discontinuation of community sponsored dances, one for colored and one for white airmen, during the town's "Air Base Days;" the cancellation of an appearance by the Air Force Band because no assurance was given that the audience would be integrated; and withdrawal of the base from the Country Club's annual golf tournament when community leaders requested a list of white golfers only from the commander.

SUMMARY

The degree of influence of the equal opportunity mission of the military on the racial customs and policies of host communities is difficult to objectively measure. While the armed forces have seldom acted as a spearhead for knocking down racial barriers

off base, they do appear to have had some impact beyond the confines of the post gate. Part of the influence stems from the
caliber of black servicemen, the working model of integration on
base, and the influx of military personnel from outside the region.

Direct action by commanders has been confined to remedying
individual problems of morale rather than waging a broad campaign
against discriminatory practices in the host community. Most of
the practices which commanders have taken action against are ones
over which they have a significant measure of control. However,
regardless of the degree of local activity, both military and
civilians know that the official policy of the Defense Department
no longer subscribes to the notion of military accommodation to
discriminatory practices off-base.

Because base commanders have been cautious in their handling
of the equal opportunity mission and showed great sensitivity to
the fears of local community leaders, the effects of the mission
on traditional military-civilian relations have been limited.
There are some indications, however, that contacts between the two
communities may have diminished because of the civil rights
directives. To that degree, the equal opportunity mission of
the military may have served to thwart somewhat the social integration of the military with the nearby civilian communities.

NOTES

Many people have contributed to this article. I am particularly indebted to John Lovell, Indiana University, for the initial
stimulus for the article and many helpful suggestions. This
writer also owes a profound debt to the many base and community
people for their hospitality, time, and information. Of course,
the study would have been impossible without the excellent cooperation of the Civil Rights Office, Department of Defense, and the
United States Air Force. Finally, the writer acknowledges the
Inter-University Seminar on Armed Forces and Society for the
financial support making the study possible. For any faults in
the work, the writer claims sole credit.

[1]New York Times, July 27, 1963, p. 1.

[2]The writer spent six weeks in the Office of Civil Rights of
the Defense Department examining directives issued by the Office
and the reports submitted by commanders concerning off-base conditions and the open housing campaign. During the field trip in
Spring 1968, the author visited seven Air Force bases in North
Carolina, South Carolina, Georgia, Florida, Alabama and Lousiana.
The number of military personnel stationed at the bases ranged
from 1,830 to 13, 696 and the number of black personnel from 126
to 1,370. The population of the host communities varied from
20,592 to 42,635. In five of the communities, blacks constituted
over one-third of the population.
At each base interviews were held with the wing or base commander, the judge advocate, the information officer, the off-base
housing referral officer, and the equal opportunity officer. In
the host communities, interviews were sought with the mayor or city
manager, the president and the manager of the chamber of commerce,
the editor or publisher of the major newspaper, the president of
the local real estate board, and the president of the ministerial
association. As time permitted, the writer also talked with other
military personnel, active and retired; members of command-community
concils, civil rights leaders; USO directors, and others. Altogether the writer interviewed 98 military and cilivian people.
Although the interviewer had a standardized questionnaire, the
questions only served as guide lines for the interviewing.

[3]Emmett J. Scott, Scott's Official History of the American
Negro in the World War, Chicago: Homewood Press, 1919, pp. 97-98.

[4]Letter from Secretary of War, Henry L. Stimson to Congressman
Leonard Allen of Louisiana, September 20, 1944, quoted in John P.
Davis, "The Negro in the Armed Forces of America," American Negro
Reference Book, Englewood Cliffs, New Jersey: Prentice-Hall, 1966,
p. 657.

[5]For accounts of racial integration and its consequences in the armed forces, see Lee Bogart, Social Research and the Desegregation of the U.S. Army, Chicago: Markham Publishing Company, 1969; Richard M. Dalfiume, Desegregation of the U.S. Armed Forces, Columbia, Missouri: University of Missouri Press, 1969; Charles C. Moskos, Jr., "Racial Integration in the Armed Forces," American Journal of Sociology, Vol. 72, September, 1966, pp. 132-148; Lee Nichols, Breakthrough on the Color Front, New York: Random House, 1954; and Richard J. Stillman, Integration of the Negro in the U. S. Armed Forces, New York: Frederick A. Praeger, 1968.

[6]See President's Committee on Equal Opportunity in the Armed Forces, Initial Report: Equality of Treatment and Opportunity for Negro Military Personnel Stationed Within the United States, June 13, 1963; United States Commission on Civil Rights, "The Negro in the Armed Forces," Civil Rights '63, Government Printing Office, Washington, D.C., pp. 169-224.

[7]President's Committee on Equal Opportunity, op. cit., p. 45.

[8]Washington Evening Star, September 8, 1967, p. 3B.

[9]New Orleans Times-Picayune, July 17, 1963, p. 1; New York Times, August 8, 1963, p. 13.

[10]New York Times, July 17, 1963, p. 1.

[11]President's Committee on Equal Opportunity, op. cit., pp. 51-52.

[12]The Vietnam War may explain the Defense Department's decision in 1967 to take a more aggressive role against segregated housing. McNamara and other senior defense officials said it was intolerable for the large number of Negro servicemen returning from Vietnam to have to accept such discrimination. Moreover, the war revealed to many Americans the obligation owed the black soldier. Statistics in 1966 showed that in the previous four years of fighting 18.3 per cent of the Army's combat dead were Negroes, a figure 5 per cent higher than the percentage of Negroes in the Army, and seven per cent more than their percentage in the population. See New York Times, November 8, 1967, p. 29; and Gene Grove, "The Army and the Negro," New York Times Magazine, July 24, 1966, p. 5.

[13]Robert S. McNamara, The Essence of Security, New York: Harper and Row, 1968, pp. 122-140.

[14]President Kennedy's instructions to the Committee on Equality of Opportunity were made in a letter to the Committee's Chairman Gerhard A. Gesell, June 22, 1962. Also see Leadership Conference on Civil Rights, Federally Supported Discrimination, New York: Futuro Press, 1961.

[15]Each service issued instructions to commanders for assuring equal treatment and opportunity. See Army Regulation No. 600-21, Navy Instruction No. 5350.6, and Air Force Regulation No. 35-78.

[16]Memorandum, Secretary of Defense to Service Secretaries, March 8, 1963; Memorandum, Cyrus Vance, Deputy Secretary of Defense, to Service Secretaries, April 11, 1967.

[17]An Air Force base in South Carolina reported that it had exceeded its United Fund quota by more than fifty percent. Another base in Florida contributed about forty five per cent of the total county-wide goal. Reports of commanders revealed two instances where the military withdrew from participation in campaigns because of the refusal of agencies to comply with equal opportunity requirements.

[18]In four of the seven towns studied, the base was the largest single employer in the area. Most of the bases employed approximately 500 civilian employees, although one had almost 19,000.

[19]The figures of the South Carolina superintendent seem representative of the towns studied. An assistant superintendent in a Georgia community said that ten retired airmen from the base were teaching in the school system and between 50 and 75 wives of active military personnel.

[20]In every community visited, the combined military-civilian payroll, ranging from $12 million to $175 million, represented the town's largest payroll.

[21]Robert S. McNamara, op. cit., p. 124.

[22]Richard J. Stillman, op. cit., p. 117.

[23]These challenges to the unity of an organization are suggested by Herbert Kaufman in his excellent study of administrative behavior in the Forest Service. See Herbert Kaufman, The Forest Ranger, Baltimore: John Hopkins Press, 1960, pp. 66-87.

[24]Vernon Pizer, The United States Army, New York: Frederick A. Praeger, 1967, p. 19.

[25]The small volume of complaints is illustrated by a memorandum of the Navy Department for the Deputy Assistant Secretary of Defense for Civil Rights. The report showed a total of 38 complaints in 1965 and 35 in 1966 from the Navy's approximately 100 activities in the United States having 500 or more personnel attached.

[26]Congressional Record, 88th Congress, 1st Session (1963), p. 13011.

[27]The President's Committee on Equal Opportunity in the Armed Forces, op. cit., p. 63.

[28]Army Times, September 4, 1963, p. 1.

[29]Army Times, May 24, 1967, p. 3.

[30]<u>Army Times</u>, May 22, 1963, p. 4.

[31]<u>Army Times</u>, August 2, 1967, p. 1.

[32]<u>Army Times</u>, December 14, 1966, p. 12.

[33]For Congressional reaction to the McNamara directive, see <u>Congressional Record</u>, 88th Congress, 1st Session (1963), pp. 13005-13014, 13548-13599.

[34]<u>Congressional Record,</u> 88th Congress, 1st Session (1963), p. 13005.

[35]<u>Ibid.</u>, p. 13009.

[36]Memorandum, Fitt To Service Under-Secretaries, May 25, 1964.

[37]New Orleans <u>Times-Picayune</u>, August 30, 1963, p. 1.

THE ARMED FORCES EXAMINING STATION:

A SOCIOLOGICAL PERSPECTIVE

Leon Bramson

It is a well-known fact of the 19th century social theory that
the fathers of modern sociology regarded military institutions
and war itself as an archaic survival in an industrial society.
St. Simon, Comte and Spencer among others argued that there was a
necessary antithesis between the military society on the one hand
and industrial society on the other. The former was homogenous,
ascriptive, authoritarian, hierarchical and self-sufficient; the
latter was heterogenous, achievement-oriented, egalitarian,
democratic and interdependent. The military was identified with
what Durkheim called a society based on mechanical solidarity.
Comte and Spencer predicted that with the flowering of industrial
society, military institutions would wither away and war itself
would become anachronistic. The basis for this prediction lay
in the notion that the industrial system carried with it its own
ethos—the ethos of work, of social stability, and of constantly
increasing wealth. As this ethos came to dominate modern society,
and as political, social and religious institutions gradually
changed their character in the age of the democratic revolutions,
new forms of solidarity would arise which would preclude inter-
tribal and international strife. Free trade would encourage
economic interdependence, and a global society would emerge which
would not fail to perceive that its best interests lay in the
avoidance of military conflict. Under the impact of this

185

realization and the spread of the ethos of work, the military establishment itself would shrivel and disappear. There would no longer be any meaningful function which it could fulfill.

The history of the past century gives no good grounds for optimism regarding this prediction, though Raymond Aron has argued that the conditions of industrialism visualized by Comte and Spencer have not yet been realized and that therefore the argument must still be regarded as at least not disproven.[1] As I have written elsewhere,[2] what actually ensued was in fact the partial militarization of industry and, more important, the industrialization of the military. Yet the military establishment in modern society still retains elements which Spencer contrasted sharply with industrialism, though it has been quick to adapt the achievements of the industrial system in the technological sphere to military purposes. If the 19th century social theorists were right there is a profound inconsistency between the military and the industrial sectors of society, or between the military and the civilian world. But, as Albert Biderman said recently in a thoughtful paper on the subject: "What is Military?"[3] More and more, civil society and military establishment alike have had to cope with the same basic problems: organizing large numbers of people for a wide variety of economic and social purposes. There is an important sense in which civil society has borrowed techniques of rational organization from the military and adapted them to its own purposes. As for the uniqueness of the military institution today, Biderman argues that neither conventional nor strategic warfare present the kinds of problems which have given the military establishment its distinctive character throughout history. "It is a matter of complete irrelevance in the event of missile war whether the men in the missile silo or the Polaris submarine perform their duty in uniform or in their underwear. The thrust of technology is to make them obsolete in any event. Most of the key functions that can culminate in the delivery of the weapon on target have been performed earlier by civilians in industrial plants, in R & D

laboratories, computer centers, Washington cubicles. . . . On
the target side, the receiving end, militariness is even more
inappropriate. Uniformed status has nothing whatsoever to do
with being eligible to be killed. In short, the old distinctions
between combatants and noncombatants, along with many of the old
rules of the game, become irrelevant."[4] The vast majority of
jobs in the U.S. Army are noncombatant support roles; only about
14 per cent of the troops are in combat posts. Furthermore, it is
paradoxical that the chances of a man's being killed or wounded
in combat might be greater if he is a civilian who is conscripted
than if he is a member of the regular Army.[5]

The question "What is military?" helps us to break through
the crust of our accepted usages and examine the actual functioning of institutions. To what extent are military institutions
like the Armed Forces Examining and Entrance Stations (AFEES)
involved in tasks which are not "military" at all? How military
does the AFEES have to be? How much anticipatory socialization
is necessary in order for AFEES to fulfill its system functions?
Such a question might be viewed in the context of ex-Secretary of
Defense McNamara's decision to replace 75,000 military personnel
with 60,000 civilians; or in the context of Army Regulation
601-270, Paragraph 11 (e) which says: "Civilians will be used in
staffing of AFEES to the maximum practical extent, and will be
provided by the Army as Executive Agent of AFEES." Few studies
of military institutions have asked questions such as Biderman's;
nor have they emphasized the problem of how military and civilian
institutions are articulated. Recent anthropological studies
have developed the concept of "interface institutions "[6] to
designate this type of situation. Such institutions are viewed
as key elements in the social structure of a plural society.
Individuals who play a role in such institutions are regarded as
brokers (Eric Wolf) or gate-keepers (Robert Redfield). Whether
this concept of "interface institutions," developed on the basis
of Meso-American anthropological field work is relevant to the
situation of the AFEES is an open question. But it might prove

useful in looking at the consistencies and inconsistencies between the military and the civilian sectors, those instances where the two sectors touch and interpenetrate--at the borders, where they have a mutual frontier. The comment of a former commander of infantry on the AFEES gives a useful perspective from the military side of the border: "What is most remarkable to me is the extent to which these stations are divorced from the real gut life of military organization. They may indeed be "interfaces" between military organization and the larger society; but insofar as military organization is concerned, they would appear to be very largely remote and strange kinds of establishments. The staff of the AFEES has only marginal participation in military organization, lives in the civilian community, has no direct contact with the kinds of experiences to which their clientele will ultimately be exposed. There also seems to be a tendency in assignment policy for the administrative officer personnel to assign people of rather marginal qualifications. The administrative officer personnel are either at the command level those who are committed to early retirement, or very recently inducted into military organization. The same great discrepancy exists among the enlisted personnel. There are the very senior sergeants whose combat credentials are considered exemplary, and, on the other hand, the very clever clerks and psychology technicians who administer the tests. There are also, of course, the very senior medical corps officers, and, on the other hand, the very fortunate and junior medical corps officers, who conduct the medical examinations. Thus the point of contact with a newly inducted or enlisted person is likely to be with a staff member who is not entirely committed to military organization."[7]

In this paper the sociological significance of AFEES will be viewed from a number of standpoints:

1. The AFEES may be seen as the prototype of an institution with "intake" functions on the border of two institutional complexes. There are in fact many such institutions in our society; they might appropriately be called "vestibule institution."

Erving Goffman has discussed aspects of such institutions in connection with "processing" in mental hospitals.

2. I propose to examine the actual experience of individuals
undergoing "processing" at AFEES from the standpoint of their
definition of the situation. This will include a consideration of
the larger societal context insofar as it affects their experience. I also propose to examine the notion that experience at
the AFEES might constitute a rite de passage or initiation
ceremony in our society. These discussion will bear on questions
of legitimacy and solidarity in the contemporary United States.

3. Taking up the theme of these meetings, "the gap between
social science and social policy," I hope to suggest that new
functions might be assimilated to the AFEES in addition to the
ones they already serve. Although our society is very unlike
that visualized by Comte and Spencer, there is always the possibility that we might help to move it in the direction which they
prophesied.

The Armed Forces Examining and Entrance Stations (AFEES) have
the manifest function (as defined in AR 601-270) of giving physical and mental examinations to all volunteers and draftees for all
branches of the armed forces and determining their eligibility.
They are responsible for all the clerical work associated with
these examinations. Although theoretically members of all the
armed forces work in these stations and the commanding officer may
be from any branch, headquarters responsibility rests with the
Army and most military personnel attached to AFEES are Army. There
are 74 AFEES in the continental United States, Hawaii and Puerto
Rico. During fiscal year 1968 the cost of operating the AFEES
was about 35 million dollars, with a military personnel authoriza-
tion of 2,121. In addition, 2,051 civilians perform various
duties connected with AFEES "processing;" half of all those
employed at AFEES in fiscal 1968 were civilians. This writer was
a participant observer at an AFEES in Memphis, Tennessee for seven-
teen months from August, 1953 to January, 1955. The opportunity
to study the operation of the AFEES as an Army enlisted man in the

Mental Testing Section was granted through the courtesy of the
Selective Service System. More recently, through the cooperation
of the Department of the Army he was permitted to refresh his
memory of AFEES procedures and observe changes which have taken
place since 1955 at the AFEES in Philadelphia, Pennsylvania.[8]

In one of the few papers in the entire sociological literature which is relevant to the situation of the AFEES, Erving
Goffman speaks of the moral career of the recruit in the total
institution and the significance of its initial stages. "The
recruit comes into the establishment with a conception of himself
made possible by certain stable social arrangements in his home
world. Upon entrance, he is immediately stripped of the support
provided by these arrangements. In the accurate language of
some of our oldest total institutions, he begins a series of
abasements, degradations, humiliations and profanations of self.
His self, is systematically, or often unintentionally, mortified.
He begins some radical shifts in his moral career, a career composed of the progressive changes that occur in the beliefs that
he has concerning himself and significant others. The processes
by which a person's self is mortified are fairly standard in
total institutions; analysis of these processes can help us to
see the arrangements that ordinary establishments must guarantee
if members are to preserve their civilian selves."[9]

Note that the final sentence of this quotation uses the term
"civilian" as a generic term, to distinguish the world outside
the total institution, be it Army barracks, monastery, convent,
boarding school, work camp, ship, colonial compound, penitentiary,
concentration camp or mental hospital. This suggests the extent
to which the distinction between the soldier and the civilian is
prototypical, and the degree to which the Army is the total institution par excellence. The self-concept of the recruit or inmate
has its roots in the civilian world; something must happen to him
in the "vestibule" to facilitate his transition to another self-
concept and his participation in another social context. "The
inmate . . . finds certain roles are lost to him by virtue of the

barrier that separates him from the outside world. The process
of entrance typically brings other kinds of loss and mortification
as well. We very generally find staff employing what are called
admissions procedures, such as taking a life history, photograph-
ing, weighing, fingerprinting, assigning numbers, searching, listing personal possessions for storage, undressing, bathing, dis-
infecting, haircutting, issuing institutional clothing, instruct-
ing as to rules, and assigning to quarters. Admission procedures
might better be called "trimming" or "programming" because in
thus being squared away the new arrival allows himself to be shaped
and coded into an object that can be fed into the administrative
machinery of the establishment, to be worked on smoothly by
routine operations. Many of these procedures depend upon attributes such as weight or fingerprints that the individual possesses
merely because he is a member of the largest and most abstract of
social categories, that of human being. Action taken on the
basis of such attributes necessarily ignores most of his previous
bases of self-identification."[10]

In the Army, which is the most relevant example for discussion
here, the admissions procedures are divided between the AFEES and
the reception center on an Army post to which the newly inducted
soldiers are sent immediately after being sworn in at the AFEES.
A serial number is assigned at AFEES after a man has been inducted.
Some aspects of Goffman's discussion, such as the assignment of
new clothes and even a new name (in the form of a rank joined to
the last name) come only after the individual leaves the AFEES.
Goffman observes: "The admission procedure can be characterized
as a leaving off and a taking on, with the midpoint marked by
physical nakedness. Leaving off of course entails a dispossession
of property, important because persons invest self-feelings in
their possessions. Perhaps the most significant of these possessions is not physical at all, one's full name; whatever one is
thereafter called, loss of one's name can be a great curtailment
of the self."[11]

Although Goffman's observations are extremely helpful as an

introduction to the nature of the experience at AFEES, a symbolic
interactionist analysis of the AFEES would be inconceivable without reference to the peculiar circumstances, engendered by the
cold war. These circumstances have a profound effect on volunteers and conscripts alike. Here the main point is that the
larger societal context which frames the experience at AFEES
affects not only the men passing through, but the functioning of
the Army itself. Two factors, broadly speaking should be distinguished which are important here for AFEES as an interface
institution: the nature of the cold-war Army, and the existence
of a peacetime draft.

THE COLD-WAR ARMY

The peculiarity of the military context today is, as Eugene
Uyecki points out, that "the structural requisites of the cold-
war Army are different from other armies, specifically from the
peacetime volunteer army or the total-war mass army."[12] He cites
Huntington's observation regarding the change in attitude of the
men who fought in Korea by contrast with that of soldiers in
World War II. This was symbolized by the rotation policy, under
which a man was sent home after nine months of combat duty
rather than being committed until the end of the war. "In World
War II, soldiers were in for the duration; they could only
achieve their personal goal of getting home when the government
achieved its political goal of military victory. In Korea,
however, rotation divorced the personal goals of the troops from
the political goals of the government. The aim of the soldiers
was simply to endure his nine months at the front and then get out.
The war was a necessary evil, and he acquiesced and accepted it
as such. His attitude was brilliantly summed up in that
classic expression of Stoic resignation which emerged from the
front lines: "That's the way the ball bounces." For the first
time in American history the common soldier fought a major war
solely and simply because he was orderd to fight it and not
because he shared any identification with the political goals for
which the war was being fought."[13] Uyecki emphasizes the

differences between the cold-war army and the other two types,
arguing that during the cold-war period the marginal and ambiguous
status of the cold-war army has been institutionalized. Uyecki
sees the effects on the draftee as emphasizing a modal adjustment
which is segmental, individualistic and detached. Among the
factors which he deals with here are the inadequacies of the
reward system, the two year limitation of service, and the indi-
vidualization and routinization of the army career. Uyecki also
argues that this detached and segmented participation on the
part of civilian-oriented citizen soldiers who have been conscripted is accepted and taken for granted by the regular army
men. This tends to weaken primary-group support within the cold-
war army by contrast with both the total-war mass army and the
peacetime voluntary army. The draftee thus regards his service as
very much like an eight-hour job, though the pay is ludicrous--
below the Federal minimum wage. The drafted soldier tends to give
little of his "real self" to the army, does his duties in an
impersonal way, and is "psychologically AWOL," while the regular
army volunteer "implies a soldier who has chosen the military life,
who enjoys taking orders, who lacks independence and initiative,
and who adheres to the spit and polish of army rituals." The
ratio of conscripts to volunteers in the American Army in recent
years since 1960 has been about one to one. Thus the orientation
Uyecki describes has a profound effect on day-to-day operations
and on the morale of regular soldiers as well.

THE DRAFT

It should not be overlooked that the increased sociological
significance of the AFEES is partly a result of the fact that the
United States has a peacetime draft and that all young men must
pass through its portals. The draft has been used by all modern
nation-states as a means of mobilizing military manpower, and was
used by the United States as early as 1777 during the war for
independence. The operation of the present Selective Service
system as a peacetime draft has a large part in determining the
definition of the situation on the part of the individuals being

"processed." One obvious factor is the well-known function of "channeling" which the Selective Service System has taken upon itself.[14] Educational and occupational deferments are granted on the basis of their contribution to "the national interest," and conscription is used as a threat to guarantee that men will choose occupations in which there are shortages of manpower. Educational deferments are currently swelling the ranks of college students as well. Critics have pointed out that the peacetime draft is inconsistent with fundamental American ideals, as suggested by the question: "Should government take life and liberty from selected innocent persons for the public good?"[15] The President's Advisory Commission on Selective Service concluded that there were real problems of inequity in the draft, and recommended fundamental changes including the elimination of arbitrary decentralized decision-making through a lottery, reversal of the order of call so that younger men would go first and men could plan their futures, and elimination of student deferments.[16] The fact that serious questions have been raised regarding the equity of the present draft system is indicated symbolically in the title of the Report of the National Advisory Commission on Selective Service: "Who Serves When Not All Serve?" Such questions suggest that there are problems of legitimacy involved, particularly in the light of widespread criticism of the American military posture abroad by persons in the highest positions of authority in government and elsewhere. Opponents of the American military posture and critics of the draft system have been quick to seize on the AFEES as the symbolic target of their protest. Anti-war demonstrators and critics of the Selective Service System have frequently engaged in peaceful picketing and leafletting at AFEES in the past few years. Such protests are symbolic in that they illustrate that some elements of the public are questioning the legitimacy not only of the Selective Service System, but also of the fundamental consensus which makes possible its operation, and which one sociologist, following Rousseau, has called an American "civil religion."[17]

THE CIVIL RELIGION AND THE CONTEXT
OF MILITARY SERVICE

It is instructive to look at what happens at AFEES from the
standpoint of the civil religion. Even in our secularized and
bureaucratized society, as will be seen below, there are still
attempts at ceremonial and ritual which find their way into the
"processing" at AFEES. Behind these elements stands the civil
religion, which, as Bellah has pointed out, is of fundamental
importance in linking the Judeo-Christian tradition and American
nationalism. "Behind the civil religion at every point lie
biblical archetypes: Exodus, Chosen People, Promised Land, New
Jerusalem, Sacrificial Death, and Rebirth. But the civil religion
is also genuinely American and genuinely new. It has its own
prophets and its own martyrs, its own sacred events and sacred
places, its own solemn rituals and symbols. It is concerned that
America be a society as perfectly in accord with the will of God
as men can make it and a light to all the nations."[18]

It is easy to lose sight of the spiritual significance of
nationalism but equally easy to demonstrate the all-pervasive
character of the national state in the life of the individual. A
number of observers have commented on the degree to which
nationalism is reinforced through ceremony and ritual in the civil
religion. Carleton Hayes, for example, has argued that nationalism has become a functional equivalent for the medieval Christian
world view, providing a framework of self-transcendance for the
individual. Not only the intellect but the emotions are called
into play, and the individual locates himself within an historically continuous experience identified with the national past and
the national destiny. Among the interesting parallels between
contemporary nationalism and medieval Christianity are the fact
that "the individual is born into the national state, and the
secular registration of birth is the national rite of baptism.
Thenceforth the state solicitously follows him through life,
tutoring him in a national catechism, teaching him by pious schooling and precept the beauties of national holiness, fitting him for

life of service, (no matter how exalted or how menial) to the
state, and commemorating his vital crises by formal registration
(with a fee) not only of his birth but likewise of his marriage,
of the birth of his children, and of his death. If he has been
a crusader on behalf of nationalism, his place of entombment is
marked with the ensign of his service. The funerals of national
heroes and potentates are celebrated with magnificant pomp and
circumstance. . . ."[19]

Membership in the national state is really compulsory. An
individual may withdraw but it is practically impossible for him
to establish himself in a country which does not practice some
form of nationalistic "religion." And membership in any national
society involves compulsory financial support in the form of
taxation, often used to support "missionary" activities associated with the national destiny. The ritual of modern nationalism, Hayes points out, focuses on the national flag; but por-
traits of the national leaders "adorn both the sumptous clubs
of the wealthy and the simple cottages of the poor." It is in
this sense in which the proceedings at AFEES may be regarded as
linked, in their ceremonial aspects and the basic assumptions
relfected in "processing," with the civil religion. It is also
because of its relationship to the civil religion that the
problem of legitimacy associated with Selective Service is so
crucial. One distinguished economist has argued recently that the
inequities of the peacetime draft and related problems associated
with our military posture are actually undermining the legitimacy
of the national state.[20] Robert Bellah suggests that the situation constitutes a crisis for the civil religion.[21] This has
important consequences for the experience of young men at AFEES.

At the age of 18 all American males must register with the
Selective Service System at their local draft boards. Most of
the men who are subsequently examined at AFEES fall into one of
two categories. They are volunteers for service in one of the
branches of the armed forces, or they are Selective Service
registrants being examined for the draft. Because men are

encouraged to explore alternatives to being drafted, e.g., volunteering for service in a special branch with a guarantee of an
opportunity to attend technical schools, many individuals are
"channeled" into volunteering who would otherwise not do so.
They volunteer in order to avoid the randomness of the draft,
the uncertainty attending draft eligibility, and for positive
reasons associated with the desire for preferential assignments
and special training. Many men who "volunteer for the draft"
or who volunteer for service in one of the branches are thus
only semi-voluntary members of the armed forces who would not
volunteer if there were no draft. It is very difficult to ascer-
tain the facts, since no impartial studies exist at this time.
Department of Defense studies indicate that four out of every
ten officers, about four out of ten of all enlisted volunteers,
and seven out of ten Reserve enlistees would not have entered
the services if there had been no draft.[22] The important point
is that of men who pass through the AFEES some are voluntary,
some are semi-voluntary and some are involuntary participants.
As Goffman observes: "Recruits enter total institutions in different spirits. At one extreme we find the quite involuntary
entrance of those who are sentenced to prison, committed to a
mental hospital, or pressed into the crew of a ship. It is perhaps in such circumstances that staff's version of the ideal
inmate has least chance of taking hold. At the other extreme,
we find religious institutions that deal only with those who
feel they have gotten the call, and, of these volunteers, take
only those who seem to be the most suitable and the most serious
in their intentions. (Presumably officer training camps and
some political training schools qualify here, too.) In such
cases, conversion seems already to have taken place, and it only
remains to show the neophyte along what lines he can best discipline himself. Midway between these two extremes we find
institutions, like the Army in regard to conscripts, where
inmates are required to serve but are given much opportunity to
feel that this service is a justifiable one required in their own

ultimate interests. Obviously, significant differences in tone
will appear in total institutions, depending on whether recruitment is voluntary, semi-voluntary, or involuntary."[23]

The fact of different degrees of voluntarism tends to com-
plicate the aspect of AFEES processing which is significant as a
rite de passage, to which I will now turn. Since 1948 all
American adolescent males have had to take account of the draft.
For those who are volunteers and who actively desire to become
members of the armed forces, AFEES can represent a traumatic
experience culminating in a humiliating failure. I will discuss
failure and the "cooling-out" process in a final section of this
paper, but here it is important to realize that for every 100
men examined at AFEES, about 33 are labelled as mental, medical
or moral failures. Of the remaining 66, almost half can be considered semi-voluntary or involuntary examinees, if we extrapo-
late from the Defense Department figures cited above. This is a
very high proportion of involuntary participants and suggests
that this particular rite de passage must be viewed with more
than the usual amount of ambivalence by participants. It also
suggests that there are limits to any analysis which attempts to
show that experience at AFEES constitutes an initiation rite in
American society today.

AFEES EXPERIENCE AS RITE de PASSAGE

I would like to give critical consideration to the idea that
the experience at AFEES has elements of a rite de passage. At
least one student of initiation rites has argued that "neither
physiologically, socially nor legally is there a clear demarca-
tion between boyhood and manhood in our society."[24] He demonstrates a relationship cross-culturally between the presence of
stringent initiation rites at puberty and intense mother-son
relationships during infancy. The resultant emotional dependence
and identification leads to a "cross-sex identity crisis" at
puberty, frequently attended by compensatory "protest masculinity."
This crisis accounts for the widespread existence of stringent
initiation rites which serve the purpose of resolving the dilemma

by reaffirming male identity and thus precluding open rivalry
with the father and "Oedipal" approaches to the mother. The
authors note the widespread emphasis on exclusive mother-child
relationships in lower class situations characterized as "broken
homes" in our society, but also not unknown in the middle classes.
They observe that one way of dealing with the problem of male
identity is to establish a formal, institutional way of coping
with adolescent boys of this type and suggest that "the present
institution of selective service would perhaps serve this purpose
were the boys to be drafted at an earlier age and exposed to the
authority of responsible adult males."[25] The Job Corps may represent an attempt to deal with a similar problem in a non-military
context.

Without in any sense endorsing the suggestion of Whiting,
et al., it is possible to examine the degree to which AFEES
processing functions as an initiation rite. Anthropologists and
sociologists have pointed out that among the changes attendant
on the rise of urban, industrial societies has been an increase
in secularization and a decline in the importance of sacred
ceremonialism. As Solon Kimball observed: "Rites of passage were
often, but not necessarily,tied to supernatural sanctions and to
the activity of priestly intermediaries. Although such rites
focused on the individual, they were also occasions for group
participation--as in the initiation ceremonies of the Australian,
or burial or marriage rites in an agrarian community. There is
no evidence that a secularized urban world has lessened the need
for ritualized expression of an individual's transition from
one status to another. Obviously, ceremonialism alone cannot
establish the new equilibrium, and perfunctory ritual may be
pleasant but also meaningless. One of our problems is that we
are lacking the empirical studies of ritual behavior and its
consequences for life-cycle crises upon which we might assess the
relation between crisis and ritual in its current setting."[26]
Such observations should be viewed in the context provided by

Bellah's work on the American civil religion, or Warner's study
of Memorial Day as a sacred ceremony.

An early student of rites of passage, Arnold van Gennep, distinguished between three phases of such rites. The phase of
separation from the old state of things; the marginal period or
rites of transition; and the integration in a new condition or
re-integration to the old, rites of incorporation. Van Gennep
stressed that one of these three stages might be emphasized
according to the situation: thus rites of separation are stressed
at funerals, rites of incorporation at weddings, and rites of
transition in initiation ceremonies. He also emphasized the
importance of "transitional periods which sometimes acquire a
certain autonomy"[27] which might be relevant to the case of AFEES.
A recent commentator on van Gennep has pointed out that "changes
in social relations involving movements between groups, or alterations of status, in semi-civilized societies with their concep-
tions of magico-religious bases for groups, disturbed both the
life of society and the life of the individual, and the function
of rites de passage was to reduce the harmful effects of these
disturbances."[28] Regarding initiation ceremonies, Gluckman
points out that they "mark and organize the transition from
childhood to socially recognized adulthood. . . . They are the
means of divesting a person of his status as a child in the
domestic domain and investing him with the status of actual or
potential citizen in the politico-jural domain."[29] By this
criterion it would seem as if elements of the AFEES experience
would definitely constitute initiation ceremonies in terms of the
cultural norms of American society. Furthermore, as Gluckman
himself points out, "The social order is so impregnated with
moral judgments that it can be disturbed by any failure to fulfill an obligation."[30]

Thus it is difficult to see why Gluckman ultimately adopts a
point of view which tends to argue that "rituals of the kind
investigated by van Gennep are incompatible with the structure
of modern urban life."[31] Gluckman is saying that the highly

bureaucratized context of modern industrial society does not encourage the rise of such rites of passage. Indeed, the highly rationalized environment characteristic of the American urban context is viewed as positively discouraging for the rise of such ceremonials and rites. "Ritual, and even ceremonial, tend to drop into desuetude in the modern urban situation where the material basis of life, and the fragmentation of roles and activities, of themselves segregate social roles."[35] In order to see whether a case can be made for the existence of elements of initiation ritual or rites de passage at AFEES, we will first have to take up the details of the experience at AFEES.

TWO TYPES OF AFEES "PROCESSING"

There are two categories of examination procedure: pre-induction examinations, and induction examinations and processing.

Pre-Induction. What follows is a brief description of pre-induction processing although there are obviously important differences in how the situation is defined according to socio-economic class, degree of voluntarism, race and other variables. A typical individual will have been notified by Selective Service of the date of his examination. The notification is usually mailed. He is to appear at the AFEES early in the morning, or if he is in an outlying district, he must foregather with others at an even earlier hour at his draft board for transportation to the AFEES. A group leader is appointed by Selective Service from among the people who are to be examined. The early hour (frequently prior to 7:00 AM) the occasionally foregone breakfast and the apprehension which accompanies the examination process usually conspire to generate a mild anxiety. There is sometimes horseplay and tension release in the group, though in the big city draft boards most of them are strangers to one another. They are received at the station in a room usually set aside for the purpose, and there is a roll call in alphabetical order. What follows is an "orientation," which is described in AR 601-270, Chapter 2, p. 2-1ff. as follows: "After the rollcall, registrants will be given an orientation by a commissioned or noncommissioned officer.

The attitudes of the pre-inductees toward military life will be
influenced by the manner in which they are treated during pre-
induction processing. All phases of preinduction processing will
be conducted in a dignified and professional manner. Registrants
will be treated with courtesy and maximum attention will be given
to the pre-inductees welfare and to those personal preferences
consistent with military requirements. Pre-inductees will be
given an opportunity to ask questions and all questions will be
answered courteously. Personnel in charge will never be arrogant,
flippant, or sarcastic no matter how absurd questions seem. . . .
Pre-inductees will be identified by their names. Cards, use of
stamps, or other such means of identification are considered
unnecessary. The orientation will cover the following subjects:
(1) steps in pre-induction processing, (2) instruction regarding
mess and quarters while at the induction station, (3) approximate
time and method by which registrants will be notified of results of
pre-induction examination . . . (etc.)."

It is important to see that the orientation constitutes a
situation in which individuals are made aware of the fact that
what happens to them that day at AFEES is fateful, that it will
determine their future in some important respects, that they are
confronting the ineluctable authority of the state, but also that
there might be something they can do to alter this imbalance of
power and control their own destiny. For example, those found
acceptable for induction are given a talk (based on Appendix 24,
AR 601-270) urging them to consider a career in the Army, Navy,
Air Force or Marine Corps by voluntary enlistment. What follows
the pre-induction orientation is an interview, where the individual sits at a desk and is queried by either a soldier or a
civilian typist regarding personal information already entered
on the form DD 47. This also includes question determining
moral eligibility—e.g., court convictions, felonies, criminal
charges filed, etc. Thus one of the first situations in which a
man finds himself in AFEES processing is one in which his past
is being explored for possible evidence of criminality. For many

individuals who pass through the AFEES this is sufficient to evoke
considerable anxiety and guilt. The Regulations state that "A
registrant who has been convicted by a civil court (of a felony)
or who has a record of adjudication adverse to him by a juvenile
court, for any offense punishable by death or imprisonment for a
term exceeding one year is morally unacceptable for service in
the armed forces unless such disqualification is waivered by the
Armed Forces Moral Waiver Determination Board, which is appointed
by the Commanding General, U.S. Army Recruiting Command." (AR
601-270, Chapter 2, C2, p. 2-4). Administratively disqualified
men tested under Selective Service included 3.9 per cent of the
total in a study of disqualifications between August 1958 through
June 1960. This was 3,643 men out of 271,601.[33]

What follows the pre-induction interview is either a mental
test, the AFQT, or a physical examination. AFEES have a great
deal of flexibility in how they handle their workloads, but they
have been beset by difficulties in work flow which is very uneven.
They have also been criticized for inefficiency, though it is
difficult to see the grounds for such criticisms given the fact
that some physical defects are difficult to detect and many
lower-class registrants have had little previous medical attention.[34]

The Physical Examination. The physical is an extremely impersonal example of "mass processing" since the individual must
undress in the company of strangers and wait in lines at the
various stations where he is tested. As Goffman points out,
many of the usual identifying attributes of the self are stripped
away and what is recorded are attributes common to him only as
"human being." It is important to realize, however, that this
will often be interpreted differently by middle-class and lower-
class individuals. A lower-class youth might interpret the processing as attention being lavished on him, particularly if he
were a volunteer with a positive orientation toward the proceedings. A middle-class individual who is an involuntary participant
facing the possibility of conscription stands at the opposite pole

of an alienation continuum with regard to AFEES. The physical
begins with a group filling out their Form 89, (Medical History)
while they are still clothed. This form is then used as they go
through the processing clad only in their shorts, moving from room
to room. They are weighed and measured, visual acuity is tested,
color vision, auditory acuity, electrocardiogram, blood pressure,
pulse rate are taken. Blood samples are drawn for the serology
tests, which include blood typing and tests for veneral disease.
A surprisingly large number of men experience nausea either before
or after the drawing of a blood sample. Testimony from enlisted
personnel and personal experience at Memphis indicates that faint-
ing is not uncommon and a technician at the Philadelphia AFEES
reported that 10 per cent of the men passing through his section
either fainted or showed extreme signs of nausea. Blood is drawn
with a syringe from a vein by a corpsman dressed in white fatigue
uniform. The "blood room" accentuates the elements of rite de
passage and serves to underscore the fact that this experience
is typically one which carries a high load of anxiety for the
individuals passing through.

In addition to the above, urine samples are taken, X-rays,
eyeglass prescriptions recorded, and a medical interview follows
detection of any physical irregularity or problem which is
brought to the attention of the examining physician either by
notations on the Form 47 filled out by the pre-inductee or through
his examination itself. Civilian doctors are hired on a fee basis
since there are not enough Army doctors to do all the examinations
at AFEES. A psychiatric interview is carried out when there is
any indication that it might be appropriate.

So far as the physical examination is concerned, the rate of
deliberate malingering is difficult to determine. There is some
evidence that in at least one large urban area of the Northeast
more men from the upper-middle and middle-classes are found
physically disqualified than from the medically underprivileged
lower classes. This is not surprising in view of the fact that
middle-class men are able to call the attention of AFEES physicians

to ailments which are disqualifying and bring letters from their personal physicians as evidence. Many lower-class registrants are unaware that they are medically disqualified, since they typically have had little medical attention during their life-times. Occasionally a disqualifying defect will escape the notice of the AFEES physician during mass processing, unless it is specifically called to his attention. In this regard, see note 34.

At the end of the physical examination (or the mental test if it came first) the pre-inductees are usually taken to lunch. By midday, because of the stress many of them have encountered, including the early rising and the anxiety of the processing, many of the men are physically and emotionally tired. Lunch is served cafeteria style at or near the AFEES and the men are moved to their meal in military style, as a group, accompanied by a noncommissioned officer.

The Mental Test. More than 10 million men have taken the Armed Forces Qualification Test; it is the basic screening instrument of the American armed forces. The test has a hundred questions and is divided into four parts: vocabulary matching, arithmetic, tool matching, and blocks and pattern matching questions. The score is rendered as a percentile, and the results are grouped into five categories, group I the highest and group V as failure. Scoring in the 9th percentile or below means that the candidate is not qualified for service in the armed forces. A candidate who scores in the 30th percentile or below is in mental group IV, and since August, 1958 these men must take an additional test called the Army Qualification Battery. Requirements regarding the AQB have changed several times, most recently in response to the Vietnam crisis. These changes are detailed in a recent article on test failures by Dr. Bernard Karpinos.[35] It takes a little more than an hour to administer the AFQT. The instructions include test questions and men are encouraged to do as well as they can on the grounds that their assignments in the Army will be affected by their test scores.

Tests are proctored by enlisted men or officers associated with
the Mental Testing Section, and proctors roam about, checking
papers to see that men understand how to use the multiple-choice
materials and that they have filled out the forms correctly. This
"academic" situation is often completely foreign to men who have
had little or no schooling and they often find it terrifying.
Readability tests on the AFQT indicate that what counts as fourth
grade reading comprehension in the northern states frequently may
require as much as 8 grades in "culturally deprived" areas.

The experience of different types of men is obviously variable
in this testing situation according to amount of education, socio-
economic class, cultural background, degree of voluntarism and
other factors. Prejudiced whites who live in racially segregated
communities are frequently shaken to find themselves in such
close proximity to Negroes or members of other minority groups
on both the AFQT and the physical examination. Highly educated
men often regard the test as a farce and as further evidence
that the armed forces will represent a degrading experience for
them. Functional illiterates who wish to volunteer for the
armed forces are terrified by the test which they fail, but try
to return again and again in the vain effort to pass and improve
their life-chances by social mobility into the armed forces.
This is particularly true of southern Negroes, for many of whom
the Army represents the only hope. At the Memphis AFEES young
Negro volunteers from Tennessee and Mississippi who failed the
test would plead tearfully with the Mental Testing personnel to
let them into the Army.

All Selective Service registrants who fail the test receive
an interview in the Mental Testing Section. The primary purpose
of this interview is to determine whether or not they were
malingering. There are a tiny number of deliberate malingerers.
Far more difficult is the case in which men malinger who could
not pass the test even if they were not malingering. Practices
vary from station to station regarding informing pre-inductees
of the test results. In any case the scores are recorded on the

forms which the men will eventually see, if they know how to
interpret them.

These various crises constitute the essence of pre-induction
processing at AFEES, and they usually take the better part of a
day. When men must be held over because of scheduling problems
or overload, they are usually housed in a local YMCA or similar
facility.

Induction Processing. The actual process of induction has
two parts: one is the required induction ceremony, the other is
the optional oath of allegiance ceremony. In a secular,
rationalized and bureaucratic society these ceremonies seem quite
unceremonious indeed; nevertheless many induction stations have
special "ceremonial rooms" decorated with flags and other
symbols of national authority in which men are inducted.

Before the induction ceremony, however, men must undergo a
physical inspection. If more than a year has elapsed since their
pre-induction physical, they must have a complete reexamination.
The first phase of induction processing involves an orientation
talk. This includes "the purpose and significance of induction"
and an account of the processing steps he will take during the
day. His reserve obligations will be explained, and questions
regarding insurance, etc., are taken up. There is a roll call
and individual records are issued which each man carries around
with him during his processing. Sometimes inductees need a
mental test too if processing has been irregular, records have
been lost, etc.

Then they must fill out DD Form 98, the Armed Forces Security
Questionnaire under the supervision of a commissioned officer.
The serious nature of this questionnaire may be gleaned from the
following excerpt: "This security questionnaire is one of the
most important forms you will ever be required to complete during
your military service. Its importance has to do with both the
security of the United States and your own future welfare as a
citizen of the United States and as a member of the United States
Armed Forces. For these reasons you must execute your question-

naire with the utmost care. Before doing so, you must fully
understand its purpose and the meaning of the statements you will
make in Section IV.

Why Must You Sign a Security Questionnaire? The fact that
you are required to sign a security questionnaire at this time
does not call into question your loyalty to the United States nor
your intention to serve in the Armed Forces with the honor and
fidelity traditional to the American soldier. The questionnaire
is simply a means of helping the federal government protect itself
and you against those who undermine and destroy our nation and
individual freedom.

As a member of the Armed Forces you will occupy a position of
honor and trust. It is vital to our national security that all
such positions of honor and trust be held by persons of complete
and unswerving loyalty to the United States.

Among the thousands of men and women coming into the Armed
Forces each month, we must recognize that there might be a
certain number of subversives and spies working for the Communist
enemy or groups hostile to our democratic form of government.
This is part of the "boring" from within tactics of the Communist
conspiracy . . ."[36]

After they have filled out the Security Questionnaire, files
of all men being inducted must be completed and checked. After
this they are allocated to a specific branch of the service,
usually the Army in the case of Selective Service registrants.

Induction Ceremony. When registrants to be inducted are
assembled, the induction officer is required to say to them: "You
are about to be inducted into the Armed Forces of the United
States, in the Army, the Navy, the Air Force, or the Marine Corps,
as indicated by the service announced following your name when
called. You will take one step forward as your name and service
are called and such step will constitute your induction into the
Armed Forces indicated."[37] After the roll has been called, the
inductees are informed that each and every one of them is a
member of the Armed Forces, using the following language: "You

have now been inducted into the Armed Forces of the United States
indicated when your name was called. Each one of you is now a
member of the Armed Forces concerned, and amenable to the regulations and the Uniform Code of Military Justice and all other
applicable laws and regulations."[38]

Oath of Allegiance Ceremony. The oath of allegiance is not a
part of the induction ceremony. It is optional and is administered
by a commissioned officer as soon as praticable after the induction ceremony. The oath of allegiance reads as follow: "I,
_____, do solemnly swear (or affirm) that I will support
and defend the Constitution of the United States against all
enemies, foreign or domestic; that I will bear true faith and
allegiance to the same; and that I will obey the orders of the
President of the United States and the orders of the officers
appointed over me, according to regulations and the Uniform Code
of Military Justice. So help me God."[39]

Outprocessing. This is the Army term for the final phase
of the work at AFEES. It includes the highly significant assignment of a service number to each individual (drafted men have the
prefix "US" before their numbers, while volunteers have the prefix
"RA" for Regular Army. The sociological significance of this
distinction is noted by Uyecki, op. cit.). Records are completed
and travel orders are assigned for the reception centers. Men are
now soldiers in some respects but not in others; they have no
uniforms, are still wearing civilian clothes, and are usually
entirely ignorant concerning the actual details of military life.
One individual is usually placed in charge of the group and
carries the records; the men proceed to the trains, busses or
airplanes which will carry them to their duty stations.

Rite de Passage? We are now in a position to review the
evidence regarding those aspects of pre-induction and induction
processing which might be considered comparable to an initiation
rite. It seems to me that it is possible to make a case for the
existence of a "quasi-rite" of the transitional type. The argument rests on the following considerations:

1. There is an actual passage or movement from the home or dwelling place to the AFEES, sometimes under mild conditions of stress and occasionally over considerable geographical distances.

2. There is a high degree of ambivalence present among the initiates because a large proportion are involuntary participants; this argues, however, for a "quasi-rite" rather than initiation ritual because they are not looking forward to the achievement of their new status.

3. The background of legitimacy and authority symbolized by the military in association with the civil religion is manifest. To the extent that legitimacy is questioned, however, the rite will fail to fulfill its functions.

4. The medical testing and examination gives some evidence of the physical manliness, since negative status is still attached to the "4-F" classification, though this must be qualified too to take account of involuntary registrants.

5. The mental test constitutes a real hurdle for a considerable proportion of the examinees; 10 per cent of whom fail the test outright and 21 per cent of whom fail contingent on the taking of the AQB. A Negro youth is four times as likely to fail as a white youth.

6. Ritual elements also include the certification of loyalty in the filling out of the DOD Form 98; failure to comply correctly is punishable by perjury charges and a jail sentence on conviction.

7. The drama of the ceremonial room in induction processing with its symbols of national flag and patriotism constitutes an obvious element of rite de passage and the incorporation of a new roll.

8. The ritual elements of processing such as the "blood room," fingerprinting, and the criminal record check all tend to generate a certain anxiety in the participants.

9. The implicit power of the national authorities to deprive one of one's liberty evokes both mild anxiety and an accommodating attitude among most pre-inductees and inductess, and the remainder regarding the jurisdiction of military law (as well as civilian

law) in the induction ceremony only help to accentuate the fact
that "they've got you."

10. Finally, the rhetoric of duty and obligation merges with
the rhetoric of the "privilege" of service as volunteers and
Selective Service registrants who fail the tests are actually
excluded.

To the extent that this evidence seems to point to the rise of
a "quasi-rite" in connection with the Armed Forces Examining
Station, to that extent does it contradict Gluckman's skepticism
regarding rites de passage in contemporary industrial society.

The AFEES Experience as Failure: The "Cooling-Out" Function.
To recapitulate: the rite de passage element, however attenuated,
which is represented by this experience at AFEES has been part of
the American scene since 1948. Over a period of 20 years, all
adolescent males have had to take account of the draft, of the
possibility of conscription, and the experience of "processing" at
AFEES. Furthermore, roughly a third of the men who are processed
as Selective Service registrants are disqualified for service;
thus, for many who wish to become members of the Armed Forces, as
well as for the disqualified volunteers (whose failure rates are
somewhat lower) AFEES processing can be a traumatic experience.
In a culture which is success-oriented and mobility-oriented, and
in which the Army beckons as one of the sole avenues of mobility
to culturally disadvantaged youth, failure at AFEES can be
devastating. As Goffman observes: "A person may be involuntarily
deprived of a role under circumstances which reflect unfavorably
on his capacity for it. The lost role may be one that he had
already acquired or one that he had openly committed himself to
preparing for. In either case the loss is more than a matter of
ceasing to act in a given capacity; it is ultimate proof of an
incapacity. And in many cases it is even more than this. The
moment of failure often catches a person acting as one who feels
that he is an appropriate sort of person for the role in question.
Assumption becomes presumption, failure becomes fraud. To loss
of substance is thereby added loss of face. Of the many themes

that can occur in the natural history of an involvement, this
seems to be the most melancholy. Here it will be quite essential
and quite difficult to cool the mark out."[40]

What kinds of "cooling-out" functions are fulfilled at AFEES?
Until recently nothing was done about the volunteer failures who
were confronted with the fact that they "hadn't made it" and
"didn't measure up." Some of these volunteers in Memphis would
return again and again in a vain effort to pass the AFQT. Failures
on the AFQT are typically functional illiterates and it would have
been very easy to establish a local community program, paid for in
part by the Department of Defense, in which such individuals
could get special instruction in reading. Such programs have never
been established, although the Army trained illiterates and
taught reading during World War II (in 1944) when the manpower
pool was depleted.

The Economic Opportunity Act of 1964 provided for the release
of rejected Selective Service registrants' test scores to the
Manpower Conservation Unit of the U.S. Employment Service. This
"cooling-out" of rejected registrants emphasized taking positive
action which might lead to better opportunities for employment,
training and/or medical care. The official orientation text
states: "One of the purposes of this program is to help young
Americans choose the kind of work which suits their interests and
abilities. Another is to help young men with the education and
training needed to find and hold the right job. For those of you
who have physical defects this will offer an opportunity to have
those defects helped or corrected so that you may live a more
useful and happy life.

Your participation in this program is entirely voluntary--that
is, it is entirely up to you whether you participate or not. However, we strongly urge you to do so. It may mean the beginning of
a new life and that opportunity you have long been waiting for."[41]

The results of this program have been very poor. The type of
vocational guidance which is conventionally employed with middle-
class groups had little impact on this special population. A

recent assessment indicates that a different approach might be
more productive.

"Underemployed and unemployed rejectees are invited by letter
to visit unemployment service counselors in their offices to talk
about jobs and career planning. Of the 234,000 rejectees so
invited, of whom 78,000 were unemployed, only 42,000 showed up
for interviews, and, of those, 32,000 were unemployed or underemployed. Thus the majority--46,000--failed to respond. And of
the 42,000 who did respond, fewer than 13,000 were referred to
jobs; fewer than 7,000 of these hired, and some only for a few
days."[42] The U.S. Employment Service has begun a program of
stationing Employment personnel in the induction center themselves,
but during my recent visits to the Philadelphia AFEES I was
informed that a representative of the Employment Service who had
been working at the station had been withdrawn and that no one
had been sent to replace him.

Another approach is represented in the Department of Defense
special program, Project 100,000. Here the Army lowered its
entrance requirements and accepted men who would otherwise have
been rejected. They did not segregate them but used the military
experience itself as a motivating force. What follows is based on
a report given at the Inter-University Seminar on Armed Forces and
Society, June 9-10, 1967. Of 28,000 men who had been taken into
the Army under this program, 40 per cent were volunteers, 60 per
cent were draftees; Negroes represented 40 per cent of the group.
Attrition in basic training was 3 1/2 per cent compared to 2 per
cent for regular trainees; only 6 per cent were reported as needing special help. (About 60 per cent of the attrition was for
disqualifying medical defects during basic training.) No additional cadres were laid on to teach men to read; the philosophy of
the program was to incorporate the men into the military, raise
their self-confidence and motivation, and try to move them through
the basic training cycle. Re-cycling was widely used in cases of
failure. Project 100,000 represents an ambitious effort on the
part of the DOD to utilize the desire of rejected individuals for

self-improvement even though they might be below the regular
requirements for enlistment on the AFQT. It is hard to determine
to what extent it may be regarded as an experiment in basic education, or as an extension of the "cooling-out" functions of AFEES.

On the whole, then, it must be said that there is very little
"cooling-out" at the AFEES though there is ample justification
for doing so, considering the positive orientation of many
rejected Selective Service registrants and volunteers. (I
assume that volunteers are given some kind of post-test interview
with a recruiter, though this may have changed since 1955.) One
of the basic elements of the work drama at AFEES consists in a
subtle conflict of interest between recruiters and testing personnel. Recruiters do have quotas and it is in their interest
to find and enlist (preferably) high quality volunteers. Since
volunteers are not always of high quality from the standpoint of
the mental testing section, and recruiters are under pressure to
produce enlistments, there is a certain tension which develops
between recruiting and testing. It is also true that $70,000,000
is spent annually in the effort to obtain new recruits by the
Armed Forces, presumably on advertising publicity and special programs. This conflict of interest has resulted in a firm directive
to the effect that no individual involved in recruitment may have
command functions at an AFEES. DOD Directive 1145.2 of June 3,
1965 states, in part V: "Operational control of AFEES will not be
bested in anyone who is responsible for the recruiting activity
at the station level." This probably makes the "cooling-out"
functions somewhat more difficult though co-ordination with
recruiters is essential in AFEES operation and appropriate arrangements for terminal interviews with rejected examinees among both
registrants and volunteers would not be difficult to arrange.

A final paradox with regard to the "cooling-out" function is
the situation of the involuntary Selective Service registrant who
hopes for and anticipates that he will be rejected on the physical
examination because of defects real or imagined though often supported by letters from a physician. If such an individual is

classified as physically acceptable, he is confronted with
another kind of "failure"--the failure to fail. He experiences
considerable cognitive dissonance. There is no "cooling-out" for
this individual--he is "cooled-in" instead.

IMPLICATIONS FOR POLICY

We must now return to the question with which we began this
discussion: "What is Military?" One assumption which will guide
us here is that, in spite of discontent with the draft and interest
in the concept of the volunteer army, there is a strong possibility
that some form of the peacetime draft will remain a permanent
feature of American society for the foreseeable future. This is
not, in my opinion, a satisfactory state of affairs, and represents
a profound contradiction of our own highest ideals and traditions
of individual freedom.

Given this assumption, however, it could be argued that if
young men were to continue to register with Selective Service at
age 18 and to be examined at the AFEES, that the process might
take place in a wider, nonmilitary context which would emphasize
the assessment of the nation's human resources. The AFEES is a
unique collector of data and it could become part of a system of
"social indicators" which would not only be of positive value in
developing the potentialities of individuals. It would also
function as a check on the level of health facilities and the
output of educational systems in state and local communities. The
cause of social justice for the disadvantaged might be aided
through a demonstration that educational and health services were
below the national standard. Indeed, comparative data from the
Office of the Surgeon General are already available which show
shocking rates of failure on the AFQT among 18 year olds in
certain regions of the country and in specific minority groups.

If the draft were eliminated, the AFEES stations could function as a clearing-house and testing center serving a wide variety
of voluntary national service programs, as well as the volunteers
for the armed forces.[44] But this would mean that the sharp line
between the military and the civilian sector would be blurred, and

that the AFEES would be functioning within a larger societal context in assessing human resources. This points toward greater "civilianization" of the AFEES and a deemphasis of their strictly military role. It is this conception which represents a return to the vision of Comte and Spencer regarding the character of the modern society.

Finally, if the draft were eliminated it could also lead to the development of new kinds of ritual and ceremony consistent with the American civil religion and its nonmilitary aspects. What is now a secular "proto-ritual" in a draft system whose legitimacy is being widely questioned could become a real rite of passage and manhood ceremony in a society where men volunteered for a wide variety of national and international service programs (including military service) as a matter of course.

NOTES

[1]Raymond Aron, War and Industrial Society, London, Oxford University Press, 1958.

[2]Leon Bramson and George W. Goethals (eds.) War: Studies From Psychology, Sociology and Anthropology , New York: Basic Books, 1964, pp. 295-96.

[3]Albert D. Biderman, "What is Military?", in Sol Tax (ed.) The Draft: A Handbook of Facts and Alternatives, Chicago: University of Chicago Press, 1967, pp. 122-37.

[4]Ibid., p. 125.

[5]Cf. ibid., p. 132: "With respect to the current scene of combat, the Army calculated that a draftee currently entering the system has a one-in-three chance of serving in Vietnam, as compared with a one-in-seven chance for a man currently in the regular army. . . If by militariness we mean putting oneself in the position of being killed or wounded in combat, we are faced with the paradox that those who are most military with respect to this attribute most often are also the ones who are least military when it comes to their socialization into the Armed Forces. I am referring here to the new recruit, or relatively recent commissioned officer."

[6]Cf. Robert and Eva Hunt, "Education as an Interface Institution in Rural Mexico and the American Inner City," Midway Magazine Vol. 8, No. 2, 1967, pp. 101 ff.

[7]Personal communication.

[8]The assistance of Dr. Harold Wool, Director for Procurement Policy and General Research, Office of the Assistant Secretary of Defense (Manpower), and of Commander Edward O'Malley and his staff at the Philadelphia AFEES are gratefully acknowledged. The following people read this paper and provided helpful comments: they are in no way responsible for any of the contents and perhaps I should add these reflections were sponsored and financed by no one but myself.

[9]Erving Goffman, "On the Characteristics of Total Institutions," Asylums, New York: Doubleday Anchor, 1961, p. 14.

[10]Ibid., p. 16.

[11]Ibid., p. 18.

[12]Eugene S. Uyecki, "Draftee Behavior in the Cold War Army," Social Problems, VIII, 1960, pp. 151-58.

[13] Samuel P. Huntington, The Soldier and the State, Cambridge: Harvard University Press, 1953, pp. 388-89.

[14] Cf. the Selective Service statement on "channeling" (1965) which is reprinted in Sol Tax, "War and Recruitment for a War System," in M. Fried, M. Harris, and R. Murphy (eds.) War: The Anthropology of Armed Conflict and Aggression: New York: Doubleday, 1968, pp. 203-4.

[15] Ibid., p. 196.

[16] Who Serves When Not All Serve? Report of the National Advisory Commission on Selective Service, Washington: Government Printing Office, 1967.

[17] Robert N. Bellah, "Civil Religion in America," in Donald R. Cutler, (ed.) The Religious Situation: 1968, Boston: Beacon Press, 1968, pp. 331-56.

[18] Ibid., p. 354. Cf. also W. Lloyd Warner, "The Function of Memorial Day," in The Living and the Dead: A Study of the Symbolic Life of Americans, New Haven: Yale University Press, 1958, pp. 278-79.

[19] Carleton Hayes, Nationalism: A Religion, New York: Macmillan, 1960, p. 165.

[20] Kenneth Boulding, "The Impact of the Draft on the Legitimacy of the National State," in Sol Tax, (ed.) The Draft, op. cit., pp. 191-96.

[21] Robert N. Bellah, "The Third Time of Trial," in "Civil Religion in America," op. cit., pp. 351-54.

[22] Review of the Administration and Operation of the Selective Service System, Hearings before the Committee, on Armed Services, 89th Congress, 2nd Session, June, 1966. United States Government Printing Office, 1966, pp. 9935-36.

[23] Goffman, op. cit., p. 118.

[24] J.W.M. Whiting, Richard Kluckhohn, and Albert Anthony, "The Function of Male Initiation Ceremonies at Puberty," in Maccobby, Newcomb and Hartley, Readings in Social Psychology, 3rd edition, New York: Holt, Rinehart and Winston, 1958, p. 359.

[25] Ibid., p. 370.

[26] Solon T. Kimball, Introduction to Arnold van Gennep, The Rites of Passage, Chicago: University of Chicago Press, 1960, pp. xvi-xvii.

[27] Arnold van Gennep, ibid., p. 191-92.

[28] Max Gluckman (ed.) Essays on the Ritual of Social Relations, Manchester: Manchester University Press, 1962, p. 3.

[29] Ibid., p. 16.

[30] Ibid., p. 29.

[31] Ibid., pp. 36-37.

[32] Ibid., p. 38.

[33] Bernard D. Karpinos, Qualification of American Youths for Military Service, Medical Statistics Division, Office of the Surgeon General, Department of the Army, 1962.

[34] A recent report criticizing AFEES medical examinations pointed out that "during a two month period at 9 AFEES selected for review, the daily workload deviated significantly from the station capacity about 50 per cent of the time. The workload ranged from a low of 24 per cent of station capacity to a high of 175 per cent, and the problem was attributed to inadequate scheduling and control of daily input to the AFEES." (p. 13, Report On Matters Relating to Enlisted Personnel Discharged Because of Physical Defects that Existed Prior to Entrance into Military Service, Department of Defense, March 21, 1968, by the Comptroller General of the United States.

This study, which was requested by Rep. Richard Schweiker of Pennsylvania, found that in fiscal year 1967 the Pentagon enlisted or drafted some 20,000 men physically unfit for military duty at a cost of over $19.6 million. . . . "The investigation found that the Pentagon had spent $19.6 million for the pay, allowances, uniforms and travel of 20,087 servicemen who were subsequently discharged shortly after entering the military because they were physically unfit when they entered." Quotation is from news release, April 21, 1968. See also New York Times, April 21, 1968, p. 36. Representative Schweiker attacked the preinduction physical examinations as "approaching being an outrageous sham" and these charges received widespread newspaper publicity.

[35] Bernard D. Karpinos, "Mental Test Failures," in Sol Tax (ed.), The Draft, op. cit., pp. 35-53.
The chart below is reproduced from Bernard D. Karpinos, "Mental Test Failures," op. cit.:

Mental Groups	Required Net Correct Answers	Percentail Score	Per Cent Within Population of Each Group
I	89-100	93-100	7
II	74-88	65-92	28
III	53-73	31-64	34
IV	25-52	10-30	21
V	24 or less	9 or below	10

"The disqualification rate for mental test failures among Negro examinees was four times as high as among white examinees. While one out of seven white draftees failed the mental tests, about 3 out of 5 Negro draftees failed--a disturbing cultural and socio-economic phenomenon." Ibid., pp. 46-47.

[36]AR-6o1-207, Appendix IV, p. A4-1.

[37]AR-601-270, Paragraph 37.

[38]Ibid.

[39]Ibid.

[40]Erving Goffman, "On Cooling the Mark Out: Some Aspects of Adaptation to Failure," in Arnold Rose (ed.), Human Behavior and Social Processes, Boston: Houghton Mifflin, 1962, p. 489.

[41]AR-601-270, p. A24-4.

[42]Jesse E. Gordon, "Project Cause, The Federal Anti-Poverty Program, and Some Implications of Subprofessional Training," American Psychologist, May, 1965.

[43]Dr. Harold Wool, during discussion on the voluntary Army, University of Chicago Conference on the Draft. His statement may be found in the transcript of the Conference, in Sol Tax, (ed.) The Draft, op. cit., p. 386.

[44]Leon Bramson, "The Sociological Significance of Voluntary National Service in Modern Society," in Donald J. Eberly (ed.) National Service, New York: Russell Sage Foundation, 1968.

DISAFFECTION, DELEGITIMATION, AND CONSEQUENCES:
AGGREGATE TRENDS FOR WORLD WAR II,
KOREA AND VIETNAM

Robert B. Smith

In this paper public opinion trends and Selective Service
records are used first to establish that the limited Korean and
Vietnam wars engendered more disaffection and delegitimation than
World War II, a war of total national involvement. After this,
the consequences of this malaise on aggregate rates of domestic
turmoil are discerned.

DISAFFECTION

Disaffection is defined as the absence or withdrawal of affection or loyalty, discontent or disloyalty, especially toward the
government.[1] It connotes alienation, estrangement, and dislike.[2]
In this analysis the level of disaffection of American society is
first gauged by public opinion trends, then by indexes derived
from Selective Service records.

The Public's Disaffection. The public's disaffection from the
war policies of the United States government is gauged by two
indexes: dissent from war, and disapproval of the incumbent president.

Dissent During Three Wars. Before World War II broke out in
Europe the American public supported England and France against
Germany and Italy. On May 27, 1938, the American Institute of
Public Opinion (AIPO) released the following data:[3]

Which side would your sympathies be with if

221

England and France have a war with Germany and
Italy?

England and France	65%
Germany and Italy	3
Neither Side	32

After the war began in Europe the actual events became consonant
with the pre-existing sentiment; this helped to mitigate dissent
after America entered the war.

Dissent during World War II can be guaged by using two
questions about disagreement with the goals of the war. Before
Pearl Harbor AIPO regularly asked the following question:[4]

Which of these two things do you think is the
more important--that this country keep out of
war, or that Germany be defeated.

Defeat Germany
Stay Out

For this question the percentage dissenting index

$$=100x \frac{\text{Stay Out}}{\text{Defeat Germany and Stay Out}}$$

averaged over a time period. After Pearl Harbor AIPO regularly
asked this question:[5]

If Hitler offered peace now to all countries
on the basis of not going any father, but
leaving matters as they are now, would you
favor or oppose such a peace?

Favor
Oppose
Undecided

For this question the percentage dissenting is

$$=100x \frac{\text{Favor}}{\text{Favor and Oppose}}$$

averaged over a time period.

The World War II trend line in Figure 1 based on these items
suggests that dissent decreased during this war. The average percentage dissenting for the year prior to Pearl Harbor was 34 per
cent compared to an average of about 8 per cent during the war in
Europe--a decrease of 26 per cent (see Figure 1).

During the Korean War (June 25, 1950-July 27, 1953) dissent
increased. Throughout this war AIPO regularly asked the following
question which is used to gauge dissent:[6]

> Do you think the United States made a mistake
> in going into the war in Korea or not?
>
>> Yes, made mistake
>> No, did not
>> No opinion

Dissent means to disagree. This meaning is rendered by the percentage of the public who say that United States involvement in Korea was a mistake, averaged over a time period. The index

$$= 100 \ x \ \frac{\text{Yes, made mistake}}{\text{Yes, made mistake and No, did not and No opinion}}$$

$$= 100 \ x \ \frac{\text{Yes, made mistake}}{\text{Total in sample}}$$

The AIPO trend line in Figure 1 reports that an average of only 20 per cent dissented at the beginning compared to 50 per cent at the end--an increase of 30 percentage points.[7]

This shift is corroborated by National Opinion Research Center (NORC) surveys. During Korea, NORC regularly asked the following question:

> Do you think the United States was right or
> wrong in sending American troops to stop the
> Communist invasion of South Korea?
>
>> Right
>> Wrong
>> Don't Know

After taking the percentage of those saying "Right" to the total and and averaging over a time period, the NORC trend line reports that on the average only 17 per cent dissented at the beginning compared to 33 per cent by mid-1952--an increase of 16 per cent.[8] Consequently, both indexes point to increased dissent during the Korean war.[9]

During the Vietnam war, AIPO regularly asks a similar question:[10]

> In view of the developments since we entered
> the fighting in Vietnam, do you think the U.S.
> made a mistake sending troops to fight in Vietnam
>> Yes, mistake
>> No
>> No opinion

Using an index similar to those above, the Vietnam trend line (Figure 1) reports that an average of only 24 per cent dissented

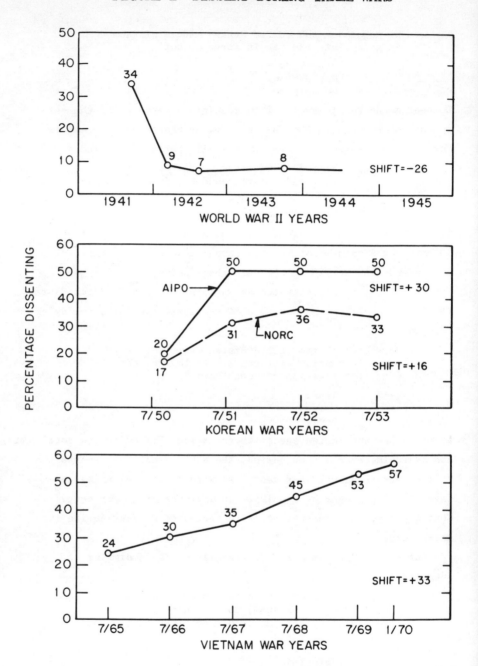

FIGURE 1   DISSENT DURING THREE WARS

during the first year after the Bay of Tonkin.[11] However, by
January, 1970, dissent increased to 57 per cent--an increase of
33 per cent. Comparing the aggregate pattern of dissent during
the three wars it appears that the two limited wars, Korea and
Vietnam, have very similar increasing dissent patterns which are
in sharp contrast to the decreasing dissent pattern of World War
II, the total war.[12]

Table 1 brings into even sharper focus the similarities and
differences in public opinion during these three wars. The table
reports the percentage dissenting toward the end of each of the
three wars gauged by almost identical questions. Korea and Vietnam have similar aggregate effects on public opinion--54 per cent
and 63 per cent, respectively (of those with an opinion), dissented toward the end of each war--compared to only 15 per cent
(of those with an opinion) toward the end of World War II. This
represents an average difference in dissent of 43 per cent between
the limited and total war (see Table 1).

Disapproval of the President during three wars. This difference is corroborated by data about the public's disapproval of
the President who was incumbent at the onset of each war. Table 2
reports that a President's popularity will increase at the start
of a war if he orders decisive retaliation for an enemy attack.[13]
During the year prior to Pearl Harbor President Roosevelt's popularity had slowly increased--by November 25, 1941, about 72 per
cent of the public approved the way he was handling his job as
President. His popularity jumped another 12 per cent immediately
after his decision to declare war against the Axis because of the
attack on Pearl Harbor[14](see Table 2).

Prior to the North Korean invasion of South Korea, President
Truman's popularity had decreased to only 37 per cent approval.
His decision to defend Korea temporarily boosted his popularity
to 46 per cent, an increase of 9 per cent.[15]

During the first six months of 1964 President Johnson's
average popularity was about 76 per cent (AIPO). On August 2 and
August 4, 1964, North Vietnamese torpedo boats were reported to

TABLE 1

DISSENT TOWARD THE END OF THREE WARS

	WORLD WAR II (AIPO)	KOREA (AIPO 11/16/52)	VIETNAM (AIPO 1/15/70)
	Do you think it was a mistake for the United States to enter World War II?	Do you think the United States made a mistake in going into the war in Korea?	In view of the developments since we entered the fighting in Vietnam, do you think the United States made a mistake sending troops to fight in Vietnam?
	2/2/44		
YES	14%	YES 43%	YES 57%
NO	77	NO 37	NO 33
DON'T KNOW	9	NO OPINION 20	NO OPINION 10
YES – NO =	−63%	YES – NO = +6%	YES – NO = +24%
$100 \times \dfrac{YES}{YES + NO} =$	15%	$100 \times \dfrac{YES}{YES + NO} =$ 54%	$100 \times \dfrac{YES}{YES + NO} =$ 63%

have unjustly attacked United States destroyers in Tonkin Bay.
Johnson immediately escalated the war by ordering air action
against gun boats and supporting facilities in North Vietnam.[16]
The Harris data reported in Table 2 indicate that Johnson's popularity jumped 12 percentage points because of his decisive retaliation. Consequently, at the onset of all three wars the popularity of the incumbent President increased because of his mili-
tancy. However, only President Roosevelt was able to maintain
his popularity--disapproval of Truman and Johnson increased as
the two limited wars dragged on (see Figure 2).[17]

Figure 2 presents trends describing disapproval of these three
Presidents during each of the three wars. These trends are based
on the AIPO question below:

> Do you approve or disapprove of the way (Roosevelt,
> Truman, Johnson) is handling his job as President?
>
>> Approve
>> Disapprove
>> No opinion

The index of the percentage disapproving is

$$= 100 \times \frac{\text{Disapprove}}{\text{Approve} + \text{Disapprove} + \text{No Opinion}}$$

averaged over a time period. Using this index disapproval of
President Roosevelt was low during World War II. During 1941
prior to Pearl Harbor his average disapproval was 23 per cent.
Soon after Pearl Harbor it dropped to only 13 per cent. Toward
the end of the war in Europe it was 19 per cent--a decrease of 4
per cent compared to 1941.[18] During the Korean war disapproval of
President Truman increased. During the six-month period prior to
the North Korean invasion Truman's average disapproval was only
44 per cent compared to 56 per cent when he left office in
January of 1953--an increase in disapproval of 12 per cent.[19]
During Vietnam disapproval of President Johnson also increased.[20]
From January, 1964 to mid-1965 his average disapproval was only
8 per cent compared to 48 per cent by January, 1969, when he left
office. This represents an increase in disapproval of 40 per cent
which was mostly caused by his handling of Vietnam.[21]

TABLE 2

AT THE ONSET OF TOTAL OR LIMITED WAR, DECISIVE
RETALIATION AGAINST THE ENEMY INCREASES
A PRESIDENT'S POPULARITY?

World War (AIPO)	Korea (AIPO)	Vietnam (Harris)
Do you approve or disapprove of the way Roosevelt is handling his job as President today?	Do you approve or disapprove of the way Truman is handling his job as President?	In this situation in North Vietnam, who would you trust more in the White House--Johnson or Goldwater?
Nov. 25,1941 Just Before Pearl Harbor	June 1950 Just Before Korean Invasion	Just Before Gulf of Tonkin
Approve 75%	37%	Johnson 59%
Disapprove 19	45	Goldwater 41
No Opinion 9	18	
Jan. 4,1942 Just After Pearl Harbor	July 1950 Just After Korean Invasion	Just After Gulf of Tonkin
Approve 84%	46%	Johnson 71%
Disapprove 9	37	Goldwater 29
No Opinion 7	17	
Shift in Approve = +12%	Shift in Approve = +9%	Shift in pro-Johnson = +12%

This is suggested by the parallel shift in disapproval of Johnson's handling of Vietnam. During the Johnson years, AIPO regularly asked:

> Do you approve or disapprove of the way President Johnson is handling the situation in Vietnam?
>
> > Approve
> > Disapprove
> > No Opinion

The Vietnam disapproval index is

$$= 100 \times \frac{\text{Disapprove}}{\text{Approve + Disapprove + No Opinion}}$$

averaged over a time period. The trend in Figure 2 reports that disapproval of Johnson's handling of Vietnam increased 25 per cent from July, 1965, to July 1968.[22]

In sum, the data about dissent and disapproval of the President suggest that the public's disaffection from war increased to high levels during the two limited wars, but support was maintained for the duration of World War II, a total war against a clear-cut enemy disliked prior to the war.[23] The subsequent analysis of Selective Service records corroborates this pattern.

DISAFFECTION OF SELECTIVE
SERVICE REGISTRANTS

The disaffection of Selective Service registrants is gauged by two indexes: evasiveness of class I-A registrants, and perceived strictness of the draft board.

Evasiveness During Three Wars. Except for the use of the lottery and deferment policies, the Selective Service System has remained relatively unchanged since its inception in 1940. Until 1970 it was headed by the same man, General Louis Hershey. During all three wars it has operated with the same decentralized organizational structure. Upon reaching the age of eighteen every male is required to register with his local draft board and to provide information so that the draft board can classify him into one of three broad classes in accordance with Selective Service regulations. These classes are: (1) available for service, (2) deferred from service, or (3) not liable for service. If the registrant is

FIGURE 2 DISAPPROVAL OF PRESIDENT DURING THREE WARS

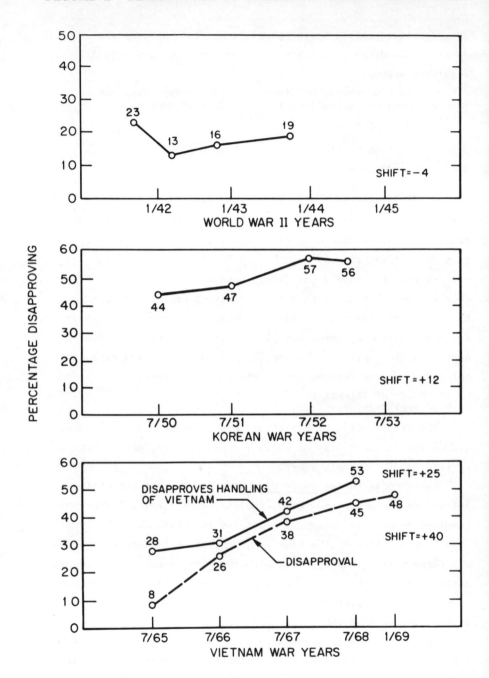

dissatisfied with his local board's classification, he can appeal
to a state appeal board which will reconsider his classification
status--most appeals are initiated after registrants are classified I-A (available for service) by their local board. If the
registrant is also dissatisfied with his appeal board's classification, he can appeal to the President if the vote of the appeal
board is not unanimous. The classification of the Presidential
appeal board is final.[24]

Because most appeals originate from I-A registrants, evasiveness is best gauged by the ratio of K-A registrants who voluntarily
appeal to the total number of I-A registrants.[25] That is, the
index of evasiveness (per thousand I-A registrants) during a particular time period is

$$= 1,000x \frac{\text{Number of voluntary appearls during a time period}}{\text{Number in I-A during the time period}}$$

Figure 3 reports the evasiveness trends during the three wars.[26]
Evasiveness decreased during World War II. For the time period
prior to Pearl Harbor there were 26 voluntary appeals per thousand
I-A registrants compared to only 3 per thousand at the end of the
war--a decrease of 23 appeals per thousand I-A registrants.[27] In
contrast, evasiveness increased during the Korean war. For fiscal
1950 (July 1, 1949-June 30, 1950) there was only 1 voluntary
appeal per thousand I-A registrants compared to 47 per thousand at
the end of the war--an increase of 46 appeals per thousand I-A
registrants.[28] Evasiveness during Vietnam increased to even higher
levels. Prior to large-scale American participation (bombing of
North Vietnam and non-advisory American troop commitments) there
were only 4 appeals per thousand I-A registrants compared to 102
per thousand by mid-1969--an increase of 98 appeals per thousand
I-A registrants (this increase is twice the Korean rate).[29] Comparing evasiveness during the three wars we find that evasiveness
increased to high levels during the two limited wars, but decreased
to a very low level during the total war.

Strictness of Draft Board. The trends below describing the
strictness of the draft board also conform to this pattern. There

FIGURE 3   EVASIVENESS DURING THREE WARS

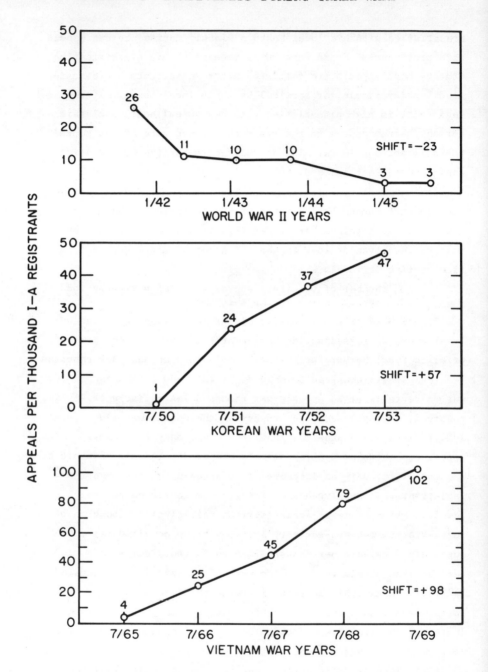

are two legitimate avenues of evasion for a dissatisfied registrant classified I-A by a local board: (1) conscientious objection;
and (2) other deferred classifications.

Conscientious Objection to War. Until very recently, because
of the stringent criteria, very few registrants were able to obtain conscientious objector (CO) status. The applicant had to be
a religious pacifist. This meant that his conscience had to be
religiously informed and he had to object to war in any form (all
wars).[30]

Figure 4 presents trends on the number of registrants who
obtained conscientious objector status in each of the three wars.
Throughout World War II there were only 4 CO's per 10,000 classified registrants. At the onset of Korea there were 13 CO's per
10,000 classified registrants compared to only 5 per 10,000 at the
end. During Vietnam, through fiscal year 1969, about 8 per 10,000
are CO's.

The Korean and Vietnam trends point out a major inflexibility
in the system. Toward the end of a limited war when disaffection
is highest, it is not easy to obtain conscientious objector status.[31] Conscientious objection does not act as an escape valve
for disaffection--in effect, disaffected registrants can only
appeal, they can't become CO's. Besides, even if granted CO
status, the life of a CO is not very satisfactory. CO's are
forced to perform alternative service for the country which, no
doubt, they would not do if they were not compelled. Most probably, even successful CO's are still dissatisfied with their
Selective Service classification.

Appeals for Deferred Classifications. The dissatisfied
registrant who appeals his local board's decision will probably
be disappointed because the vast majority of classifications are
sustained by the state appeal board--Selective Service records
show that about 65 per cent were sustained during World War II
and about 80 per cent during Korea. There is no information in
print for Vietnam.[32] Consequently, appeals for deferment also do
not provide as escape for disaffected I-A registrants. Since

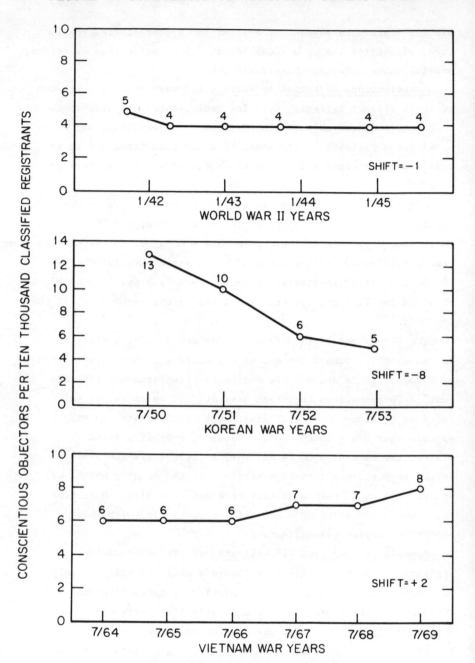

FIGURE 4 CONSCIENTIOUS OBJECTORS DURING THREE WARS

there is no escape valve, registrants would be more likely to perceive their draft board as strict during limited wars. The strictness of the draft board can be gauged by the ratio of unsuccessful voluntary appeals to total dissatisfied registrants. That is, strictness per 100 dissatisfied registrants is

$$= 100 \quad x \quad \frac{\text{Unsuccessful voluntary appeals}}{\text{Total dissatisfied registrants}}$$

$$= 100 \quad x \quad \frac{\text{Unsuccessful voluntary appeals}}{\text{Total voluntary appeals + CO's}}$$

Figure 5 presents strictness trends for the three wars.[33] Strictness, gauged by the above index, decreased during World War II. Prior to Pearl Harbor there were 65 unsuccessful appeals per hundred dissatisfied registrants compared to only 26 per hundred at the end of the war--a decrease of 39 per hundred. In contrast to World War II, strictness increased during the Korean war. At the beginning of the war there were only 13 unsuccessful appeals per hundred dissatisfied registrants compared to 70 unsuccessful appeals per hundred at the end of the war--an increase of 57 per hundred. The Vietnam pattern is very similar to Korea. At the time of the Bay of Tonkin incident there were merely 25 unsuccessful appeals per hundred dissatisfied registrants compared to 67 per hundred by mid-1969--an increase of 42 per hundred.[34] Comparing strictness during the three wars we find that the two limited wars have very similar high strictness patterns in contrast to the low strictness pattern of World War II.

Public opinion data corroborate this pattern. Table 3 describes the public's evaluation of the fairness of their local draft board. At the end of World War II 79 per cent said their draft board was fair compared to 60 per cent for Korea (1953) and 43 per cent for Vietnam (June, 1966).[35]

In sum, the evidence on evasiveness and strictness of the draft board suggests that the disaffection of Selective Service registrants increased to high levels during both limited wars, but was not a problem during World War II, a war of total national involvement. Consequently, all four indexes of disaffection--dissent, disapproval of the President, evasiveness of Selective

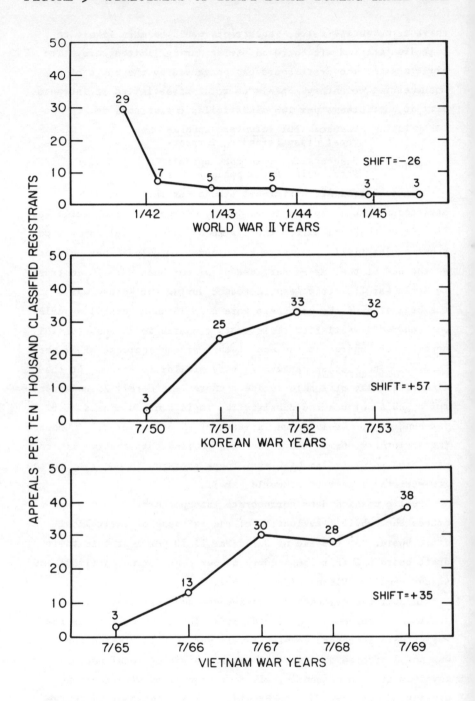

FIGURE 5   STRICTNESS OF DRAFT BOARD DURING THREE WARS

Service registrants, and strictness of draft board--point out the
high disaffection engendered by limited wars. During these
limited wars there was also delegitimation of authority.

Legitimacy. Lipset has defined legitimacy to mean the capacity of a social system to engender and maintain the belief that
the existing political institutions are most appropriate for the
society.[36] Legitimacy is a very important variable because it is
related to both conformity and rebellion.[37] When the legitimacy
of a political system is high people will conform without the use
of threats or coercion. But when legitimacy is low, when there
is delegitimation, rebellion is likely. In this situation, the
leadership of the political system will either have to change
their policies, becoming responsive and effective, or they will
have to resort to manipulation, co-optation or force in order to
obtain compliance.[38]

TABLE 3

FAIRNESS OF DRAFTBOARD TOWARD THE END OF THREE WARS

World War II (AIPO) Do you think the draft is being handled fairly in your community?	Korea (AIPO) Do you think the present draft system is fair, or not?	Vietnam (AIPO) Do you think the present deaft system is fair, or not?
June, 1945	1953	June, 1966
*Yes 79%	Fair 60%	Fair 45%
No 21	Not Fair 11	Not Fair 38
	No Opinion 29	No Opinion 19

*Of those with an opinion

Legitimacy of Governmental Authority. Boulding suggests that
legitimacy of governmental authority can be gauged by the extent
of the sacrifice people are willing to make:

> In the rise and decline of legitimacy, as we have
> seen, we find first a period in which sacrifices are
> made, voluntarily and gladly, in the interests of the
> legitimate institution, and indeed, reinforce the
> legitimacy of the institution. As the institution
> becomes more and more pressing in its demands,
> however, voluntary sacrifices become replaced with
> forced sacrifices.[39]

For most young men military service is a sacrifice; some men

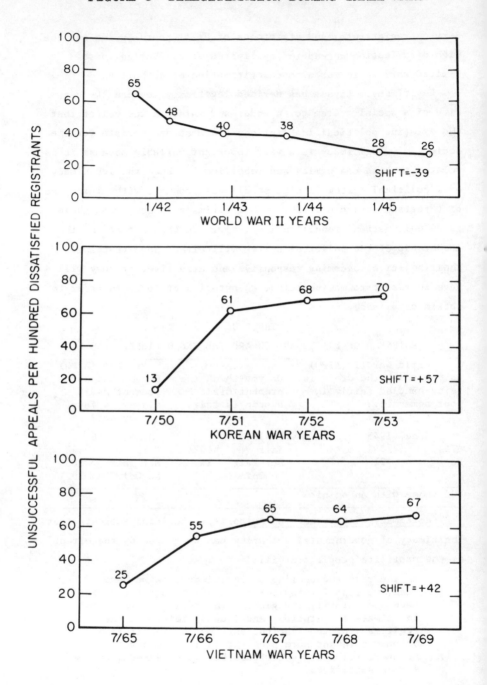

FIGURE 6   DELEGITIMATION DURING THREE WARS

willingly make this sacrifice, while others try to evade. Consequently, delegitimation of national authority can be gauged by
the Selective Service registrants' unwillingness to serve. The
index of delegitimation per 10,000 resistrants is

$$= 10,000 \times \frac{\text{Number of voluntary appeals during a time period}}{\text{Total number of classified registrants during a}}$$
$$\text{time period}$$

The delegitimation trends for the three wars are presented in
Figure 6. During World War II, delegitimation decreased. Prior to
Pearl Harbor there were 29 voluntary appeals per 10,000 classified registrants compared to only 3 per 10,000 at the end--a
decrease of 26 per 10,000. By way of contrast, during the Korean
war the loss in legitimacy was high. At the beginning there were
only 3 voluntary appeals per 10,000 classified registrants compared to 32 per 10,000 at the end--an increase in delegitimation
of 29 per 10,000. The Vietnam delegitimation pattern is similar.
In mid-1965 there were only 3 voluntary appeals per 10,000 classified registrants compared to 30 per 10,000 by mid-1969--an increase
in delegitimation of 35 per 10,000.[40] Consequently, both limited
wars are characterized by a decline of legitimacy in contrast to
the rise of legitimacy during World War II.

These trends are corroborated by the public opinion data of
Table 4 which describes the public's approval of compulsory military service, an indicator of high legitimacy. The data suggest
that approval of compulsory military service increased during
World War II but decreased during Korea and Vietnam.[41]

CONSEQUENCES

The differences in disaffection and delegitimation which
differentiated World War II from the two limited wars are reflected
in differences in domestic turmoil and electoral punishment.
Table 5 reports aggregate trends for the three wars.

During World War II, and soon after, there was very little
disaffection and delegitimation. As a consequence the Democratic
Presidents were not punished by the electorate. Roosevelt was
re-elected in 1944, and after his death, Truman was re-elected

TABLE 4

APPROVAL OF COMPULSORY MILITARY SERVICE
IN THREE WARS

(% Approving of Compulsory Military Service)					
World War II (AIPO)		Korea (AIPO)		Vietnam (AIPO)	
June–Oct. 1940	During War 1941–1945	August 1950	March 1952	October 1966	January 1969
63%	67%	78%	60%	69%	62%
October–December 1945 71%					
Shift = +8%		Shift = -18%		Shift = -7%	

in 1948. After the attack on Pearl Harbor there were virtually no
antiwar protests. Except for the widely supported unjust treatment
of Japanese-Americans on the West Coast, and the strict treatment
of conscientious objectors, there was very little official or
unofficial repression of the public during World War II.[42]

Contrariwise, during the Korean war, largely as a consequence
of the malaise engendered by the war, the Democrats were voted out
of office. The American public supported Eisenhower, the Republican candidate, and increasingly approved of Senator Joseph
McCarthy's attacks on liberals and "communists." Table 5 reports
that support for McCarthy increased 25 per cent from 1951 to 1954.
This support for repression was in part a consequence of disaffection from the Korean war.[43] It was not a backlash response
because there were no salient anti-Korean war demonstrations,
Black rebellions, nor student protests during this war.[44]

After President Johnson escalated the war in Vietnam the
public's disapproval of his actions eventually increased to such
an extent that he decided not to stand for re-election. His Vice-
President, Hubert Humphrey, eventually became the Democratic candidate and was defeated by Richard Nixon, a Republican. Most probably, a crucial element in Humphrey's defeat was the lack of sup-

TABLE 5

AGGREGATE TRENDS IN ELECTORAL PUNISHMENT,
REBELLION, AND REPRESSION DURING THREE WARS

WORLD WAR II

Electoral Punishment   None, Democrats Retained Presidency

Rebellion   No Salient Pattern

Repression   Incarceration of Japanese-Americans

KOREA

Electoral Punishment   Democrats Lost Presidency

Rebellion   No Salient Pattern

Repression

  Support for Radical Right
  (McCarthyism)[a]

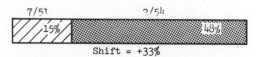

7/51   2/54   15%   48%

Shift = +33%

VIETNAM

Electoral Punishment   Democrats Lost Presidency

Rebellion

  Antiwar Protests

    Number of Participants in
    Antiwar Demonstrations
    Involving 1,000+ persons
    (in thousands)[b]

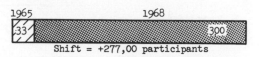

1965   1968   33   300

Shift = +277,00 participants

    Number of Participants in
    Antiwar Protests (in
    thousands)[c]

1965   1968   222   329

Shift = +107,000 participants

  Black Protests

    Urban Riots or Clashes[c]

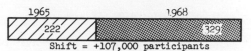

1964   1968   16   65

Shift = +49 riots or clashes

    Participants in Non-Violent
    Civil Rights Demonstrations
    (in thousands)[c]

1965   1968   117   42

Shift = -75,000 participants

  Student Protests (at UCSB)

    Number of Reported Protests[d]

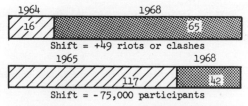

1967-1968   1969-1970   22   114

Shift = +92 protests

    Per Cent of Reported
    Protests[d] That are Non-
    Violent, Non-Forceful

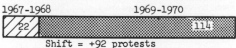

1967-1968   1969-1970   100%   75%

Shift = -25% in non-violent
protests

TABLE 5
(continued)

VIETNAM (continued)

Repression

"Hard-line" Against Criminals

Advocates Death Penalty[e]
for Murderers (National)

1966	1969
42%	51%

Shift = +9% in advocates death penalty

Advocates Death Penalty[e]
for Murderers (California)

1965	1969
51%	65%

Shift = +14% in advocates death penalty

Resistance to Racial Change

Negroes Have Tried to Move
Too Fast (Whites)[f]

1964	1966
34%	85%

Shift = +51% in moving too fast

Punitive Actions Against
UCSB Students

By Police[d]

1968-1969	1969-1970
14	43

Shift = +29 in reported punitive actions

---

[a]AIPO (8/17/1951); AIPO (1/14/54)

[b]Jerome Skolnick, The Politics of Protest (Washington, D. C.: U.S. Government Printing Office, 1969), Chart I, p. 24.

[c]Raymond Tanter, "International War and Domestic Turmoil," in Hugh Davis Graham and Ted Robert Gurr, eds., Violence in America, Volume 2, (Washington, D. C.: U.S. Government Printing Office, 1969), Table 16-1, p. 426.

[d]Coded from reports in El Gaucho, the University of California, Santa Barbara (UCSB) student newspaper.

[e]Public Opinion Quarterly, 34 (Summer, 1970), pp. 291-295.

[f]Public Opinion Quarterly, 32 (Fall, 1968), p. 522.

port from antiwar Democrats who disliked his middle-of-the-road stance on Vietnam.

In Addition to this electoral punishment, the disaffection and delegitimation engendered by the Vietnam War has severely strained the social fabric of American society.[45] Table 5 reports some sharp aggregate shifts in rates of protest and in turn repressive attitudes during this war. As disaffection and delegitimation increased, rebellious antiwar protests, urban riots, and student violence became over the short run commonplace. Conversely, participation in non-violent civil rights demonstrations and the percentage of non-violent student protests decreased. At the same time, as during the Korean war, attitude support for repression increased. The public increasingly approved of a "hard-line" against criminals, resisted social change, and supported police actions against students and ghetto residents.[46] Hopefully, these anti-democratic trends will be reversed by an end to the war.

NOTES

[1] Webster's New World Dictionary, College Edition, 1954.

[2] American College Dictionary, 1958.

[3] Handly Cantril, Public Opinion 1935-1946 (Princeton: Princeton University Press, 1949), p. 1061.

[4] The responses to this questionwere gleaned from various AIPO press releases on file at the American Institute of Public Opinion.

[5] Cantril, Public Opinion, p. 1166.

[6] For a concise review of public opinion and the Korean war, see Gallup Opinion Index, Report No. 3 (August, 1965), p. 23.

[7] Dissent in Korea was in large part a consequence of the rapid increase in the costs of the war due to the entry of the Chinese Communists. AIPO reported this trend (ibid., p. 26):

	After Chinese Entered	August 1950
Yes, we made a mistake	49%	20%
No, we did not	38	65
No opinion	13	15

The shift in disapproval is 29 per cent.

[8]The NORC trends are reported by Hazel Erskine, "The Polls: Is War a Mistake?" The Public Opinion Quarterly 34 (Spring, 1970), pp. 134-150.

[9]Waltz noted that the decision to defend South Korea was widely approved but the implementation of that decision was not. This resulted in electoral punishment for the Democratic Party, many voted against their interest on domestic matters for Eisenhower because he was thought to be able to make peace. See Kenneth N. Waltz, "Electoral Punishment and Foreign Policy Crisis," in Domestic Sources of Foreign Policy, etc., by James N. Rosenau (New York: Free Press, 1967), p. 274.

[10]For concise summaries of public opinion and the Vietnam war, see Gallup Opinion Index, Report No. 30 (December, 1967),Report No. 52(October,1969) and Report No. 54 (December, 1969).

[11]Writing in mid-1966 Lipset correctly noted that opposition to Vietnam was less than for Korea. However, since August, 1968, dissent has surpassed Korean levels. For Lipset's comparison, see Seymour Martin Lipset, "The President, the Polls, and Vietnam," Trans-action (Sept.-Oct. 1966), p. 24.

[12]John T. Campbell and Leila S. Cain systematically compared support for World War II and for Korea in their attempt to validate one of Richardson's mathematical models. See John T. Campbell and Leila S. Cain, "Public Opinion and the Outbreak of War," Journal of Conflict Resolution, IX (September, 1965), pp. 318-333. For a comparison of Vietnam and Korean Trends based on University of Michigan Survey Research Center surveys, see Philip E. Converse and Howard Schuman, "'Silent Majorities' and the Vietnam War," Scientific American, 222 (June 1970), pp. 17-25.

[13]Waltz makes the same point. See Waltz, "Electoral Punishment and Foreign Policy Crises," p. 272.
President Kennedy also improved his popularity as a result of the Cuban Missile Crisis. AIPO reported these statistics in the Gallup Opinion Index, Report No. 56 (February, 1970), p. 13:

	Prior to Missile Crisis (Oct.1962)	After Missile Crisis (Nov.1962)
Approve	62%	74%
Disapprove	22%	15%
No Opinion	16%	11%

The shift in approval was +12 per cent.
However, President Nixon's escalation of the war into Cambodia, late in the Vietnam war, did not improve his popularity—the withdrawal of the troops did. AIPO reported these trends (July 31, 1970):

	Just Before Invasion	Just After Invasion	Just After Troops Withdrawn
	April 17–19 1970	May 2–5 1970	July 10–12 1970
Approve	56%	57%	61%
Disapprove	31	31	28
No Opinion	13	12	11

His popularity improve +1 per cent because of the invasion and another +4 per cent because of the withdrawal.

[14]Cantril, Public Opinion, p. 756.

[15]Gallup Opinion Index, Report No. 3, p. 23.

[16]Gallup Opinion Index, Report No. 30, p. 9.

[17]It is unlikely that the decreases in popularity were caused by Truman and Johnson's limiting of the Korean and Vietnamese wars. Rather, the costs of both wars increased creating a difficult problem. Truman and Johnson's inability to solve their respective problems caused the drop in their popularity. Red China's entry into the Korean war (an increase in cost) increased disapproval of Truman:

	After Chinese Invasion January, 1951	Before Chinese Invasion October, 1950
Disapproval	49%	42%
Approval	36	39
No Opinion	15	19

The shift was 7 per cent.

Source: Gallup Opinion Index, Report No. 12 (May, 1966), p. 25.

Moreover, Johnson's order to limit bombing of North Vietnam (an attempt to de-escalate the war) increased his popularity:

	After Peace Offensive April 1968	Before Peace Offensive March 1968 (late)
Approve	41%	26%
Disapprove	48	63
No Opinion	11	11

The shift in approval was 15 per cent.

Source: Gallup Opinion Index, Report No. 35 (May, 1968), p. 17.

Gallup also reported that the public approved Johnson's decision to reduce bombing:

Do you approve or disapprove of President Johnson's
decision to stop the bombing of North Vietnam?

	April, 1968
Approve	64%
Disapprove	26
No Opinion	

Source: Gallup Opinion Index, Report No. 35 (May, 1968), p. 18.

[18] The trends in Roosevelt's popularity are reported in Cantril,
Public Opinion, p. 756.

[19] The trends in Truman's popularity are reported in Gallup
Opinion Index, Report No. 56.

[20] Ibid., pp. 14-16. The trends for Truman and Johnson are
compared in Gallup Opinion Index, Report No. 18 (November-
December, 1966), p. 3.

[21] Gallup noted that Vietnam was a major reason for Johnson's
loss of popularity. He stated:

> There are a number of factors that account for the
> decline in Johnson's popularity, but a chief reason
> is the Vietnam situation, considered by the public
> to be the top problem facing the nation.

See the Gallup Opinion Index, Report No. 12 (May, 1966), p. 20.

[22] Party affiliation also affected approval of Johnson's handling of Vietnam. The zero order effect of party affiliation
is below:

	Party Affiliation	
	Democrat	Republican
Favors Johnson's	69%	51%
Handling of Vietnam	(654)	(305)

This effect is interpreted by vote in the 1964 election:

	Democrat		Republican	
Vote 1964 Election:	Johnson	Goldwater	Johnson	Goldwater
Per cent who Favor	71%	30%	67%	45%
Johnson's Handling	(608)	(56)	(80)	(225)
of Vietnam				

Average Effect of Democrat Affiliation = -2%
Average Effect of Vote Last Election   = 27%

Consequently, this causal mechanism holds:

Democrat	+	Voting for	+	Approval of
Affiliation		Johnson		Johnson's Handling
				of Vietnam

Source: Sidney Verba, Richard A. Brody, Edwin B. Parker, Norman
H. Nie, Nelson W. Polsby, Paul Ekman, and Gordon S. Black, "Public
Opinion and the War in Vietnam," The American Political Science
Review, LXI (June, 1967), Table 2.

[23]There are indications that Nixon's inability to end the
Vietnam war is eroding his popularity. Comparing disapproval
after two years in office for the last four Presidents, Nixon's
disapproval has increased the most. The trends are below:

Per Cent Disapproval (of Total)

	After 6 Months	After 1 Year	After 18 Months	After 2 Years	Shift in Disapproval
Eisenhower	9%	19%	21%	22%	+13%
Kennedy	8	12	14	20	+12
Johnson	8	16	18	21	+13
Nixon	11	22	28	30	+19

The trends are reported in the Gallup Opinion Index, Report No. 56.
The Nixon trend was updated in the Gallup Opinion Index, Report
No. 66.

[24]Lt. General Lewis B. Hershey, "A Fact Paper on Selective
Service," in The Draft: A Handbook of Facts and Alternatives, ed.
Sol Tax (Chicago: University of Chicago Press, 1967), pp. 3-6.

[25]During Korea, General Hershey stated that: "Most personal
appearances and appeals, as might be expected, take place after
men are classified I-A, available for service, by their local
boards. See Lewis B. Hershey, Annual Report of the Director of
Selective Service for the Fiscal Year 1952, (Washington: U. S.
Government Printing Office, 1953), p. 36.
During Vietnam, General Hershey stated that: "Most of the
registrants requesting appeals are those found available for military service or assignment to civilian work in lieu of induction,
but feel entitled to deferment or exemption. See Lewis B. Hershey,
Annual Report of the Director of Selective Service for the Fiscal
Year 1967 (Washington: U. S. Government Printing Office, 1967),
p. 26. I am indebted to Sigmund Diamond for suggesting how this
index might be constructed.

[26]The Selective Service data for these trends and for the other
trends reported below were gleaned from Selective Service reports
during World War II, Korea, and Vietnam:

World War II

Lewis B. Hershey, Selective Service in Peace Time, 1940-1941
(Washington: Government Printing Office, 1942).

Lewis B. Hershey, Selective Service in Wartime, 1941-1942 (Washington: Government Printing Office, 1943).

Lewis B. Hershey, Selective Service as the Tide of War Turns, 1943-1944 (Washington: Government Printing Office, 1945).

Lewis B. Hershey, Selective Service and Victory, 1944-1947 (Washington: Government Printing Office, 1948).

Korea

Lewis B. Hershey, Selective Service Under the 1948 Act (Washington: Government Printing Office, 1951).

Lewis B. Hershey, Selective Service Under the 1948 Act Extended, July 9, 1950-June 19, 1951 (Washington: Government Printing Office, 1953).

Lewis B. Hershey, Annual Report of the Director of Selective Service (Washington, Government Printing Office).

> Fiscal Year 1951
> Fiscal Year 1952
> Fiscal Year 1953
> Fiscal Year 1954

Vietnam

Lewis B. Hershey, Annual Report.

> Fiscal Year 1960
> Fiscal Year 1961
> Fiscal Year 1962
> Fiscal Year 1963
> Fiscal Year 1964
> Fiscal Year 1965
> Fiscal Year 1966
> Fiscal Year 1967 (Semi-Annual)
> Fiscal Year 1968 (Semi-Annual)

Statistics supplied by the National Headquarters of Selective Service were used to extend the Vietnam trends beyong July, 1968.

[27] The numerator for the World War II trend was gleaned from Table 14 and Table 15 of Lewis B. Hershey, Selective Service and Victory, pp. 134-135. From October 16, 1940 to November, 1942 about 58 per cent of the appeals were voluntary (originated with registrant or dependent). During the next year, about a third of the appeals were voluntary. For the subsequent years, the number of voluntary appeals are tabulated in Table 15.

[28] During Korea, about 86 per cent of the total appeals were made voluntarily (personal communication from the information clerk of the Ohio State Headquarters, Selective Service System).

[29] During Vietnam, it was assumed that 86 per cent of the total appeals were made voluntarily. The information clerk of the Ohio

State Headquarters, Selective Service System, suggested that this
percentage be used.

The evasiveness rate for fiscal 1970 is lower than the 1969
rate.   It is 66 per 10,000 I-A registrants.   This decrease is
probably due to the use of the lottery system which has created
"safe" numbers.   This reduces the risk of being called for about
a third of the registrants nominally classified I-A.   Consequently,
these registrants are not motivated to appeal.

[30]See John de J. Pemberton, Jr., "Equality in the Exemption of
Conscientious Objectors" in The Draft, edited by Sol Tax (Chicago:
University of Chicago Press, 1967).

[31]During discal 1970, probably due to policy changes, the
number of CO's increased to 10 per 10,000 classified registrants.

[32]For the World War II data, see Lewis B. Hershey, Selective
Service as the Tide of War Turns, Table 121, p. 500. For the
Korean War data, see Lewis Hershey, Annual Report, 1954, p. 29.
It was assumed that the Vietnam record of sustaining local board
appeals was the same as that for Korea.

[33]Strictness is the frequency probability of being disappointed
by the draft board, given that you are dissatisfied with your
deaft status.

[34]Strictness increased during fiscal 1970. By July 1, 1970
there were 72 unsuccessful appeals per hundred dissatisfied registrants.

[35]All three percentages are from AIPO tabulations. The World
War II data is reported in Cantril, Public Opinion, p. 462 . The
Korean and Vietnam data are presented in the Gallup Opinion Index,
Report No. 13 (June, 1966), p. 11.

[36]Seymour Martin Lipset, Political Man(Garden City, New York:
Doubleday and Company, Inc., 1960), p. 77. Boulding offers a
similar definition:

>   Legitimacy may be defined as general acceptace by all
>   those concerned in a certain institution, role, or
>   pattern of behavior that it constitutes part of the
>   regular moral or social order within which they live.

See Kenneth E. Boulding, "The Impact of the Draft on the
Legitimacy of the National State," in The Draft, ed. by Sol Tax
(Chicago: University of Chicago Press, 1967), p. 191.

[37]For an interesting discussion of legitimacy, see Richard
Flacks, "Protest and Conform: Some Social Psychological Perspectives on Legitimacy"; Kenneth E. Boulding, "Preventing Schismo-
genesis"; Amitai Etzioni, "Beyond a Hollow Legitimacy: What";
and Herbert C. Kelman, "Is a New Pattern of Legitimacy Emerging,"
all in The Journal of Applied Behavioral Science 5(April/May/June,

1969), pp. 127-156.

[38]For an insightful analysis of compliance structures and the transformation of unresponsive societies, see Amitai Etzioni, The Active Society (New York: The Free Press, 1968).

[39]Boulding, "The Impact of the Draft on the Legitimacy of the National State," p. 195.

[40]In Selective Service fiscal year 1970 delegitimation dropped to the 1967-1968 levels--about 29 voluntary appeals per 10,000 classified registrants.

[41]The trend for the Universal Military Training question is presented in the Gallup Opinion Index, Report No. 17 (October, 1966). The data for Vietnam are incomplete.
Delegitimation can also be gauged by complaints about income taxes. The AIPO data below indicate that complaints about taxes were high during the two limited wars and increased as the wars progressed. By way of contrast during World War II complaints were low and did not increase as the war progressed.

COMPLAINTS ABOUT TAXES

WORLD WAR II (AIPO) Do you regard the income tax which you will have to pay this year as fair?			KOREA (AIPO) Do you consider the amount of Federal income tax which you have to pay as too high, about right, or too low?		VIETNAM (AIPO) Do you consider the amount of Federal income tax which you have to pay as too high, about right, or too low?	
	2/23/43	3/45		1950 1952		1964 1969
No	15%	15%	Too High	56% 71%	Too High	55% 69%
Yes	85	85	Not	44 29	Not	45 31
Shift = 0%			Shift = +15%		Shift = +14%	

[42]Support for the incarceration of Japanese in America and Japanese-Americans was very high. In March, 1942, 93 per cent supported the relocation of Japanese who were not citizens and 59 per cent, the relocation of United States citizens of Japanese ancestry. Sixty-five per cent thought the internment camps should be guarded strictly. See Cantril, Public Opinion, pp. 380-381.
Cantril (p. 135) also reports that in 1940 only 13 per cent of the public would exempt CO's from service and that 76 per cent approved jail sentences for some students who were studying for the ministry and who refused to register for the draft because of their religious beliefs.

[43]For an insightful analysis of the relationship between the Korean war and McCarthyism see Michael Paul Rogin, The Intellec-

lectuals and McCarthy: The Radical Specter (Cambridge: The M.I.T. Press, 1967). Rogin's analysis is based on ecological correlations and aggregate trends, but is very convincing.

[44] Robin Brooks, "Domestic Violence and America's Wars: An Historical Interpretation," in Hugh Davis Graham and Ted Robert Gurr, editors, Violence in America, Volume 2 (Washington, D.C., United States Government Printing Office, 1969), p.p. 415-416.

[45] Ibid., pp. 416-418.

[46] There is some evidence from surveys that indicates that Blacks who are disaffected from war are more likely to participate in riots. The following data was reported by the National Advisory Commission on Civil Disorders (New York: Bantom Books, 1968), p. 178.

Disaffection and Riot Participation

Country worth fighting for in major world war	Detroit Survey (1967)		
	Rioters	Not Involved	Counter Rioter
Worth fighting	53.3%	75.0%	86.9%
Not Worth fighting	39.4	15.5	3.3
Don't know	5.3	9.5	9.8
	100.0%	100.0%	100.0%
	(38)	(264)	(56)

Country worth fighting for in major world war	Newark Survey (1967)	
	Rioter	Not Involved
Worth fighting	33.0%	50.8%
Not Worth fighting	52.8	27.8
Don't know	14.2	21.4
	100.0%	100.0%
	(106)	(126)

Support for a "hard-line" against riot participants is strong. Fifty-four per cent of the public want the police to shoot on sight anyone found looting stores during race riots (AIPO, May, 1968).

The majority of the public do not perceive that America is a racist society. Fifty-four per cent believe that Negroes themselves are responsible for their present position (AIPO, May, 1968); sixty-five per cent believe that businesses do not discriminate in their hiring policies (AIPO, May, 1968), seventy per cent think Negroes are being treated the same as whites (AIPO, May, 1968), and 50 per cent think that labor unions do not discriminate. These findings were reported in the Public Opinion Quarterly, 34 (Winter, 1968-1969), pp. 696-703.

Part III.

THE EMERGENT MILITARY ESTABLISHMENT

THE EMERGENT MILITARY

Morris Janowitz

How can one speak about the military profession in the post
1970's when one can not readily anticipate the outcome of immediate and crucial events? It has become popular to skip over
current uncertainties and make bold projections into the longer
range future. Often such forecasting is not only highly inaccurate but it may be self-defeating. It can be self-defeating if
predictions become self-fulfilling prophecies because they inhibit
creative thinking and limit options.

To speak of the military profession of the post 1970's is to
identify those institutional policies and practices that require
change. Rather than becoming enamored with predicting the future,
I prefer to focus on the changes that men must accomplish in order
to manage by rational means the human environment. Prediction
based on extrapolations of current trends are particulary dangerous in international relations since change does not evolve
gradually and at a uniform rate. Both in the deployment and use
of conventional weapons by the major powers and in the evolution
of nuclear weapons systems, the last years of the decade of the
1960's may well be one of basic transformation comparable to the
period of 1945. The phase of American foreign policy from 1945 to
1970, a phase of a quarter of a century, can be thought of as a
distinct period.

Changing Politico-Military Context

First, during this last 25 year phase, the prospects of
nuclear war were very remote indeed. It has been argued that
during this period nuclear technology developed a delicate balance
of terror, which was perhaps not so delicate as relatively stable,
because its dimensions could be calculated. Political leadership
and political arrangements accounted for the absence of major war,
or rather accounted for the ability of the Soviets and the Western
bloc to work out an arrangement to exist under the threat of
accidental and premeditated nuclear war. The essential political
formula was that the Soviet bloc believed that the United States
political leaders firmly controlled their military establishment
and that the United States had ruled out a preemptive nuclear
attack on the Soviet Union. In short, the political initiative
and political posture of the United States was crucial, during
this period as the Soviet Union expanded its nuclear weapons
system.

As 1970 came to an end, this political formula was being
fundamentally strained by the uncertainties that MIRV type weapons
introduce. Political communications must become more mutual and
two way; but currently neither side was able to extend to the
other the essential political guarantees, although it was abundantly clear to each that any nuclear initiative remains self-
defeating. In addition, the nuclear balance was gravely compli-
cated because the United State and the Soviet Union independently
or in concert cannot extend the political formula of the last
twenty-five years to include relations with China as she develops
her nuclear weapons.

Second, during the last twenty-five years, conventional
military forces were employed by the United States to implement
two increasingly divergent foreign policies: one in Western Europe
and one in the Far East. In Western Europe, the stationing of
American troops and the system of defense alliances were reasonably compatible with European national political aspirations. In

the Far East the stationing of troops and their direct involvement
were relatively compatible with local national aspirations until
the end of the Korean War. Progressively the tasks of American
forces have become more and more difficult because of opposition
they encountered from local nationalist political forces; especially the nationalist sentiments of the developing nations. Vietnam represented the epitome of the stalemate of military force
and nationalist political elements.

In exploring the tasks of institution building for the military profession during the next two decades, it is possible to
make very grim or merely grim assumptions about international
relations. In the nuclear arms race, it might well be assumed
that the Strategic Arms Limitation Talks (SALT) will fail and MIRV
weapons will become standard equipment. In South East Asia, it
could be assumed not only that peace negotiations will fail but
that in the process of disengagement of American forces the result
will be to incorporate into the National Liberation Front, significant portions of the present South Vietnamese military poten-
tials (less manpower and more weapons). In short the domino
theory could be made to work if American efforts contributed to
the development of a Vietnamese military potential which would
threaten neighboring states.

My observations about the future of the military profession
are not based on any particular assumptions about the outcome of
specific international negotiations. They are based on a more
general assumption. Namely the crucial issue facing the military
profession rests on whether it has the ability to recognize the
paradox that nuclear weapons and contemporary nationalist movements raise; that the growth in the destructive capacity of both
conventional and unconventional weapons has been paralleled by an
extension in the limitation of the political effectiveness of
force. The use of force has traditionally operated within circum-
scribed limits and contemporary political considerations have
served only to narrow the limits. This is what is emphasized in
the "constabulary concept", a notion of military force as defined

in The Professional Soldier. "The military establishment becomes
a constabulary force when it is continuously prepared to act,
committed to the minimum use of force, and seeks viable international relations, rather than victory, because it has incor-
porated a protective military posture." (P.148) In other words,
the outbreak of general war is no longer inevitable in the calculus of political leaders.

The military profession believes that it has unique characteristics because of its responsibility for the management of the
instruments of violence. Rationality in the military profession
means that it must, in the contemporary scene, accept the notion
that a successful officer can be one who does not fight, but
contributes to deterrence and the resolution of international
conflict. It is truly unique to be trained to perform tasks
that one hopes never to perform. Therefore, the basic question
is whether I am justified in making the radical assumption that
in the decades ahead the military profession will increase its
capacity to understand the limitations on military force and will
be able to incorporate such an understanding into its doctrine,
training and organization.

Of course, such an assumption must be seen in the light of
the lessons to be drawn from the Vietnam war. These lessons deal
not only with a host of tactical and organizational issues, but
involve the questioning of fundamental strategic concepts. For
example, in 1961 and 1962, ground force planners concluded that
the limitations on military force in Vietnam were such that one
million to one million two hundred thousand men would be required
for a land engagement. How was that reality denied first by U.S.
political leaders and then by the military professionals themselves?

The Emerging Military Format

But the impact of Vietnam on the future of the military profession has already been felt. First, the political definition
of the national interest has come to include the public demand
that future engagements similar in scope and strategy to the

Vietnam conflict be avoided. Second, the frustration of Vietnam, plus the inequalities and rigidities of Selective Service have created a crisis in the legitimacy of the current system of manpower. The result is that the demand for a volunteer armed force will be a persistent and increasing theme in the years ahead. In the near future United States military posture will be conditioned, and limited, by a changing manpower system. The professional military is likely to emerge as (a) a smaller establishment, (b) recruited more and more on an all volunteer basis and (c) organized predominantly on a force "in being" basis with a deemphasis of the older tradition of a cadre for mobilization.

All of these three elements articulate with one another. The pressure for and the need for a smaller size force does not guarantee proportionate reductions in manpower costs. Economists have committed themselves to estimates and there is good reason to anticipate that like most military budgeting they are understatements of actual expenditures.

But the trend toward a fully volunteer force is not merely a matter of cost and efficiency. It has emerged as an ideological goal for a variety of groups in the United States. For some, it is a desirable objective, because it is an expression of individual freedom. Those who speak of the need for individual initiative in business enterprise system are the same ones who urge the end of selective service and who are opposed to all forms of national service. At the same time, many of the sharpest critics of the current economic system also agree that the military service should be organized without the draft. For these, despite practical and moral objections, the "volunteer army" is offered as a basis for producing greater consensus in a society divided by a range of social and political issues.

An armed force "in being" which is highly transportable has a strong appeal to the military profession seeking a solution to competing pressures. While professional officers prefer to build such a force on a modified selective service system, they will, of course, accept the trend toward an all volunteer service.

The initial implication of these policy directions are abundantly clear; the result will be to reverse the pattern of civilian-military relations of the last two decades. To reduce reliance on or to eliminate the draft, to recruit a fully volunteer force with longer tours of duty for officers and enlisted personnel and to shift from a mobilization to a force "in being" format will make the military much more of a self-contained establishment. Clearly, the military will not revert to the professional isolation of the period between World War I and World War II. The resources and skills which the military require, and the central importance of military operations in current affairs will prevent such a gross transformation. But much civilian pressure on the military profession will have the effect of emphasizing the organizational autonomy and the separate character of the armed forces. However, the task of effective institution building will have to be the opposite. The task will be to develop a military profession which is closely articulated with civilian society. The underlying issue is not merely the danger of military opposition to civilian political leadership, but rather the question of professional vitality and legitimacy as well as sensitivity to the need for change.

The great danger will be if the military profession comes to be seen as a distinct and separate establishment by civilian society and in turn if the military profession begins to see itself as alienated from civilian society. To prevent such developments and to increase the military's understanding of the limitations on the use of violence in international relations, institution building in a wide range of areas is required, as for example, recruitment, education and career development.

My focus will be on officer personnel although the issues of enlisted manpower are real. It is essential to keep in mind the format under which the military profession operated during the post-World War II period. The professional officer corps is characterized by a) a very broad base of recruitment, that is, in terms of social class, educational background, geographical

region and even in terms of more intangible social personality.
There is no specific social type which tends to make up the bulk
of the recruitment; b) a significant, but declining number of the
officers served as enlisted personnel (in the early 1960's over
one-quarter of the ground officers had some enlisted experience,
including the National Guard; c) the bulk of the officer corps is
composed of personnel with relative short term career commitments.
This includes not only the bulk of the junior officers with two
to four years of obligated tours of duty, but many middle level
officers whose careers end after five to ten years of duty.
Although the senior posts are dominated by academy trained officers
with long term career commitments, the personnel mix of the armed
service currently operates with a constant inflow and outflow of
civilian oriented officers; d) a significant portion of the
officers, but again a declining portion, are men who held civilian
posts before they entered the armed forces or were mobilized as
reservists and then chose to remain in the armed forces. Although
this system might contribute to higher training costs it also has
economic and social relevance for the officer's civilian employment after retirement. But the issue at hand is not only the
economic costs but the character of civilian-military relations
and the type of armed force that such emerging manpower system
will produce. The trend toward a smaller, fully volunteer standby
force will alter this personnel mix and change the pattern of
recruitment.

    Recruitment. Movement toward an all volunteer force is
certain to narrow the base of recruitment into the officer corps.
First, the number and range of ROTC units from which the bulk of
the officer corps is drawn is certain to contrast. This is not
mainly a matter of agitation at selected college campuses against
ROTC units. The pressure on ROTC units will be to produce a
supply of officers and an emphasis will be placed on a smaller
number of successful units. These will tend to be located in
rural areas and in the South and West where the tradition of
entrance into the military profession is the strongest. Often

these ROTC units will be at universities with more modest academic standards.

Second, the armed forces will seek a higher component of officers who are trained in the service academies, a step which has already been taken by increasing the size of the student body at these institutions. While such a step may be necessary, it is an additional trend toward social separation, if more officers are trained at the academies in contrast to ROTC and OCS units. While the system of selection into the service academies is broadly based, increased use of academic graduates will also in the future narrow recruitment because military family background is likely to become even more important in academy selection. It is important to note that the pool of such military families and the number of their offspring are increasing because of the expansion of the armed services during the last twenty years. Some such increase is acceptable because the percentage of officers whose fathers were in the military profession is still below the amount of occupational inheritance of other professions, for example, the medical profession. But excessive recruitment from military families--officers and enlisted--would not only serve to narrow the basis of social recruitment, but would also contribute to a separation of the officer corps from civilian society. Any increased reliance on government sponsored military preparatory schools or even privately sponsored preparatory schools would also specialize social and geographical background.

Third, there is a danger that recruitment from the ranks into the officer corps may decline. As the military place greater and greater emphasis on a college degree, the trend will be to recruit from college graduates rather than train and promote from the ranks. Of course, the services have shown considerable ability to offer a college education to highly motivated enlisted personnel.

The issue at stake is not only a broadly based military officer corps, but its academic, creative and leadership potential. To focus on academic test scores which have come to

characterize American university life is to miss basic elements.
How can we account for the extraordinary leadership and statesman-
like cadres of higher officers who rose to prominence during
World War II? They were not selected by means of psychological
or academic tests; self-selection was crucial. The pool of outstanding officers was in part the result of the attraction of an
academy education for the sons of respectable families without
financial resources. This was the strength of the academies in
the 1920's and 1930's, especially during the depression. The rise
of the state universities and the opening up of the talent search
by the prestige universities has weakened the relative position
of the service academies for recruiting outstanding leadership
potential.

Institution building for the professional officer corps will
in the future require extensive lateral entry if recruitment is to
remain representative and vigorous. The professional military
since the end of the Civil War, and especially since the turn of
the century, has opposed lateral entry with great vigor. But it
seems impossible to cope with a fully volunteer service and its
emerging skill requirements without opportunities for lateral
entry. Lateral entry can involve limited tours of duty, and in
this respect is close to reserve status. The difference would
be that an active duty assignment would be a routine event and
not only in an emergency. Lateral entry includes the opportunity
to take up an extended career in the professional military, two,
five, and even ten years after graduation from a civilian university. Such lateral entry would be crucial both for a variety of
technical assignments, and also for specialists in area and
language work.

Education and Career Development. In the emerging armed
forces, the education of the professional military man is designed
not only to supply him with essential skills but to provide him
with the necessary linkages with civilian society. Education
emerges as one of the main mechanisms for articulating the military with civilian social structure. The tasks of the constabu-

lary force requires increased awareness of the larger society. However, the training and operational realities of much of the emerging military force along with its recruitment process will tend to separate the military from larger society. The education of the officer, which, of course, cannot be thought of independently from his career development will have to carry the main burden of meaningful relations with the larger society.

In the past, the ground forces have had the major responsibilities for politico-military affairs and have supplied the cadre of officers for these tasks. Not only the mission of the ground forces, but their style of life have predisposed them in this direction. But in the future the ground force "in being" with its heavy emphasis on air transportability will become more like the current air force. Its organizational life will be contained mainly within the confines of a military base. Given the limited supply of uniformed personnel, the pressure will be to remove military personnel from logistical roles and thereby opportunities for civilian experiences will be diminished. Higher headquarters will be removed from metropolitan centers and placed on military bases or in remote areas. The trend will be toward garrison life in which each military professional will strive for the high prestige assignment of an operational role. Even residence and social contacts will be more and more garrison based since fewer personnel will be living off base. Preparation for military duties will separate the armed force both in residence and daily existence from the larger society.

A more detailed examination of career lines is required. As the military establishment moves toward a constabulary format with an overriding emphasis on deterrence, the range of tasks to be performed increases. The traditional ideas of a standard or prescribed career comes to have less and less meaning. The effectiveness of the military profession will depend on its ability to reward and integrate a wide range of careers. But this is not an easy task. First, the military are certain to continue to define the unit commander of manned conventional forces as the central role, and to think of such assignments as being at the heart of the professional prestige system. However, the dilemma of the commander at each level in the military hierarchy is that training, experience and concern with the internal management of the system does not necessarily increase his understanding of the politico-military context of higher command and of the consequences and limitations of force. Moreover, he must learn to live with the idea that he is really successful, national objectives can be achieved by his sheer existence and not by his involvement in actual operations.

Second, the tasks of manning the automated system of mass destruction and their counterdefenses will consume a large portion of the personnel of the future military profession. The need to prevent nuclear accidents and the responsibility for managing the disposal of nuclear garbage and dangerous or obsolete weapons prevents these tasks from becoming routine. They are essential tasks but ones which do not necessarily develop military statesmen.

Third, the military see a broad range of specialized tasks as falling under the rubric of politico-military affairs, for example, the management of military alliances, military assistance programs and involvement in arms control. The importance of these tasks are clear and increasing. However, it is a fundamental error to think of these assignments as constituting a set of specialized staff assignments. Every task and responsibility of the armed force--no matter how tactical "military" or routine, has its politico-military implication. The ineffective and disruptive disposal of obsolete chemical weapons, the uncalled for use of bayonets for local security around an overseas base indicate the fusion of tasks and career lines in the military profession. It has not been and will not be the case in the future, that only high ranking officers are involved in politico-military affairs. It is no longer the case that an officer first learn his purely military skill and then in mid career requires exposure to the consequences of force in international relations.

These tasks are now diffused throughout the entire structure. Even the command of tactical military units--both at home and abro abroad--needs to be seen as the symbolic presence of American goals rather than concrete and specific force levels.

Institution building for the future will involve both educational and career changes. Like professional development in a wide area of contemporary civilian society. the officer will require both higher degrees of expertise in his particular area of competence and at the same time heightened consciousness of the responsibility of the military establishment as a whole. An all volunteer force may well, despite its disadvantages, supply a unique opportunity for restructuring the military profession.

It will be necessary to eliminate the world wide personnel system which periodically distributes, rotates, and redistributes military personnel. Instead a modern equivalent--and I say equivalent--of the old fashioned regimental system could well be developed both for the Army and Air Force. The Navy could strengthen and make realistic the notion of a home base. The experience with gyroscope units is a step in this direction. Such a system would permit each officer to have a basic affiliation with an operational, planning, logistical or education unit, and would represent his primary affiliation. It could make possible a higher degree of cohesion and solidarity and the conservation of the best element of military tradition, which has been weakened by constant rotation. It would help to reduce family disruption and to increase career satisfaction.

Such a system would also permit and in fact enhance rotation of assignments required for professional development. It would make possible a greater degree of geographical specialization essential both for operational units and for personnel with area and language skills. It would increase effectiveness in those functions which require long term contacts with foreign governments and alliance organizations which today suffer from endless rotation of personnel.

A greater degree of career and geographical specialization in

a personnel system of increased stability could articulate with
an educational system designed to strengthen both civil-military
relations and increase the awareness of the military about the
limits of force in international relations. First, there should
be no objection to starting professional officer education at an
earlier age. It is well recognized that youngsters mature earlier,
that a good part of high school is a waste of time and that much
of current unrest is the result of prolonged dependence that
youngsters must endure in high school and college. It should be
possible for the academies to permit entrance after three years
of high school. (In addition, one element in handling ROTC recruitment would be to make it possible for ROTC cadres to serve on
active duty as enlisted personnel for a period of one or two years
when they find college too boring and too confining. For this
time, they would receive constructive service credit if they
elected a long term professional career.)

Academy instruction should include the junior year of instruction at a civilian university. This would be the equivalent to
the junior year abroad and would supply an important educational
experience. The military profession is already moving toward a
larger and larger number of officers with higher degrees, and
there should be a corresponding emphasis of obtaining these degrees
at civilian universities in order to maintain effective civilian
linkages.

But the basic transformation of professional education must
focus on increased sensitivity to the consequences of the use of
force. It is the case especially that junior officers need to be
introduced to the broad professional educational objectives that
are supposed to be the responsibilities of the advanced level
schools (command and general staff colleges and service war colleges). But it must also be recognized that both the curriculum
and the approach of such instruction at all levels requires a
recasting. Much of current instruction involves generalized discussion of current issues. The study in depth of politico-military affairs with concern for concrete details is required.

At the academy level, basic instruction in the social sciences is not enough. The social science analysis of tactical and strategic issues needs to be developed with a concern for political and economic and social aspects of military operations. For example, at West Point such an approach would involve joint endeavor by social science faculty, the office of Military Psychology and Leadership and the tactical department to present realistic and simulated problems. The same type of instruction would be appropriate at the command and staff level. Yet it should be kept in mind that there are limits to the role of class room instruction in developing a statesman-like approach to the management of military affairs. Actual apprenticeship is an essential ingredient. It could well be that the war college level of instruction could be curtailed or even eliminated. During this time period, officer instruction could include a host of new experiences such as assignment to a civilian government agency, in community work or as participant observer with an outstanding military officer.

Basically the evolution of military education is designed not only to prepare the officer for higher commands, but to assist him in the transition to civilian life. The emerging military career line will involve a second career in civilian life. The advocates of a volunteer army speak of the reduction of personnel turnover but the military profession, despite the hope of the economists, will continue to be a young man's game. The future armed forces, because of strains and tension, will have to make possible the exercise of authority in the prime of life. The vitality of the armed forces depends on its age grading system, and this point is well recognized by the Israeli army. Even if the armed forces permit a significant number of officers to remain on duty outside of the promotion system, early retirement and the second career is and will remain crucial.

Military Authority. Finally, institution building for the emergent military requires continual attention to the issues of military authority and discipline, particularly as it relates to

internal management. Because of the equalitarianism of American
society and the emphasis on informal personal relations, civilian
society views with suspicion the practices of military authority.
The military profession had engaged in considerable self-scrutiny
about its authority relations, and has slowly adapted itself to
the requirements of technical and team management. But there can
be no doubt that the gap between garrison life and the realities
both of operations and of combat is very great. Under conditions
of operational duty and especially under the requirement of stress
combat, there emerges the close fraternal authority required for
group solidarity.

The military profession must recognize that many civilians
view with suspicion a fully volunteer armed force because they
fear a retrograde in authority, with harsh and unfunctional discipline, unrelated to the realities of modern military life. There
is belief that with the removal of the reluctant draftee, and the
pressure he places on the system, the style of life dramatized in
From Here to Eternity, would return. These fears may be unfounded
but they exist for many American civilians who recall or exaggerate the excessive formalism and arbitrary discipline which they
have experienced in garrison life. There can be no doubt that a
cultural factor is here at work; the professional military seems
to assume that informality weakens leadership and limits response
to direct commands.

It will not suffice to claim that civilian fears are unfounded;
the military profession will have to confront this issue and
expose its practices to full public scrutiny. Any misunderstanding
as to how the armed forces operate would greatly weaken civil-
military relations. The professional military will, in the future,
be concerned with strategic concepts, and realistic military
doctrine, and it will hope to be judged on these issues. However,
it will be judged by civilian society in part on the patterns of
discipline and authority it uses in its daily and operational life.
The military profession of the future must also be prepared to participate in discussions of fundamental questions of human goals

and to explore hypothetical issues including the military format of a world without war. There is no reason why the military profession should avoid such an analysis, since a world without war would not be without its equivalent peace officers.

ARMED FORCES AND AMERICAN SOCIETY:

CONVERGENCE OR DIVERGENCE?

Charles C. Moskos, Jr.

Two apparently contradictory characterizations of the contemporary military establishment have widespread currency. On the
one hand, there is the viewpoint that the institutional forms of
the military are converging with those of civilian society. On the
other hand, there is the perspective which emphasizes the sharp
differentiation between military and civilian structures. The war
in Vietnam, the domestic reactions to that war, and the movement
toward an all-volunteer force have served to heighten rather than
bridge these contrasting interpretations.

The view that the armed forces are increasingly sharing the
attributes common to all large-scale bureaucracies has been a
leitmotiv in most social science and scholarly studies of military
organization. It is typically argued by students of the armed
forces that the administrative mechanisms, social forms, and definitions of professionalism of the military are becoming more like
those of all institutions in a modern complex society.[1] Concep-
tually related (but often at variance ideologically) to the convergent theorists are those commentators who express deep concern
over the "militarization" of civilian society; a phenomenon which
in one way or another is regarded as a near inevitable accompani-
ment of a massive military establishment.[2]

The contrary viewpoint is that which sees the armed forces as

quasi-feudal organizations with features quite unlike those found
in the community at large.[3] This portrayal has been especially
prevalent in the popular culture and mass media treatments of
service life.[4] Likewise, literary and jouranlistic accounts of
military society tend to place much stress on the total institutional qualities of the military organization.[5] A variant of the
divergent-military school has been the recent emphasis on the
increasing alienation of career military personnel from the
putative values of civilian society.[6]

Though sometimes posed as such, the convergent versus divergent hypotheses of military and civilian social organization are
not mutually exclusive. In fact, much of the antinomy can be
reconciled by specifying what within the military is the referent
for the generalization. By and large, studies dealing with the
officer corps are most likely to discuss trends in the armed forces
along the lines of convergence with civilian society, while des-
criptions of enlisted life typically focus on the peculiar
qualities of the military system. There are also the distinctions
to be made between war and peacetime duty, between stateside and
overseas assignments, and between career and single-term servicemen. Moreover, nearly all accounts agree that there are important
differences between the armed services as well. The organizational
characteristics tending toward convergence with civilian structures have been most apparent in the Air Force, somewhat less so
in the Navy, and least of all in the Army and especially the
Marine Corps.

In other words, to appreciate the scope of the changes induced
by technological and bureaucratic factors in the military of recent
times need not presume these changes have had equivalent consequences on all levels or have been equally pervasive throughout
each of the armed services. Put still another way, it is within
a dialectical context--the institutional persistencies of military
life reacting against and toward the transformations occuring
within the larger societal setting---that we are to understand the
emergent social organization of the American military.

In trying to assess the relationship of the armed forces to
American society then, it is useful to conceive of a continuum
ranging from a military organization highly differentiated from
civilian society to a military system that is highly convergent
with civilian structures. Concretely, of course, America's military forces have never been either entirely separate or entirely
conterminous with civilian society. But conceiving of a scale
along which the military has been more or less overlapping with
civilian society serves the heuristic purpose of highlighting the
ever-changing interphase between the armed forces and American
society. It is also in this way that we can be alerted to emergent trends within the military establishment; trends that appear
to augur a fundamental change in the social characteristics of the
armed forces within the near future.

The convergent-divergent model of armed forces and society,
however, must account for several levels of variation. One
variable centers around the way in which the membership of the
armed forces is representative of the broader society. A second
variation is the degree to which there are institutional parallels
(or discontinuities) in the social organization of military and
civilian structures. Differences in required skills between military and civilian occupations are a third aspect. A fourth
variable refers to ideological (dis) similarities between civilians
and military men. Furthermore, internal distinctions within the
armed forces cut across each of the preceding variables: differences between officers and enlisted men; differences between
services; differences between branches within the services; differences between echelons within branches.

Needless to add, there are formidable problems in ascertaining
the meaningful evidence on the degree of convergence or divergence
between the armed forces and society.[7] Dealing with this issue,
some of the more important findings of previous researchers along
with the introduction of new materials have been presented
throughout this study. There appears to be general agreement
among students of the subject that relationships between military

and civilian structures have gone through several distinctive and successive phases over the past generation.

Prior to World War II (1939), the military forces of this country constituted less than one per cent of the male labor force. Armed forces personnel were exclusively volunteers, most of whom were making a career out of military service. Enlisted men were almost entirely of working-class or rural origin, and officers were overproportionately drawn from Southern Protestant middle-class families. Within the military organization itself, the vast majority of servicemen was assigned to combat or manual labor positions. Socially, the pre-World War II military was a self-contained institution with marked separation from civilian society. In its essential qualities, the "From-Here-to-Eternity" Army was a garrison force predicated upon military tradition, ceremony, hierarchy, and authority.

The Second World War was a period of mass mobilization. By 1945 the number of men in uniform came close to 20 per cent of the total labor force, representing a proportionately much higher figure for young adult males. Although technical specialization proceeded apace during the war, the large majority of ground forces was still assigned to combat or service units. Even in the Navy and Air Corps--services where specialization was most pronounced--only about one-third of personnel was in technical or administrative specialties. The membership of the World War II force was largely conscripted or draft-induced volunteers. Serving only for the duration of the war, the typical serviceman was essentially a civilian in uniform; a man who found distasteful the traditional military forms of command, discipline, and social control. To put it another way, the military of World War II, while socially representative of American society, was still an institution whose internal organization contrasted markedly with that of civilian structures.

During the Cold War period the military--excepting for the buildups arising from the wars in Korea and Vietnam--accounted for between 3 and 4 per cent of the total labor force. Especially

significant, technical specialization became a pervasive trend
throughout the military during the 1950s and early 1960s. The
proportion of men assigned to combat or service units for all the
armed forces declined from 14 per cent at the end of World War II
to 26 per cent in 1963. Conversely, the proportion assigned to
electronics and technical specialities over the same time period
increased from 13 to 22 per cent. These trends were most apparent
in the Air Force which, because of the post-Korea doctrine of
nuclear deterrence and massive retaliation, was also the military
service experiencing the greatest proportional growth. In 1950,
prior to the outbreak of the Korean conflict, the Army constituted
41 per cent of total military manpower compared to 28 per cent for
the Air Force. By 1960, the figure was 35 per cent for the Army
and 33 per cent for the Air Force.

These changes in the emphases of the military's mission and
the shifts in skill requirements had major consequences on the
authority structure of the officer corps. Following the Korean
War there was a movement away from the military system based on
traditional authority to one placing greater stress on persuasion
and individual incentive. Concurrently, a college degree became
more and more a requisite for an officer's commission. There was
also an increase in the number of nonacademy graduates at the
highest levels of the military establishment, and a broadening of
the social origins of officers to include a more representative
sampling of America's regions and religious groups. More ominous,
there was at the same time a growing lateral movement of military
elites to top positions in the corporate and political world.
Even sympathetic observers of the changing nature of the military
establishment were in accord that there was a convergence in the
managerial skills required in both civilian and military organizations.

At the enlisted levels, however, the trend toward convergence
with civilian society was much more muted. Especially in the
ground forces, the inert qualities of enlisted social organization
persisted. For many draftees and single-term volunteers of the

Cold War, military life was still experienced in its traditional forms. The membership of the enlisted ranks, moreover, was only partially representative of the larger American society. Broadly speaking, the Cold War enlisted man was typically of working-or lower-middle-class background. The upper-middle-class youth was often deferred, or served as an officer. (But the small number of college-educated enlisted men was still sufficient to be defined as a special problem by many noncoms.) The lower-class youth, on the other hand, because of raised mental entrance standards, was generally excluded from military service during the Cold War period.

The war in Vietnam has ushered in another phase in the relationships between the armed forces and society. There has been the obvious increase in troop strength: from 2,500,000 in 1961 to 3,400,000 in 1971. Because of the nature of the conflict in Vietnam, moreover, the Army and Marine Corps have come to bear the brunt of the war (correspondingly diminishing the role of the Air Force and, to a lesser extent, that of the Navy as well). Concomitantly, there has been an ascendancy of the use of ground combat forces halting the long-term trend toward increasing technical specialization. The Vietnam War has also led to deviations from the Cold War policies of manpower procurement. In 1966, entrance standards were lowered to allow the induction of persons from lower mental levels—overproportionately lower class and black—formerly excluded from military service. In 1968 the manpower pool was again enlarged; this time by terminating draft deferments for recent college graduates—largely middle-class whites. For the first time since the Korean conflict, the membership of the armed forces was again bearing some resemblance to the composition of the larger society.

The immediate question is whether the Vietnam period represents a temporary aberration in the basic trends set since World War II or whether it portends a new and different type of military establishment. Put plainly, what is the likely shape of the armed forces in the foreseeable future?

TOWARD A DIVERGENT MILITARY

A major insistence of this study has been that the armed forces
at the enlisted levels have always been more disparate from
civilian structures than the officer corps. But it is further
proposed that the over-two-decade-long institutional convergence
of the armed forces and American society is beginning to reverse
itself. It appears highly likely, in other words, that the military in the post-Vietnam period will increasingly diverge along a
variety of dimensions from the mainstream of developments in the
general society. This emerging apartness of the military will be
reflective of society-wide trends as well as indigenous efforts
toward institutional autonomy on the part of the armed forces.
This is not to argue that the military establishment will occupy
a position reminiscent of the pre-World War II situation. The
sheer size of the post-Vietnam military--in all likelihood about
2,500,000 men--and the probable maintenance of Cold War policies
preclude that. But it is to say that the military is undergoing a
fundamental turning inward in its relations to the civilian structures of American society. Some of the more significant indicators of this growing divergence are summarized immediately below.

Recruitment. The long-term trend in the twentieth century in
recruitment of the American officer corps has been from a narrow
social base toward one more representative of the broader American
population. Recent evidence, however, shows that starting around
1960 this trend toward military convergence with civilian society
has reversed itself. Three measures of the growing unrepresenta-
tiveness of the officer corps in the past decade are: (1) the
overproportionate number of recent officers coming from rural and
small town backgrounds;[8] (2) the marked increase in the number of
cadets at service academies who come from career military families;[9]
and (3) an increasing monopolization of military elite positions
by academy graduates.[10]

Although the enlisted ranks have always been grossly over-
representative of working class youth, the fact remains that large
numbers of middle-class youth also served at the enlisted levels

over the past quarter-century. While the likelihood of middle-
class men to be drafted increases during times of military buildups, it is also true that even during the Cold War years between
Korea and Vietnam, the selective service system, directly or
indirectly, infused a middle-class component into the military's
rank and file. Since the end of World War II, however, there has
been a discernible and growing discrepancy between the educational
levels of officers and enlisted men.[11] (The 1968 decision to draft
a higher proportion of college graduates to meet the manpower needs
of the Vietnam War can be regarded as only a temporary fluctuation
in this trend.)

Whatever the immediate effects of the Vietnam War on enlisted
membership, it is almost certain that the social unrepresentative-
ness of the enlisted ranks will become much more marked in the
post-Vietnam period. The high probability of a curtailed draft,
if not a completely all-volunteer force, will serve to reduce significantly the degree of middle-class participation in the enlisted
ranks. Furthermore, such an enlisted membership coupled with an
almost entirely college-educated officer corps will most likely
contribute to a more rigid and sharp definition of the castelike
distinction between officers and enlisted men within the military
organization of the 1970s.

Welfare Role. Starting in 1966, the Department of Defense
initiated a program of accepting recruits from Selective Service
categories previously excluded from military service. The plan
was for the military to accept 100,000 youths each year who,
because of mental test score deficiencies, or in some cases minor
physical defects, would otherwise have been rejected. Figures
through June, 1968, show that a total of 118,000 such men were
recruited into the military. Some 40 per cent were nonwhite and
more than half had not completed high school. While the official
rationale behind "Project 100,000" is that the military is uniquely
suited to "salvage" poverty-scarred youth, the program in effect
also opened up an essentially lower-class manpower pool from which
to recruit enlisted personnel in the eventuality of an all-volunteer

military force. And in fact, from the military's standpoint, the
preliminary results of Project 100,000 have been encouraging.
Ninety-six per cent of the men entering the military under the new
program have successfully completed basic training, a figure only
2 per cent less than that of regular entrants.

Another new program having deprived youth as its primary
object is "Project Transition." This program, initiated in 1968,
is designed to provide marketable skills--through job training,
formal education, and counseling--for servicemen soon to be discharged. Once in full operation, Project Transition is to train
over 500,000 men leaving the service each year in a variety of
civilian occupations. In time Project Transition may be as significant a development for lower-class veterans (viz. vocational
training) as the GI Bill was for middle-class veterans (viz.
higher education).

Although the military has traditionally served as a career
avenue for many working-class youth, its welfare role has never
been primary, nor even officially acknolwedged.[12]   What is novel
in programs along the lines of Project 100.000 and Project Transition is that the armed forces are now manifestly being used to
prepare youth for the larger society and civilian marketplace.
What is happening is that the armed forces are being used to correct the structural failures--socioeducational and socioeconomic--
that now confront American society. The military establishment,
in other words, is being charged with massive and unprecedented
responsibilities for America's underclasses. All this at the
very same time that the post-Vietnam military appears to be heading toward less middle-class representation in its enlsited ranks.

Racial Relations. The transformation of the armed forces from
a totally segregated institution (through World War II) into a
fully integrated organization (during and immediately following
the Korean War) was an impressive achievement in directed social
change. Although the military did not become a panacea for racial
relations, it was remarkably free from racial turmoil from the
early 1950s through the middle 1960s. In its degree and quality of

racial integration the military stood in marked and favorable contrast to the racial situation in the country at large.

Paradoxically enough, though, the very integration of the armed forces can be viewed as a kind of divergence from civilian society. This is to say that the polarization of the races—at least symbolically—occurring in contemporary American society was at odds with racial developments within the military. On this point, it is also probably true that racial integration of military life has not served to increase the acceptance or prestige of the armed forces. In fact, the reverse may be the case. Those sections of the civilian community who are professedly egalitarian on racial matters are most often the least sympathetic to the military. Many of those who espouse militaristic values, on the other hand, are those who find racial integration distasteful. Put in another way, the racial integration of the armed forces has probably cost the military support among some of its traditional defenders, while not gaining any increased military acceptance among liberal-radical groups.

Nevertheless, it is also the case, that the military establishment is no longer immune from the racial and class conflicts occurring in the larger society. The armed forces—as other areas of American life—will be increasingly subject to the new challenges of black separatism as well as the persistencies of white racism. Incidents with racial overtones have become more frequent in recent years and will probably continue into the foreseeable future. That black soldiers may find they owe higher fealty to the black community than to the United States military is a possibility that haunts commanders.[13] The likelihood of such an eventuality, however, will be serious only if the Army is regularly summoned into action in black ghettos. Sensitive to the civil rights issue and the specter of black power in the military, the armed forces have been surprisingly mild in their handling of black servicemen involved in racial incidents. Most likely there will not be a widespread organized black resistance within the armed forces— barring repeated ghetto interventions—as long as the military

follows its present course of internal racially egalitarian
policies and allowing moderate leeway for manifestation of black
solidarity among troops.

Whatever the racial turn of events within the military, the
nature of black participation within the military system will be
a critical issue. As given in Table 1, we find that blacks constitute 8.7 per cent of active-duty military personnel (as of
December 31, 1969), a figure somewhat below the 11-12 per cent
black in the total population. There are important differences
in the black proportions across the services: Marine Corps, 10.7
per cent; Army, 9.9 per cent; Air Force, 9.3 per cent; and Navy
4.8 per cent. That is, blacks are overproportionately represented in the more traditional ground forces as opposed to the
more technical air and sea services. Also, from data not presented here, blacks within the ground forces are much more likely
to be found in combat and combat support units than are whites.[14]

There are also diverse patterns between the individual services as to the rank or grade distribution of blacks. Looking at
Table 1, we find that the ratio of black to white officers in late
1969 was roughly 1 to 30 in the Army, 1 to 50 in the Air Force,
1 to 80 in the Marine Corps, and 1 to 150 in the Navy. Among
officers there is the anomaly of higher black representation at
the middle levels than at the top and the bottom grades. This is
most evident in the Army where the proportion of black lieutenant
colonels and majors is over twice that of black lieutenants.
Similarly at the enlisted levels, the black overrepresentation at
middle NCO levels is readily apparent. Again with regard to the
Army, we find that one out of five staff sergeants is black, a
proportion well over three times the number of black privates.
Indeed, there are proportionately more Army sergeant majors than
there are black recruits!

What all this means is hard to appraise definitively. But
several considerations are germane to the convergent-divergent
model. First is the fact that the middle "bulge" of blacks at
both the officer and NCO levels reflects the attractiveness of a

TABLE 1

BLACKS AS A PERCENTAGE OF TOTAL PERSONNEL BY GRADE AND SERVICE

(December 31, 1969)

Grade*	Total Armed Forces	Army	Navy	Air Force	Marine Corps
Officers:					
07-10 (generals)	.1	.2	--	.2	--
06 (colonel)	.5	.9	.1	.4	--
05 (lt. colonel)	2.0	4.1	.3	1.1	.1
04 (Major)	2.7	5.2	.5	1.8	.3
03 (captain)	2.6	3.7	1.2	2.4	1.2
02 (1st lt.)	1.5	2.6	.5	1.6	.9
01 (2nd lt.)	1.5	1.7	.7	1.2	2.6
Total Officers	2.1	3.2	.7	1.9	1.2
Enlisted Men:					
E9 (sgt. major)	3.5	6.1	1.5	2.8	2.0
E8 (master sgt.)	6.6	11.1	2.7	4.0	4.9
E7 (sgt. 1st class)	9.9	16.6	5.1	5.9	9.3
E6 (staff sgt.)	13.0	20.7	6.8	9.6	13.3
E5 (sergeant)	10.6	11.0	4.6	14.1	10.9
E4 (specialist 4)	8.9	10.9	2.8	9.6	9.5
E3 (pvt. 1st class)	9.2	11.2	4.7	10.8	10.5
E2 (private)	9.8	7.6	9.8	12.7	13.8
E1 (recruit)	7.4	5.0	8.4	15.0	13.7
Total Enlisted Men	9.6	10.7	5.4	10.7	11.6
Total Military Personnel	8.7	9.9	4.8	9.3	10.7

*Army titles given in parentheses have equivalent pay grades in other services.

Source: Defense Department statistics.

military career to many black young men during the late 1950s and
early 1960s and who accordingly entered the service at the time.
Today, those blacks eligible for commissions (i.e. college graduates) are more likely to find alternate openings in civilian
careers. At the enlisted levels, the lower number of black
entrants may reflect a less favorable definition of military
service within the black community (perhaps on racial-ideological
grounds). Indirect evidence in support of this proposition is the
notable decrease in the rate of black enlistments since 1965.
Then there is also the sheer demographic fact that more whites
than blacks are proportionately being drafted in the later years
of the Vietnam buildup.

   Skill-transferability. The well-documented trend toward
increasing technical specialization within the military has already
reached its maximal point. The end of this trend clearly implies
a lessened transferability between military and civilian skills.
A careful and detailed analysis of military occupational trends by
Harold Wool reveals that the most pronounced shift away from combat and manual labor occupations occurred between 1945 and 1957.[15]
Since that time there has been relative stability in the occupational requirements of the armed forces. In fact, developments
in the 1960s resulted in a partial reversal of the long-term trend
toward greater specialization. Shortly after coming into office,
the Kennedy Administration decided to emphasize limited-war
capabilities, a decision resulting in a higher proportion of
enlisted men required for ground-combat specialties. While the
greater reliance on ground forces has been abnormally accelerated
by the war in Vietnam, limited-war capabilities will apparently
remain a cardinal tenet of this country's military posture in the
post-Vietnam period.

   Moreover, as Wool points out, it is often the technical jobs
(e.g., specialized radio operators, warning systems personnel)
that are most likely to be automated, thereby indirectly increasing the numbers of combat personnel. Another factor that will
contribute to a rising proportion of combat and manual labor

specialties within the military is the Defense Department's 1965
decision to replace servicemen with civilians in support-type
military functions, particularly in administrative and clerical
positions. By 1967 over 110,000 such formerly military positions
were scheduled for civilian replacements. The almost certain
maintenance of this policy into the 1970s will significantly
increase the proportion of traditional military occupations
within the enlisted ranks. The use of civilians in support-type
positions, moreover, can be expected to be even more notable in
the event of an all-volunteer military force.

Family Life. Before the Second World War, the military at the
enlisted levels was glaringly indifferent to family needs. In
fact, excepting some noncoms, enlisted men were typically un-
married men who spent most of their time within the confines of
the military post and adjacent "boomtowns." Indeed, prior to
1940 all enlisted men had to be bachelors at the time of their
service entry. In World War II, millions of married men were
recruited into the armed forces; except for allotment checks,
however, families of servicemen more or less fended for themselves.
Starting with the Cold War, the military began to take steps to
deal with some of the practical problems faced by married personnel. An array of on-post privileges (e.g., free medical care,
PX and commissary privileges, government quarters for married
noncoms) were established or expanded to meet the needs of military
families.

This greater concern for service families on the part of the
military became especially evident in the late 1960s.[16] Activities
such as the Army's Community Service and the Air Force's Dependents Assistance Program are recent efforts to make available a
wide range of services for enlisted families: legal and real
estate advice; family counseling; baby-sitting services; employment opportunities for wives; loans of infant furnishings, linen,
and china; and the like. In one sense, the military's belated
recognition of family needs is a movement toward paralleling
civilian society. From another perspective, however, we may

expect a diminishment of ties with civilian institutions as family
needs are increasingly met by family-service agencies within the
armed forces. In this sense, then,we encounter another indication
of an emerging divergence between the military and civilian worlds.
At the risk of some overstatement, the pre-World War II military
might be seen as a total institution encapsulating bachelors, while
the post-Vietnam military may well encapsulate the family along
with the serviceman husband-father.

Overseas Forces. In 1940 about one-fourth of America's military forces was deployed overseas--mainly in Hawaii, the Philip-
pines, and the Panama Canal Zone. Since the end of World War II,
the overseas proportion in peacetime has been about 30 per cent in
foreign locales and another 10 per cent in possessions and non-
contiguous states of the United States. The overseas proportion
of our military forces is even higher during times of war such as
in Korea and Vietnam. This is all to say that next to combat the
most distinguishing characteristic of military compared to civilian
life is the high probability of extended duty outside the continental United States.

Another important consequence of a permanent overseas military
force is the incorporation of large numbers of foreign nationals
into the broader American system. It is not so generally recognized that, unlike civilian structures, the American military has
a sizable component of foreign nationals. These include, variously,
those catering to GI hedonistic wants, the clerical and maintenance staff of overseas installations, and those persons hired by
company-level units to perform menial and service work. In all but
the narrowest of definitions, such foreign nationals must be considered an integral part of the overseas military community.

At a more significant level, there is another important non-
American element in the American military system: the foreign-
national military personnel who come under the direct operational
control of the American command. In Korea, the KATUSA (from
"Korean Augmentation to the U.S. Army") program has been in operation for almost two decades. In fact, the "Katusas"--Korean

soldiers who formally occupy Table of Organization positions and live in American units—constitute one-sixth of the "American" Eighth Army. A somewhat different use of local troops has occurred in Vietnam. The Marine Corps has what is known as "combined action platoons," that is, a squad of American Marines placed within a platoon of South Vietnamese Popular Forces. The Army's 25th Infantry Division has a variation of the above called "combined lightning teams." Whether the "integrated" model of Korea or the "fusion" pattern of Vietnam, the utilization of non-American forces under American command is a paramount indicator of a military force divergent from American society. Moreover, now that significant precedents have been set, we may find American forces being increasingly augmented by foreign nationals in future years.

The Citizen-Soldier. The troop strength of the American military consists of nonactive as well as active-duty forces. These nonactive forces in 1970 numbered about 2,300,000 federal reservists (under Pentagon administration) in the various military services, and some 500,000 men in National and Air Guard units (normally under state control in peacetime). As a general rule, nonactive military personnel attend weekly drill meetings and spend two weeks in training every summer. During certain specified times of emergency—ranging from full-scale war to quelling local violence—reservists or Guardsmen may be called into service. Practically speaking, however, only a few reserve or Guard units have been called upon for extended active duty since the end of the Korean conflict.

From a historical perspective, the concept of the citizen-soldier has been a central premise of this country's military thinking. Nevertheless, since the late 1950s and especially since 1963, there has been a determined effort by the Defense Department to reduce the role of nonactive forces. The proportion of reserve and Guard servicemen of the total military force (i.e., both active and nonactive military personnel) declined from 61 per cent in 1957 to 43 per cent in 1970. As William Levantrosser

points out in his comprehensive study on the subject, the Chief
Executive's position toward reservists has changed from one of
strong support during Truman's time, to deemphasis under the
Eisenhower Administration, to pressure for fewer but better
trained reservists under Kennedy, to concerted steps to curtail
reserve forces under Johnson.[17]   In 1964, Secretary of Defense
McNamara proposed to eliminate the federal reserves entirely by
merging them with the National Guard. Although this plan was not
carried out—owing to Congressional opposition—the Army Reserve
was subsequently reduced from eight to five divisions, a reduction in strength of 55,000 men. In 1967, the National Guard itself was reorganized—over the resistance of state leaders—by
reducing it from 23 to 8 divisions.

The post-Vietnam period promises to witness further erosion
of reserve and Guard support. For one thing, the declining role
of reserve forces is somewhat conterminous with the long-term
accretion of power by the Executive Branch at the expense of Congress and state legislatures—the traditional champions of
reserve forces. Moreover, present experience with limited wars
points to the strategic need for highly trained and readily
operational combat units thereby undercutting much of the military
justification for large reserve forces. Further, the public con-
troversies centering around reservists called to active duty have
not been favorable from the military standpoint. The complaints
of many reservists activated during the Berlin crisis of 1961 and
National Guardsmen called up in 1968 for Vietnam approached a
major scandal. Moreover, the 1970 Gates Commission Report on the
all-volunteer armed force stated that reserve strengths could
decline "without posing a serious national security problem."[18]
A variety of considerations, then, indicate that the lessened
importance of the reserve serviceman will be another factor con-
tributing to the divergence of the military from civilian society.

The impending eclipse of the citizen-soldier concept is suggested from another vantage point as well. It is relevant to
compare the conclusions of two Presidential Commissions dealing

with policies toward veterans.[19] In 1956, the Commission on
Veterans' Pensions held that military-service--whether in time
of war or peace--is an obligation of citizenship and should not
be considered inherently as a basis for future governement benefits. In particular, the 1956 report held that the veteran qua
veteran had no priorities for government assistance (as distinct
from service-connected disabilities). Instead, it recommended
the integration of veterans' needs with social programs existing
for the citizenry at large. In 1968, on the other hand, the
Veterans Advisory Commission advocated a much more separate treatment of veterans. The 1968 Commission concluded that even non-
service-connected ailments of veterans should be the special pro-
vince of the Veterans Administration. Unlike the situation of
the veteran of old, it is now recommended that the ex-serviceman
should have distinctive prerequisites in governmental assistance.
From this perspective, it appears that the emerging institutional
differentiation of the military will correspondingly carry over
into the post-service lives of many servicemen. Indeed, the very
category "veteran" may come more and more to designate not the
single-term serviceman but rather the retired career serviceman.

Antimilitarism. It is fair to assert that the original
opposition to the war in Vietnam began within this country's
intellectual and academic community. Although the antiwar movement has since come to encompass a much broader and wider support,
its main thrust remains within its original constituency. Moreover, as the opposition to the specifics of the war increased, the
very legitimacy of military service has been impugned. Intellectuals and student radicals, in particular, have vociferously
turned upon the military on a number of fronts. Illustrative of
this activity are the harassment of military recruiters on campuses, the generally successful efforts to remove the ROTC from
the curriculums of prestige colleges, and the frontal challenge
of the ties between major universities and military research.
More broadly, the cultural elites of our society have come close
to portraying the military as the bugaboo of American society. In

the cinema and on stage, military characters have achieved the
status of buffoons or grotesque malefactors. A minor industry
exists in the production of books and lectures castigating the
military mind, the military-industrial complex, the Pentagon, and
GI butchers.

It is my belief that the resurgence of antimilitarism among
intellectuals and college students will not dissipate once the
war in Vietnam is concluded--though the volume of the attack will
undoubtedly subside. Contrary to the views of many observers,
however, the emergent antimilitarism is not all that aberrant in
the American context. Quite the opposite. The anomaly lies in
the unquestioned acceptance of the military's role which started
in World War II and continued through the early 1960s. What
should not be forgotten is that the United States has normally
looked upon its military with some disfavor. In this sense, our
society appears to be moving toward its more conventional social
definition of the military. This is to suggest that the anti-
militarism engendered by the war in Vietnam may be returning this
country to its traditional low regard of the armed forces. Put
another way, while intellectuals and radicals have been in the
forefront of the antimilitary movement, it is also more than
possible that the quarter-century-old honeymoon between the
American public and the military establishment is likewise coming
to an end.

Marcus Cunliff, in his insightful study of American attitudes
toward civil-military relations in our country's early history,
delineates three diverse normative standards: (1) the "Chavelier"
or professional militarist; (2) the "Rifleman" or anti-profes-
sional militarist; and (3) the "Quaker" or anti-militarist.[20]
Applying Cunliffe's typology to the convergent-divergent model of
the armed forces and society, the Chevalier stands for a divergent military while the Rifleman represents a military infused
with civilians in uniform. What is striking in much of the current
mood is the confluence of two usually opposing schools of thought.
Thus, we find the necessity of an all-volunteer and career mili-

tary force being argued for by both the antimilitarists and the
professional militarists; the former because of the repugnance
of military service and their alienation from America, the latter
because of practical considerations and their desire to strengthen
America militarily. Curiously enough, together the supporters
and opponents of America's armed might were both establishing a
rationale for a military force highly differentiated from civilian
society.

ARMED FORCE AND AMERICAN SOCIETY

Over a quarter-century ago, Harold Lasswell first stated his
theory of modern civil-military relations in the concept of the
garrison state.[21] Forecasting a particular form of social organization, the garrison state would be characterized by the militarization of the civil order as the military system became conterminous with the larger society. The subordination of societal goals
to the preparations for war would lead to the obliteration of the
distinction between civilians and military personnel. The convergence of the armed forces and American society which began in
World War II and continued through the Cold War decades of the
fifties and sixties seemed in certain respects to confirm the
emergence of the garrison state. But the prospects for the 1970s
require a reformulation of the garrison-state concept. For we
are entering a time in which the armed forces are becoming more
distinct and segmented from civilian society.

In the enlisted component, the bases of military recruitment
are shifting away from conscription and toward ascription, from
being somewhat representative of American youth to excessively
reliant upon young men coming from our society's depressed levels.
The move toward a nonconscripted military force will effectively
end any equitable sharing of enlisted participation on the part
of America's middle classes and college-educated youth. Indeed,
much like the "civic action" theories applied by American strate-
gists to underdeveloped countries--the use of the military for
purposes of social engineering--the military is now being charged
with an analogous role regarding America's underclasses.

At elite levels, the divergence of armed forces and society will be reflected in closer and more critical scrutiny of the military's budgetary and force demands. But it is highly improbable that this new skepticism will result in any fundamental curtailment of the dominant role the military establishment has come to play in our country's economic output. It is also unlikely that the United States will basically alter what it considers to be its global politico-economic-military interests. The near future, then, points to a new phase in American civil-military relations. The character of the post-Vietnam period will be the conjunction of a military force divergent from civilian society coupled with the continuance--in its essentials--of America's worldwide strategic policies.

Rather than a Lasswellian garrison state, there will be a sharpening contrast between the internal social organization of the military and the institutional developments occurring in civilian society. Throughout the American nation of the late 1960s there was a movement toward greater control of institutional decisions by persons most affected by those decisions. There has been a shift--at least in style and probably in substance--toward a more participative or democratic model of social organization. Insensitive administrators, obsolete structures, and encumbering procedures were being challenged in unprecedented ways. Police and welfare departments, schools and colleges, political parties and labor unions, churches and hospitals, were all subjected to the growing norm of participation. What is important is that these institutions were coming under attack from the inside.

Even the military of the late Vietnam period was beginning to feel such internal pressures. Some numbers of men in uniform-- white radicals, black separatists, disgruntled enlisted men, antiwar officers--were increasingly communicating their resentments to other servicemen as well to groups in the larger society.[22] In Vietnam itself, the American military force by 1971 was plagued by breakdowns in discipline including violent reprisals against unpopular officers and NCOs. Although much of the

malaise in the ranks could be attributed to changes in youth
styles—particularly the widespread incidence of drug abuse, it
was also likely that the military's disciplinary problems reflected
in large part a general weakening of morale which seems always to
occur in an army coming to an end of a war. Even the use of sheer
coercive power on the part of commanders has limitations once the
elan of an armed force has been so undermined.

Partly in response to these internal problems, the armed forces
were beginning to experiment in allowing greater latitude in life
styles, degrees of privacy, and more individually tailored training procedures. Nevertheless, efforts on the part of the military
to "democratize" itself could turn into a self-defeating endeavor.
Steps taken in the direction of more recognition of individual
rights and less rigidity in social control would in all likelihood
seriously disaffect career personnel while making military service
only marginally more palatable to its resistant members.

In any event, the probability of sustained internal agitation
or even questioning of the military system is unlikely once the
war in Southeast Asia ends. With the advent of a curtailed draft
or all-volunteer force, the military will find its membership
much more acquiescent to established procedures and organizational
goals. Without broadly based civilian representation, the leaven-
ing effect of recalcitrant servicemen—drafted enlisted men and
ROTC officers—will be no more. It appears that while our civilian
institutions are heading toward more participative definition and
control, the post-Vietnam military will follow a more conventional
and authoritarian social organization. This partial reversion to
traditional forms may well be the paradoxical quality of the "new"
military of the 1970s.

NOTES

[1]See, for example, Morris Janowitz, The Professional Soldier
(New York: Free Press, 1970); Samuel P. Huntington, The Soldier
and the State (Cambridge, Mass.: Harvard University Press, 1957);
Jacques van Doorn, ed., Armed Forces and Society (The Hague:

Mouton, 1968); Morris Janowitz, ed., The New Military (New York: Russell Sage Foundation, 1964); Adam Yarmolinsky, The Military Establishment (New York: Harper and Row, 1971). Note, however, that in the preface to the new edition of The Professional Soldier (New York: Free Press, 1971) Janowitz speaks of "the limits of civilianization," i.e., a trend away from military-civilian convergence.

[2] See, for example, C. Wright Mills, The Power Elite (New York: Oxford University Press, 1965); Seymour Melman, Pentagon Capitalism (New York: McGraw-Hill, 1970); Sidney Lens, The Military Industrial Complex (Philadelphia: Pilgrim Press, 1970); and James A Donovan, Militarism, U.S.A. (New York: Charles Scribner's Sons, 1970.

[3] See, for example, Charles C. Moskos, Jr., The American Enlisted Man (New York: Russell Sage Foundation, 1970).

[4] Ibid., pp. 1-36.

[5] See, for example, Malcolm Cowley, The Literary Situation (New York: Viking Press, 1958), pp. 23-42; J. Glenn Gray, The Warriors (New York: Harper Torchbooks, 1967); and Ward Just, Military Men (New York: Alfred A. Knopf, 1970).

[6] William R. Corson, The Betrayal (New York: W. W. Norton, 1968) and Just, op. cit.

[7] For a somewhat different formulation than that given here of the variables involved in a convergent-divergent model of armed forces and society, see Albert D. Biderman and Laure M. Sharp, "The Convergence of Military and Civilian Occupational Structures Evidence from Studies of Military Retired Employment," American Journal of Sociology, Vol. 73 (January, 1968), pp. 381-399.

[8] See the chapter by Laurence I. Radway in this volume.

[9] See the chapter by Morris Janowitz in this volume.

[10] David R. Segal, "Selective Promotion in Officer Cohorts," The Sociological Quarterly, Vol. 8 (Spring, 1967), pp. 199-206.

[11] Moskos, op. cit., p. 196.

[12] See the chapter by Bernard Beck in this volume.

[13] See, Moskos, op. cit., pp. 108-133; and Yarmolinsky, op.cit., pp. 340-354. For a revealing insight into militant black attitudes toward military service and black separatist movements within the armed forces, see the articles by Milton White and Wallace Terry in The Black Scholar, November, 1970, pp. 7-18 and pp. 40-45.

[14]Moskos, op. cit., pp. 114-117.

[15]Harold Wool, The Military Specialist (Baltimore, Maryland: Johns Hopkins Press, 1968).

[16]Roger W. Little, "The Military Family," in Little, ed. Handbook of Military Institutions (Beverly Hills, California: Sage Publications, 1971).

[17]William F. Levantrosser, Congress and the Citizen-Soldier (Columbus: Ohio State University Press, 1967).

[18]The Report on the President's Commission on an All-Volunteer Force ("Gates Commission"), (New York: Macmillan, 1970), p. 99.

[19]President's Commission on Veterans' Pensions, Veterans' Benefits in the United States (Washington, D.C.: Government Printing Office, 1956). The 1968 report of the United States Veterans Advisory Commission is summarized in The New York Times, April 23, 1968, p. 7.

[20]Marcus Cunliffe, Soldiers and Civilians (Boston, Mass: Little, Brown and Company, 1968).

[21]Harold D. Lasswell, "The Garrison State," American Journal of Sociology, Vol. 46 (January, 1941), pp. 455-468; and Lasswell, "The Garrison State Hypothesis Today," in Samuel P. Huntington, ed., Changing Patterns of Military Politics (New York: Free Press, 1962) pp. 51-70.

[22]Although a comprehensive account of GI anti-war activity in the Vietnam period is yet to be written, informative accounts are found in Andy Stapp, Up Against the Brass (New York: Simon and Schuster, 1970); Fred Halstead, GIs Speak Out Against the War (New York: Pathfinder Press, 1970); and Fred Gardner, The Unlawful Concert (New York: Viking Press, 1970).

LIST OF CONTRIBUTORS

Bernard Beck, Department of Sociology, Northwestern University.

Leon Bramson, Department of Sociology and Anthropology, Swathmore College.

Morris Janowitz, Department of Sociology, University of Chicago.

Peter Karsten, Department of History, University of Pittsburgh.

William A. Lucas, Division of Social Sciences, National Science Foundation.

Nona Glazer Malbin, Department of Sociology, Portland State University.

Charles C. Moskos, Jr., Department of Sociology, Northwestern University.

Laurence I. Radway, Department of Government, Dartmouth College.

Robert B. Smith, Department of Sociology, University of California, Santa Barbara.

David Sutton, Department of Political Science, Appalachian State University.